Fletcher's Aces

Essex: County Cricket

OTHER BOOKS ON CRICKET AND ESSEX HISTORY BY DESERT ISLAND BOOKS

FLETCHER'S ACES AND JOKERS

ESSEX: COUNTY CRICKET CHAMPIONS
1979

IAN OXBORROW & ROB PRITCHARD

DESERT ISLAND BOOKS

First published in 2009
by
DESERT ISLAND BOOKS LIMITED
7 Clarence Road, Southend-on-Sea, Essex SS1 1AN
United Kingdom
www.desertislandbooks.com

British Library Cataloguing-in-Publication Data
A catalogue record for this book is available from the British Library

ISBN 978-1-905328-60-4

Printed in Great Britain
by
4Edge Ltd, Hockley, Essex

The publishers are grateful to Essex County Cricket Club and Essex County Newspapers for permission to reproduce the photographs in this book

ACKNOWLEDGEMENTS:
The authors would like to thank Danny Macklin for allowing us access to the Essex CCC archives, Martin McNeill for access to Essex County Newspapers picture library, Andy Pritchard for sorting out the images, Keith Oxborrow for his reading, and finally the 1979 Essex CCC squad for their joyful co-operation

Contents

Cast of Characters

PETER EDWARDS: club secretary/general manager, who played a major part in making Essex run smoothly off the pitch.

KEITH FLETCHER: the county's greatest ever captain and a fine middle-order batsman.

GRAHAM GOOCH: run machine, who starred for England in the World Cup.

MIKE DENNESS: experienced opener, who formerly won the title with Kent.

KEN McEWAN: classy South African batsman and fans' favourite.

BRIAN HARDIE: dour Scottish batsman, didn't give his wicket away.

KEITH PONT: big-hitting all rounder and prankster.

STUART TURNER: wily performer who would bowl all day.

NEIL SMITH: wicketkeeper and unorthodox batsman.

NORBERT PHILLIP: quiet West Indian fast bowler, who could also hit the ball a long way

JOHN LEVER: unstoppable left-arm opening bowler, in his pomp.

RAY EAST: joker, left-arm spinner and useful nightwatchman.

DAVID ACFIELD: Olympic fencer and off-spin bowler, who hated training.

ALAN LILLEY: aggressive opening batsman, trying to make his mark in county cricket.

MIKE McEVOY: young batsman finding first-team cricket tough.

GARY SAINSBURY: left-arm bowler, impressive in the second team.

Introduction

It is 30 years since Essex ended their century-long wait for success in the world of English county cricket. But looking back to the occasion in July 1979, when they lifted the Benson and Hedges Cup in front of their adoring fans at Lord's, and followed it a month later with the County Championship title, it is hard to imagine Essex not being a successful club.

Since the moment they finally went from nearly-men and perennial under-achievers to champions, the club has been synonymous with silverware, claiming a further five championship titles in the ensuing years, together with eight one-day trophies.

As recently as 2008, the club lifted the Friends Provident Trophy to mark the beginning of a new era under young skipper Mark Pettini, who was handed the captaincy reins at the tender age of 23, following the retirement of the colourful Ronnie Irani.

Pettini's side went on to claim the NatWest Pro40 Division Two title and reached the semi-finals of the Twenty20 Cup – a form of cricket those in 1979 could only imagine in their wildest dreams.

For Essex fans under the age of 40, it is as though the county has rarely been starved of success or big-name players, many of whom have gone on to enjoy illustrious international careers. A new can of polish needed to be brought in to keep the contents of the bulging trophy cabinet as sparkling as it deserves to be.

As cricket's history deepens and the opportunity to win trophies expands with the splitting of the championship into two divisions and the introduction of new one-day competitions, a wider spread of success among English counties is to be expected. But for Essex, their wait went on somewhat longer than most. 103 years to be exact.

From its origins in 1876, through World Wars and financial difficulties, the club was finally able to realise its ultimate ambition.

So many decades of pain, missed opportunities, and doses of bad luck were all a thing of the past, as of the afternoon of Tuesday, 21 August 1979. County champions at last. The year will live long in the memory of cricket fans nationwide, and, for those with their hearts in Essex, it will live on forever.

Chapter One

The Format of Cricket in 1979

County cricket was enjoying a boom in 1979. One of the main reasons for this was the set-up of the competitions, which encouraged attacking cricket, especially in the Schweppes County Championship. Matches were set for a duration of three days, rather than the four-day games played today.

Seventeen counties competed for the championship title, unlike today's two-tiered promotion and relegation system. Ten counties were played once and six counties were faced twice. The choice of counties played twice was made randomly.

The winning team of each match earned 12 points, plus any bonus points scored in the first innings. These had to be achieved in the first 100 overs and were retained whatever the result of the match. A maximum of four batting points were available: 150-199 runs – 1 point; 200-249 runs – 2 points; 250-299 runs – 3 points; 300 and above – 4 points. A maximum of four bowling points were also available: 3 to 4 wickets taken – 1 point; 5 to 6 wickets taken – 2 points; 7 to 8 wickets taken – 3 points; 9 to 10 wickets – four points.

In the event of a tie, each side earned six points, plus points earned in the first innings. If the scores were equal in a drawn match, the side batting in the fourth innings scored six points plus points earned in the first innings.

If play was prevented because of rain – as it quite often was in 1979 – with less than eight hours playing time remaining, a one innings match could be played. No bonus points would be accumulated, but the winning side earned the same 12 points.

The overs in which the sides could bat in the opening innings was restricted. A maximum of 200 overs between the two was permitted, of which the side batting first could bat for no more than 100 overs.

The format of the championship meant contrived declarations were commonplace. As draws earned no points, captains tried to force a result. If the weather interrupted play, time was short with the matches only lasting three days. Therefore, both teams would work towards creating a target for the side batting last to chase.

Uncovered pitches also gave cricket extra spice. That little bit more exposure to the elements gave pitches unpredictability, which led to difficulties for batsman at times, but plenty of wickets falling for the bowlers and spectators to enjoy.

The prize money for the title winners seems small today – £8,000, while second place earned £3,500.

The John Player League was played on Sundays and consisted of 16 matches, with each county being played once. Matches were 80 overs long – 40 overs each. The length of the bowler's run-up was restricted to 15 yards, measured from the wicket. Bowlers could bowl no more than eight overs each. A result was only achieved if both teams had batted for ten overs or more. If the scores were level the result was a tie – the number of wickets lost was not taken into account. If the team batting second was prevented from completing its overs because of rain and the match was abandoned before 6.40pm, the result was decided on the average run-rate throughout both innings. A bit simpler than the Duckworth-Lewis system used today! The winning team earned four points, the losers none, and a tie saw both teams earn two points – the same if no result was achieved. The winners of the John Player League were given £5,500 for their success, while the runners-up earned £2,750.

The Benson and Hedges Cup saw each side have 55 overs. All matches were to be completed in one day, if possible, but three days (four if Sunday play was possible) were allocated in case of weather interference. Matches started at 11am, meaning the players could still be out playing at 7.30pm. Bowlers were restricted to 11 overs each. Unfinished matches were judged on which side scored their runs at a faster rate, provided at least 20 overs were bowled in the second innings. The competition began with a group stage and, in the event of no result being possible, it would end as 'no result'. But in the later knockout stages, if the captains were unable to agree on an alternative method of achieving a result, it was decided on the toss of a coin. In the event of a tie, the winner was the side who took the greater number of wickets. In the group stage, a victory meant three points were earned and no result provided one point.

The Gillette Cup consisted of 60 overs per side. It began in June when the Benson and Hedges Cup was in its latter stages. Bowlers were restricted to 12 overs each. The format consisted of a straight knockout through to the final. Such one-day competitions are overshadowed nowadays by the crash, bang wallop of Twenty20 cricket. The Friends Provident Trophy – a 50-over competition similar to the Benson and Hedges Cup – still survives, but for how long?

Cricketers wore their whites for all competitions in 1979, unlike the psychedelic strips being worn now. The ball was red and floodlights stood at football grounds, not cricket grounds.

Chapter Two

The Makings of Success

The sad events of the 1978 season had summed Essex up nicely. They finished runners-up to Kent in the Schweppes County Championship by a mere 19 points, while the narrowest of defeats had been suffered to Somerset in the semi-final of the Gillette Cup at Taunton. Essex could taste success without taking a bite of the winner's cake.

RAY EAST: 'It was my benefit year and I had my best year ever. I got 90-odd wickets and it would have been nice to get 100. As it was my benefit year I was in the pub most evenings so it's extraordinary to think I took all of those wickets. Maybe because I was drunk most of the time I just let the ball go up in the air. You had to work hard if you wanted to get money. One of the things we did was put these lottery tickets in a jar. There would be about 1,000 of them in a jar and you'd take them into pubs. I'd go around the pubs seeing how they were getting on and would have to have a pint at each one. I had a driver, needless to say, otherwise I would never have made it back. We nearly made it that year. At the back of my mind I knew we had a good side. We had been close before in the John Player League and it niggled in the mind.'

East was alluding to the heartache Essex had suffered in the John Player League – the one-day competition contested on Sunday afternoons – in 1971, 1972, 1976 and 1977. In 1971, Essex were denied by winners Worcestershire by the thinnest of margins, missing out by a run-rate of just 0.003. The following year, they came third. In 1975, Essex finished fourth, before losing out to champions Kent and Leicestershire on the dreaded run-rate in 1976 and 1977.

On to 1978 and it all began to go wrong for the county as August dawned. In the championship Essex faltered badly at the last hurdle. Second was their highest ever finish, but it felt as though they had finished far lower, such was the pain on missing out.

The one-day competitions had proved equally frustrating. No progress was made in the Benson and Hedges Cup and, for the first time in four years, they failed to threaten in the John Player League.

The Gillette Cup semi-final at Taunton produced great excitement as Essex sensed how close they were to their first honour. Somerset batted first and rode their luck when West Indian legend Viv Richards was dropped at slip off the bowling of John Lever. In the next over another catch was dropped at slip and, while Essex's fielding was regarded highly, it summed up the feeling that Essex were unable to perform on the big occasion. Richards went on to smash 116, including a six driven over extra cover off East, out of 187 scored while he was at the crease. Keith Pont was hit out of the attack and Stuart Turner fared no better. Graham Gooch finally dismissed Richards, caught at deep mid-wicket, but Somerset reached 287 for 6 – a daunting total.

Essex began their chase badly when Mike Denness was out for 3. Gooch and Ken McEwan repaired the damage, though, and the South African made 70 before being bowled. Essex reached 117 from their first 25 overs. Not a position from which they were expected to cruise to victory. Joel Garner had Gooch caught behind for 61, and Brian Hardie and Keith Fletcher found the required run-rate hard to maintain. When Hardie was run out in the 42nd over, 122 were still needed, whereupon Pont and Fletcher began to score at better than six runs an over. England star Ian Botham ran out Pont and then bowled Fletcher as the tension mounted. Norbert Phillip was run out and Turner hit the boundary boards twice before he was castled.

With the last six balls to be bowled, Essex were 276 for 8. Neil Smith and East managed five from the first two balls but East was bowled by the third. The fourth ball, bowled by Colin Dredge, was a no-ball. Lever pushed it for a single and Somerset panicked, conceding two overthrows. Smith swung at the re-bowled fourth ball and missed. He scored a single off the fifth ball. It was left to Lever to face the last delivery of the match. Essex required three runs. He turned it to fine-leg and took off between the wickets. He could make two runs, but a third looked improbable and, despite Smith's dive, which produced a cloud of dust, he was run out, leaving the scores level and Essex as losers, having lost more wickets.

DAVID ACFIELD: 'I think I was probably more nervous than most of them. I've always been very nervous and that is always one of the reasons why my cricket took so much out of me. I just think we had to do it once. We had come desperately close to getting to finals – there was the semi-final in Somerset when Neil Smith got run out going for a third by an inch, otherwise we'd have been in the final. All the way though, we kept on coming up against the buffers and not quite making it. We did want to win something, particularly when we'd been so close throughout the 1970s. I think we were always going to win something in one-day cricket but, from 1976 onwards, we were starting to look like a good all-round side in the championship as well.'

Turn the clock forwards 12 months and it would be their various opponents, rather than Essex, on the wrong end of such exciting finishes.

Born and bred in the county, Francis Ponder was an avid Essex fan from the days when his father took him to matches around the county. Ponder was working in engineering for Colchester-based diesel engine manufacturers Paxman and turned 35 as the 1979 season was breaking. A few years later he found himself closer to the action than he had ever imagined when he took a career diversion and became a sports journalist for Essex County Newspapers. For the next 25 years he covered Essex's ups and downs, interviewing players, ghost-writing columns for the club's stars and gaining an insight into the everyday life of county cricket. But during Essex's magical season of seasons, he was on the outside looking in, cheering every wicket and living the roller-coaster of emotions along with every other Essex supporter.

'Essex were always regarded as something of a Cinderella club,' he said. 'They made the numbers up and played for fun, with people like Ray East in the team, being regarded as the Clown Prince of county cricket. It was as though Essex were never going to win anything.

'You realised six years beforehand when Brian Taylor was captain: he got things moving, far more professionally and disciplined. They still played for fun but there was a disciplined approach and young players like Graham Gooch and Stuart Turner, John Lever and Ken McEwan, who was the biggest giveaway ever from Sussex, were already making their mark.

'In 1973, Essex reached the semi-final of the Benson and Hedges Cup so you knew they were a bit more serious about their cricket. Then, finishing second in the John Player League and finishing second to Kent in the championship showed things were moving in the right direction. They had a younger captain in Fletcher, who was tactically astute. Having got so close you began to think Essex were never going to win anything, that they were always going to be the bridesmaids and not the bride.'

The players were even more aware of the cloak of doom they wrapped themselves in every time they sensed success.

BRIAN HARDIE: 'We choked on a few occasions. There were some we lost on run-rate and there were some that we lost on the number of wins – the rules seemed to change through the years. We had it in our hands one year and we played Yorkshire and we were winning a game that would probably have seen us top the John Player League. In the last couple of overs, we just went to pieces. It was a collective mental thing and, until we managed to win something, it was a lot more difficult to do. 1978 was the first time we knew we could win the championship. Before then, it had always been the John Player League that we thought we could win. That was the first time we were nip and tuck at the top of the championship and it was a great fight right until the end. We enjoyed that in a way, having the pressure. It helped us and gave us more confidence and belief to achieve what we did in 1979.'

KEITH FLETCHER: 'We had come close in the Sunday League under Brian Taylor. The County Championship was just one up from club cricket, or one up from minor county cricket. Yorkshire would normally come close to winning it, or Surrey would be there or thereabouts, and if somebody had a good year, a fluke season, they might come somewhere near. Nobody expected to do anything. I started as captain in 1974 and in '78 we came second in the championship. We thought "Why can't we win it?" We were a good enough side. It was really from 1977, '78 that we really felt that we could win the championship.

'Not winning for so long didn't weigh on my mind. We were still developing as a unit. Kenny McEwan and Goochie, Mike Denness came in [from

Kent] in 1978 and he was the final cog in the wheel. We needed an experienced batter up front and he gave us that experience as Kent had won things. Brian Hardie was also developing. The time was right when it happened. Before that, we were still developing.

'I didn't feel any pressure. Cricket at that time was slightly different to how it is now. The [Essex Cricket] Committee were different. They knew about the game of cricket and were quite happy being able to watch the action out on the pitch. I thought it was a squad good enough to win a championship. The sad thing was Keith Boyce had got injured and his career had to finish at a youngish age. It would have been nice to have him around.'

JOHN LEVER: 'I think the fact that in our history we had never won anything was absolutely huge. We thought we were somewhere near a good side. Being a young side, Tonker [Brian Taylor] had to mould us together, and really put the discipline into the team because it would have been very easy finishing halfway in the table in those days and just go out and enjoy yourself. But he put the discipline in.

'There was a quiet confidence we were a good side because in 1979 we had three or four medals from the John Player League – bronze or silver. We knew we were a reasonable outfit.'

STUART TURNER: 'Things were starting to come together under Fletch. Under Brian, or 'Tonker' as we used to call him, he was the catalyst that got things going, then Fletch took over and he had a terrific cricket brain. He had a group of lads who were a bit rough around the edges to start with, but we gelled into a pretty good unit. Of course, the staff was very small too and you didn't get injured. You just got on with it.

'When Ronnie Irani was captain, it epitomised the way things were when they had a committee meeting and Fletch was on it. They talked about injuries to players. Under Ronnie they had a few injury problems and a few players were out and he happened to ask Fletch what he did when players got injured. Ronnie asked him who bowled at the start of the year and Fletch said "Lever, Phillip and Turner". He asked who was bowling at the end of the year and Fletch told him again "Lever, Phillip and Turner". We just didn't get injured.'

GRAHAM GOOCH: 'We were getting better and some of those players who had been with the club during the real hard times of the late 1960s, when they cut the staff down to 12 – people like Stuart Turner, David Acfield, Ray East and Keith Pont – were all getting more experienced together. We signed Kenny McEwan, which was a big signing for us. Keith Boyce had finished and Norbert Phillip had come to Essex and obviously I had come on to the staff in 1974, so we were building a good side. Keith Fletcher had also pretty much finished playing for England so he was leading the side all the time and we put together a good team.'

The usual air of optimism surrounded the club at the beginning of 1979, but without the conviction that it was necessarily going to be their year, according to secretary Peter Edwards. The success of 1979 did not come about just by the endeavours of captain Keith Fletcher and his players, though.

It was as much about the carefully constructed organisation off the pitch, of which Edwards was the focal point. In 1978 it was decided a general manager/secretary would be appointed to undertake the daily running of the club and, from 350 applicants, Edwards was chosen.

He would stay in the role for the next 21 years, overseeing the most successful spell in the club's history. Regarded as a workaholic, Edwards rarely took a holiday and would work six-and-a-half day weeks as he strove to keep the club running smoothly.

Amazingly, he didn't take a day's holiday one year, when sportsmen all over the globe were complaining of burnout. Their heavy schedules were said to be taking a toll, despite wage packets thick enough to make sure they would never have to work again – a far cry from the lives and careers of the Essex players of 1979.

Having already been a passionate Essex fan, Edwards was able to see the shortcomings and, from his experiences with the John Laing Group, a large and successful construction company, he put into effect his proven ability in business administration. For the next two decades Edwards was, to all intents and purposes, Essex County Cricket Club.

However, it all came to a sad end on 18 February 2000 when Edwards embarked on a working holiday to South Africa and Zimbabwe to watch the England cricket team. Around 400 cricket dignitaries and enthusiasts packed into Chelmsford Cathedral to honour Edwards, who had passed away at the age of 63.

The effect Edwards had on Essex was touchingly portrayed by Irani, captain at the time of the death of the Essex chief. He paid the following tribute in the *Basildon and Southend Evening Echo*:

'Peter was the life and soul of Essex cricket and people came from all over the country to honour his life. Peter was a top man. He was Essex cricket. He would have been very proud of his send-off. It is no coincidence that the county's fortunes took off, on and off the pitch, on his arrival at the club in 1979. Those who really knew Peter will know he had a great and very dry sense of humour and professionalism second to none. He set the standards and his successor will have a lot to live up to. When I first came to Essex from Lancashire I was a nobody, who turned up on Peter's doorstep. He made sure I wanted for nothing, but he also warned me that I had a lot to live up to, as many players who had joined Essex had gone on to play for England. I achieved that for him, and his wife Sue said to me how very proud of me Peter was.'

Edwards was known as a combative committee man, who was proud to represent what was regarded as the Old Traditionalists XI. As his time with Essex wore on, he resisted four-day championship cricket, became irked by split divisions in the county game, and had little taste for the fanfare of colourful one-day cricket, with players bedecked in clothing more suitable for bedtime than going into battle on the pitch.

Having turned his back on an industry in which he could expect to earn far more than as secretary at Essex, Edwards began his new role on 1 January 1979 and was instantly allowed by senior club officials, such as Doug Insole and Tom Pearce, to administer the affairs of the club within broad guidelines.

His first act was a significant one – he changed the décor in the changing rooms from green to blue. Edwards was of the view that Essex didn't stand a chance of winning anything with green changing rooms. Did he know something which nobody else did?

Further changes off the pitch saw assistant secretary Graham Saville depart. He was appointed National Cricket Association coach for the Essex region. The MCC appointed Saville as one of five coaches across England and Scotland. He joined Rob Carter (Midlands), Les Lenham (South), and Keith Andrew (North), with a new appointment to follow for Scotland. Saville would continue to operate from the County Ground. Along with his coaching duties he could regularly be found turning out for Essex's second eleven and Colchester and East Essex CC. His association with Essex had started in 1962 when he joined the staff as a promising young batsman. He was capped the following year and, after a break of two years, during which he played for Norfolk, he returned to the administrative staff during the 1970s. At the time of his departure Saville told the *Essex County Standard*: 'I shall, in a way, be sorry to leave Essex, but the new job offers a tremendous challenge.' His coaching area was the whole of the east of England, with Essex the only first-class county.

Meanwhile, Essex denied reports they were poised to appoint a full-time team manager and that former skipper Brian Taylor was the man lined up for the job.

PLENTY IN RESERVE
At the start of 1979, the Essex squad was made up of a mixture of international stars and dependable county professionals. It was a blend of cricketers with a thirst to impress the national selectors, those whose time at the very top had maybe passed and wanted to lift some silverware, and younger players desperate for a piece of the action. It proved to be just the recipe Essex needed.

Essex were led by Keith Fletcher, a man who should not be judged by his statistics alone, impressive though they are. For Fletcher was a skilful tactician, a leader of men, and the tag 'one of the greatest servants the club has ever had, and is likely to have' can easily be bestowed upon him.

In 1985 Fletcher was invited to Buckingham Palace to be made an OBE from Her Majesty the Queen. Come the end of that season he had become the first captain to have led his county to each of cricket's four major honours,

Essex having won the John Player League and Natwest Bank Trophy to complete the set they began by winning the Schweppes County Championship and Benson and Hedges Cup six years previously. It is fitting to think that such a fine servant of the county should be the man who will always be remembered as the captain of the first Essex side to win each of domestic cricket's quartet of major honours.

Popular as an Essex player, and for his country, Fletcher went on to captain England seven times in his 59 Tests and struck more than 3,000 runs at an average of just under 40 – recognised as the benchmark of a decent Test batsman. Such was his thinking on the game and technical streak, he went on to coach England from 1993 to 1995, but the national side was going through a rocky patch and his spell was terminated early.

Nicknamed 'The Gnome', Fletcher first caught the eye at Essex when he was spotted wearing pointy shoes shortly after joining the playing staff. He made his first-team debut in 1962 and was rewarded with his county cap after just one season. His maiden century came in 1964 and he regularly passed 1,000 runs. Aside from his batting, which involved high levels of concentration and patience, Fletcher was notable for his close catching, taking 42 catches in 1966, and taking six catches in a match for Essex on three occasions.

Fletcher's England debut was not one to remember, although he managed the highest score of his career in 1968 (228 against Sussex at Hastings) and his stroke-making was winning admirers in the right places. Having been named in the 12-man squad to play Australia at Headingley, he was not expected to play. That was until Tom Graveney cut his hand and was forced to miss out. The selectors called up Yorkshire's Phil Sharpe on stand-by. Fletcher was chosen to replace Graveney, as Sharpe had not been in the original squad, but the Leeds crowd saw otherwise. Fletcher dropped three catches and failed to trouble the scorers. The crowd let him know how they felt.

Undeterred by his international baptism of fire, Fletcher took over the Essex captaincy in 1973 from Brian Taylor. Come the glory of 1979, Fletcher was turning 35, with years of experience and nous to call upon. He struck his first century for two years against Derbyshire and went on to pass 1,000 runs. Fletcher's career-best bowling figures were also to arrive during that magical summer, taking 5 for 41 against Middlesex at Colchester with his leg-spin.

But while his batting and occasional bowling were admired, it was Fletcher's captaincy that drew the highest praise from his players.

BRIAN HARDIE: 'Tactically he was the best captain I played under and probably the best on the county circuit. He did things on the cricket field that we didn't think of, like putting pressure on a batsman, and that seemed to work. He never used a set pattern. Sometimes, after just a few overs, one of the spinners would come on. He might have seen something, or that the batsman would not be able to cope with his change and a lot of it worked for him. When he went to captain in Test cricket, you tend to play the game more to a set plan. The game at that level doesn't seem to need as much manipulation as county cricket does.'

DAVID ACFIELD: 'He used to walk past me in the field and say "We haven't done very well Ackers". I'd say "No we haven't. You're going to tell me we have naughty-boy nets tomorrow" and he'd simply say "Yes, so you'd better bowl better.".

'I remember one year, and this wasn't the championship year, that we were being pulverised by Vivian Richards. He [Fletcher] put four men round the bat, Viv said "You can't do that" and then he slogged it straight up in the air and we won the game. That would have been in 1983 or 1984. Reputations meant nothing to him [Fletcher]. We were either going to lose the game or we were going to win it. He got to a position at Essex where he could do no wrong. He was the most successful captain we'd ever had and therefore he could take those sorts of risks even if we lost.

'We would never bat for longer than we had to. If we declared 150 ahead, we'd have to bowl the other team out. He didn't care. If we lost, then we'd just say "Well played". If we had to bowl teams out for 150 he'd just say "Good luck" and that was it.'

Fletcher played his last game for Essex in 1989 and is second only to the prolific Gooch as the county's highest ever run scorer. He holds the record for scoring 1,000 runs in a season the most times (19), holding the most catches (519) and making the most appearances (574). The leaders of successful sides are rarely forgotten, and Fletcher's contribution cannot be underestimated.

'In Fletcher they had one of the most tactically aware captains on the county circuit,' said Francis Ponder. 'He was the master of pulling results out of the bag. He seemed to know when to declare, when to dangle the right carrots and, at times when you didn't think sides were interested in a result, we were left thinking it is actually going to happen. He seemed to be a master at getting a team to give them however many minutes or however many overs it was and we would always score more runs from those overs than the opposition anticipated.'

Essex had more than just a multi-talented leader to call upon, however. An undoubted star wherever and whenever he played, Graham Gooch was a workaholic who would not rest until his mind and body were in perfect condition for each and every match he took part in. As testimony to that hard work, Gooch, who had made his Test debut for England as a 21-year-old in July 1975, was already an established international cricketer when the 1979 season dawned. He had made 1,254 first-class runs the previous summer at an average of 41.8, plundering two centuries and nine fifties as Essex finished runners-up to neighbours Kent in the championship.

The right-handed opener – captain Fletcher had promoted Gooch to the top of the order at the start of the 1978 season, dropping Brian Hardie to number five – was equally adept in the one-day game, making his one-day international debut for England against the West Indies at the cricketing out-post of Scarborough in August 1976. While he had lost his place in England's one-day side in 1977, Gooch was firmly back in the selectors' thoughts in both forms of the game in the spring of 1979.

At Chelmsford, Whipps Cross-born Gooch had become a stalwart at the top of the order. At the age of 25, he was still short of his prime. By the end of a glittering career, Gooch had totted up 8,900 Test runs – the highest of any English batsman in history – and 4,290 one-day international runs. By the time of his retirement in 2000 at the grand old age of 47, Gooch had scored a monumental 67,057 runs in one, three, four, and five-day cricket at an aver-age of 45.68.

Back to the summer of 1979 and Gooch was doing what he did best – scoring runs. While he was restricted to just ten championship appearances, fewer than half, due to his England commitments, he was still able to total 545 runs in 15 innings, including a valuable hundred against Derbyshire at Chesterfield, and four half-centuries.

It was in the one-day arena, however, that Gooch's light shone brightest that summer. In both the Benson and Hedges Cup, which Essex won, and the John Player League, he was imperious. Gooch stated his intentions in his sec-ond domestic one-day appearance of the season, making a vital 83 as Essex sneaked to a dramatic three-run Benson and Hedges Cup, Group 'C' victory at Northampton on 5 May. The following day, he made a patient, unbeaten 68 to lead the county past Derbyshire in the John Player League at Chelmsford.

A fortnight later, Gooch made 133 in sharing a record-breaking opening stand of 223 with Alan Lilley in the 214-run victory over the Combined Universities in the Benson and Hedges Cup – a competition he virtually made his own in 1979. In the quarter-final against Warwickshire, Gooch bettered his earlier effort by making 138, before top-scoring with 49 in Essex's nail-biting semi-final win over Yorkshire at Chelmsford.

On to the final against Surrey at Lord's on 20 July and Gooch rose to the occasion again, compiling a memorable 120 runs to lead his county to the first major silverware in its long history.

It was not just for Essex that Gooch showed his one-day prowess, howev-er. England also benefited from the opener's avalanche of runs in the shorter form of the game as he spearheaded Mike Brearley's side to the World Cup final. Gooch scored 210 runs in five innings in the tournament, picking up man-of-the-match awards for his 53 against Australia in the group stage and 71 against New Zealand in the semi-finals.

Only the brilliance of the West Indies' Viv Richards, who made 138 in the final, prevented Gooch from receiving what would have been his third win-ners' medal of the summer. Even in defeat, the England batsman had shown his class in making 32 from just 28 balls, but Richards' heroics meant that Gooch's fluent effort was in vain.

Back in the County Championship, Gooch's knock of 109 against Derbyshire paved the way for a huge innings and a 171-run win that set Essex on the road to the title in mid-May. The match saw the opener share a superb 148-run stand with skipper Fletcher, a man he would follow in captaining both his county and his country in later years.

In the following three-day game against Glamorgan at Ilford's Valentine's Park, Gooch was at it again, making an unbeaten 93 in just 27.3 overs to lead Essex to a rain-affected nine-wicket victory on 1 June.

While his subsequent championship appearances were fleeting, due to England's Test series against India and the World Cup, Gooch still found time to make 86 against Sussex at Southend and an important 70 against Hampshire at Bournemouth. He also returned to the side for the final game of the season, against Yorkshire at Scarborough – the scene of his England one-day international debut three years previously – to compile 69 as Essex completed their title-winning campaign.

JOHN LEVER: 'We always said if Gooch had [Geoffrey] Boycott's hunger for runs he would have broken all records. But [South African] Barry Richards, in my mind, would have done the same. Gooch was a great player against the real super quicks. Against the spinners, he took them on and was a bully. He was intimidating. The trademark was his straight drive just to the left of the bowler. Then, as the bowler followed through he would turn his back on the bowler and mark his leg stump out. It was arrogance but you don't get to the top without some sort of arrogance. You have to believe you are better. The stance he adopted, he had a bit of trouble with it at one stage when his head was moving and his bat was waving around. It was a minor blip and he had to go back to standing still.

'Gooch insisted on finishing his toolmakers apprenticeship. It was the single-mindedness of the guy. He was single-minded to the attention of his gear. He ended up trying to design pads, thigh pads and gloves especially just to suit what he wanted. If he came in and had got out for nought he would sit down and it was never because of a bad decision. He would put his bat down, take his gloves off, undo his pads and the next thing you know he was pulling on his shorts and a pair of trainers and he would be off for a run. I'd say "You're not going off for a run are you?" and he would say "Yeah, I shouldn't have missed it should I? Serves me right!" Off he would go, running around the park. I went with him a few times. If he got out at Lord's he would go out around Regent's Park.

'He had a good sense of humour. Sometimes it was a little bit overshadowed by his dedication. With Goochie, myself, Fletch, Easty, we were products of the state education system which now is going to struggle a bit more [to produce cricketers].'

DAVID ACFIELD: 'He [Gooch] would trundle off after making a low score. It was a penance run for getting out, but that was Goochie. I think he used to get an adrenaline rush to go running. He was a very lazy bloke when he started and got a taste for international cricket. A lot of people said he'd got too big and all credit to him because he became fit and he's remained so and he's had to because he's a very big man with very small legs, as Ian Botham always tells him. Because of that, he's had to be fit because he'd have just ballooned if he hadn't.'

At the top of the order alongside Gooch there was Mike Denness. A former Kent and England captain, Denness was the eldest member of Essex's County Championship-winning squad. The Lanarkshire-born player – widely considered to be Scotland's greatest ever batsman – was well past his 38th birthday when the 1979 season began.

A stylish batsman at his peak, Denness was a cricketer of the old school, immaculately turned out both on and off the field of play. Tall, slim and well-mannered, he had been made captain of England in 1973. That decision was not welcomed by opening batsman Geoffrey Boycott, who coveted the role and would play in only the first six of Denness's 19 Tests in charge. The absence of Boycott, who refused to play, left England short when they travelled to Australia to fight for the Ashes over the winter of 1974-75. They lost 4-1. When England lost the first Test to Australia at Edgbaston in July 1975, Denness was removed. He would never play another Test match.

In county cricket, Denness had been made captain of Kent – the county he served for 15 seasons – in 1972. During his time at Canterbury, he had been part of a hugely successful era, winning the Gillette Cup in 1967 and 1974, the Benson and Hedges Cup in 1973, and the John Player League in 1972, 1973 and 1976. It was a golden period for Kent cricket, crowned by the county's first County Championship success in 57 years in 1970. Personal recognition of Denness's achievements with his adopted county came in 1975, when he was named as one of Wisden's five Cricketers of the Year.

As his career entered its twilight period, Denness moved north of the River Thames to Chelmsford for the beginning of the 1977 season. In his first summer with Essex, he managed a more than respectable 1,343 first-class runs at 39.5, complete with three centuries. The following year, as Essex finished second to his former county in the championship, Denness showed the first signs that his age may be catching up with him, managing just 870 first-class runs at 24.85. However, despite his downturn in form, the Bellshill-born batsman still had an important role to play during Essex's glorious 1979 campaign.

A superb fielder, Denness was known as 'Will' to his team-mates and was able to contribute in both one and three-day cricket. Two first-class hundreds and four half-centuries helped him to break the 1,000 run barrier for the 14th time in his illustrious career.

Further down the batting order at number five, Brian Hardie's flourishing blade became a familiar sight during the Scot's 18-year career as an Essex player. A stroke-playing batsman, the Stenhousemuir-born Hardie hit the century that ensured Essex would lift the first County Championship title in the club's history against Northamptonshire in August 1979.

Hardie, who later became a tutor at Brentwood School – the public institution attended by county team-mates David Acfield and Keith Pont – started his cricketing career playing for his hometown club in the East of Scotland League. Hardie followed his father Millar and older brother Keith into the Scotland team in 1970 at the age of just 20. The following summer, Hardie made a century in each innings of an unofficial match against the MCC at Aberdeen. That brought him to the attention of the English counties, and it was Essex who took the plunge and brought him south of the border for the start of the 1973 season.

After scoring 483 first-class runs at an average of 24.15 in his opening summer in England, Hardie became the county's regular opening batsman in 1974. In the early part of his time with Essex, he developed a reputation for being a slow, obdurate batsman. A 142-minute innings in which he made just four against Hampshire at Chelmsford in May 1974 seemed to illustrate that perfectly. However, it would not be long before Hardie would shrug off that caution and become a thoughtful shot-maker.

RAY EAST: 'He [Hardie] could be dour but wasn't really. I think I fell asleep watching the time he scored four runs in two hours. He must have played well that day because it was a turning pitch and he didn't even edge one for four so he must have middled everything. He could hit a ball as good as anyone. The "Flashing Blade" we called him. He used to annoy [West Indies fast bowler] Malcolm Marshall by playing and missing a few times and then flay him for two fours.'

Before enhancing his reputation, however, Hardie would endure a pair of frustrating seasons during which he struggled both for form and for runs. The emergence of a young Graham Gooch allowed the Scot to drop down into the middle-order. The decision paid dividends, never more so than during the title-winning season of 1979. Against Lancashire at Ilford's Valentine's Park in the opening week of June, Hardie made a round unbeaten 100 batting at number five as Essex triumphed by an innings and 132 runs. Six weeks later, he would make 146 not out – again from number five – as the champions-elect routed Hampshire by an innings and 33 runs at Bournemouth.

Hardie's third and arguably most important century of the summer, however, came as an opening batsman. Chasing a victory target of 228 to clinch the County Championship title, Hardie shared a first-wicket partnership of 113 with fellow Scot Mike Denness and finished with 103 not out himself as Essex wrapped up a seven-wicket victory over Northamptonshire.

Aside from the batting prowess that saw him carve out 17,466 first-class runs in Essex colours, Hardie also turned his arm over on rare occasions. It was during the summer of 1979 that he would take two of his three first-class wickets for the county in a single innings, removing Glamorgan's Rodney

Ontong and then Mike Llewellyn in returning figures of 2 for 39 at Ilford on 1 June.

Number three Ken McEwan was quite simply one of the finest batsmen never to play Test cricket. Born in the small town of Bedford on the southern edge of the Winterberg mountain range in South Africa's Eastern Cape, McEwan was prevented from showcasing his undoubted batting talents on the international stage by his home nation's pro-apartheid government. Without seeking to make a political statement, that state of political affairs denied the world the chance to watch a *bona fide* run machine at work.

Instead, international cricket's loss was Essex's gain. The right-hander showed glimpses of his timing and touch in making 45, complete with six boundaries, playing as a guest during the county's tour of Scotland in July 1973. He was immediately offered a three-year contract, which he accepted readily. It could all have been so different, however.

McEwan had initially been recommended to Sussex – for whom he played second eleven cricket in 1972 and 1973 – by South African-born future England captain Tony Greig but, since the south-coast county had already filled their quota of overseas players for the 1974 season, the 21-year-old joined Essex on a permanent basis.

The signing of McEwan still represented something of a gamble for Essex, who were taking on board a batsmen who had yet to record his maiden first-class century. Indeed, he had yet to top 1,000 first-class runs in some 35 innings before heading for Chelmsford. In short, there was little sign of the torrent of big scores and vital innings that would follow in an Essex sweater.

McEwan began life as a full-time Essex player in inauspicious fashion, being dismissed 'leg before' for a duck by Nottinghamshire seamer Barry Stead on the first morning of his County Championship debut at Trent Bridge. The youngster would be removed in an identical manner by Stead in the second innings, but at least this time around he would make four before being trapped in front of the stumps by the left-armer.

While the statistics suggested McEwan would struggle in English conditions, subsequent actions would prove that those early mishaps would not shape his future. Indeed, there was no disgrace in being dismissed by the wily Stead, who would himself finish 1974 – as McEwan would nine years subsequently – as Professional Cricketers' Association Player of the Year.

1976 was the year McEwan began to make the country's cricket aficionados take notice. A Benson and Hedges Cup Group 'C' fixture against the Minor Counties East at Lakenham saw him strike 116 and compile a 172-run second wicket partnership with Brian Edmeades at Norwich.

The following summer McEwan made the first double century of his career, a chanceless 218 in the County Championship match against Sussex at Chelmsford. The innings came as he hit the batting form of his life, hitting five consecutive centuries in all forms of cricket. The day before his 218 – in between the opening two days of the Sussex fixture – McEwan smashed 104 in a John Player League game against Warwickshire at Edgbaston. The following week, McEwan made 102 and 116 against Warwickshire at the same venue in the championship. The dream run ended with the small matter of an unbeaten 106 against Gloucestershire at Southend. McEwan finished eighth in the national batting averages in 1977. In 23 first-class matches, he had scored 1,702 runs at an average of better than 51.

McEwan went into the 1979 season as one of the five reigning *Wisden* Cricketers of the Year. He had been honoured alongside Somerset all-rounder Ian Botham, Warwickshire paceman Bob Willis, Derbyshire seamer Mike Hendrick and Glamorgan captain Alan Jones, following a prolific 1978 season, during which McEwan added 321 for the second wicket with Gooch against Northamptonshire at Ilford, scoring 186 himself in just four hours.

In 1978 the South African plundered 1,682 first-class runs in 24 matches at an average of 49.47. The five hundreds and eight fifties he notched up in just 37 innings were a continuation of where he had left off during the 1977 season. That summer, McEwan's figures were even more sensational – eight hundreds and four half-centuries.

The championship-winning campaign of 1979 saw McEwan maintain his impressive form, making 208 not out against Warwickshire at Edgbaston in mid-June and a brutal 185 against Derbyshire at Chelmsford a week later. The South African saved another memorable innings – 72 from 99 balls in sharing a 124-run second wicket partnership with Gooch – for the Benson and Hedges Cup final victory over Surrey at Lord's.

By the end of that glorious summer, McEwan had piled up another 1,873 runs in all forms of the game, notching three centuries and eight fifties. It may not have been his most prolific of seasons, but Essex's adopted South African had played an influential role in what was the greatest campaign in county's history. He was a dream to watch for the spectators and Francis Ponder claims McEwan was the best he ever saw: 'If you liked classy batsman you'd like watching him. It was all about timing. Gooch was exciting in a different way. McEwan is my favourite Essex batsman. He made it look so easy and so did Fletcher on his day. Not everyone wanted to just see McEwan bat. They wanted to see Essex bat and if you saw them bat you would see McEwan and Gooch. McEwan was the more technical player, whereas Gooch would force the pace and go after the bowling.'

Aged 19, Alan Lilley was the baby of Essex's title-winning squad. Born in Ilford in May 1959, Lilley had kept wicket for Essex Young Amateurs as long ago as 1974 before making his second eleven debut the following summer. Playing against a Surrey side including England batsman Alan Butcher, again as a wicketkeeper, the 16-year-old made 35 and 20 with the bat but did not take a catch. It would be three more years before Lilley would be handed his chance in first-class cricket but, when it came, he took it with both hands.

Facing Nottinghamshire at Trent Bridge in early September 1978, the 19-year-old was asked to open the batting alongside England's Graham Gooch. In the first innings, after losing his illustrious opening partner for a duck, Lilley showed admirable composure in putting together a stand of 50 with Ken McEwan before perishing for a patient 22.

It was in the second innings, however, that Lilley's talent shone through. He and Gooch put on 159 for the first wicket before the latter was dismissed for 97. Lilley, though, continued through to make his maiden first-class century on his debut, hitting an unbeaten 100 to lead Essex to a nine-wicket victory.

While that innings was unfortunately not a portent of things to come – Lilley would make just three more centuries in 189 first-class innings spanning his 13-year career with Essex – it did ensure the youngster would be part of the county's squad for the 1979 season.

After appearing in the annual pre-season fixture at Cambridge University, however, Lilley was consigned to second eleven cricket until mid-June, when he returned to make a duck in the drawn County Championship match against Derbyshire at Chelmsford. Lilley retained his place for the following match against Kent at Tunbridge Wells, only to be dismissed for six in a rain-affected draw. Lilley would make just one further championship appearance that title-winning summer, making 35 and 5 in a 46-run win over Nottinghamshire at Southend's Southchurch Park in July – a match in which he also caught South African batsman Clive Rice off the bowling of Ray East.

The young opener also struggled for form later on in one-day cricket. Handed the chance to make a name for himself in the Benson and Hedges Cup semi-final against Yorkshire at Chelmsford, Lilley was caught behind by David Bairstow off the bowling of Graham Stevenson without troubling the scorers.

It was not all doom and gloom for Lilley that season, however, as he managed a career-best 119 in the Benson and Hedges Cup Group 'B' match against the Combined Universities at the County Ground on 19 May.

Following his retirement from first-class cricket in 1990, Lilley joined the Essex backroom staff, becoming the county's director of cricket operations.

The other young man vying for a batting place was Mike McEvoy. Sadly for McEvoy, he never fulfilled the potential many in and around Essex believed he possessed going into the 1979 season.

McEvoy, who was born in Jorhat, in India's Assam province, in January 1956, had shown glimpses that he might be able to force his way into Essex's strong middle-order by scoring a half-century in each of the previous three seasons. During the same period, he was also a consistent figure for the county's second eleven. However, with Brian Hardie dropping to number five and the prolific Ken McEwan, captain Keith Fletcher and batting all-rounder Keith Pont filling out the top six, the 23-year-old was always likely to find his opportunities limited.

The major problem facing McEvoy, however, was that when those opportunities came along, he failed to take them. In seven County Championship appearances during the title-winning season, he made 108 runs at an average of just nine. McEvoy's highest score that summer was 28, coming in the second innings of the crushing innings and 22 runs defeat by Worcestershire in early August.

MIKE McEVOY: 'I had just finished my teacher training and came off a first job down in London. I was trying to get myself established. I played a few games in 1976, '77 and '78 and it was a difficult side to get into. To try and stay in it was also quite difficult. I started '79 on the fringe hoping to get a look in and play the odd game. I got my chances when Gooch was away on Test duty, which was difficult psychologically sometimes because I felt I was going in for just that game and regardless of how I did I would be going out again, though it is no excuse. Sometimes I batted at number ten in one-day games and literally played as a fielder. I rated myself as a fielder. I could field in the slips and in the covers and had a good arm.'

Following Essex's title-winning campaign, McEvoy became a more regular figure in the first eleven in 1980, playing 16 matches. However, he still managed just 600 first-class runs at an average of a smidgen over 20. After leaving Essex at the end of the 1981 season, McEvoy joined Cambridgeshire for a single season of Minor Counties cricket before linking up with Worcestershire in 1983. At Worcester, he again failed to make his mark on the first-class game, although he did manage to compile his one and only century, against Warwickshire, that summer.

McEvoy left New Road at the culmination of the 1984 campaign and settled for a career in the Minor Counties, this time with Suffolk. There, the right-handed batsman enjoyed moderate success, helping the county reach the Minor Counties Championship final against Cheshire in 1985. By the end of his career, McEvoy had scored 2,128 runs in 69 first-class matches at an average of 19.17. As his Essex captain Keith Fletcher put it, he was 'not quite good enough' to enjoy a successful career at the highest level.

Following his departure from the first-class game, McEvoy turned his hand to teaching and coaching young players, later becoming head of PE and Games at Colchester Royal Grammar School and also coaching the Under-15 team at the County Ground.

Every great side has a great all-rounder, and Essex were fortunate enough to have more than one. The moustachioed Stuart Turner, who would later go on to teach at Forest School in Chigwell, was a pivotal figure in Essex's wonderful summer of 1979.

STUART TURNER: 'I grew my moustache back in 1976 when I went to South Africa. I played for Durban Collegians and also for Natal as one of their professionals. All the players except for me had moustaches so I grew one and that was it. I kept it until 2006 when I took my school first eleven to Barbados and all the boys told me to shave it off. I had a bet with my wife as she was smoking a little bit at the time. She said if I shaved it off, she would stop. It made me look ten years younger! It was my trademark. Goochie had one as well.'

A mark of Turner's skill comes with a glance at his career statistics in first-class cricket – four hundreds and 41 half-centuries and nearly 9,500 runs with the bat and 821 wickets at exactly 26 apiece with the ball. Indeed, it is somewhat of a surprise that the Essex man never forced his way into the England selectors' thinking in either one-day international or Test match cricket.

Born in Chester in July 1943, Turner joined Essex in 1964, appearing in 14 second eleven championship matches before making his first-class bow in the County Championship match against Yorkshire at the Park Avenue Cricket Ground in Bradford on 24 July 1965.

Turner's initial experience of first-class cricket was unusual as Barry Knight and Trevor Bailey bowled out Yorkshire for 75 in 42.1 unchanged overs. Knight finished with figures of five for 41, while Bailey delivered 13 maidens in taking five for 27. After making just a single, batting at number ten in Essex's reply, Turner was thrown the ball during Yorkshire's second innings and did reasonably well, returning figures of nought for 31 from 12 overs, as the home side held out for a dogged draw.

Turner retained his place for the next match at Derby, but would have to wait until his third game – against Northamptonshire at the wonderfully named Vista Road Recreation Ground in Clacton-on-Sea – to finally take his first championship wicket. The victim was opening batsman Brian Reynolds, trapped 'leg before' for 22. From then on, Turner would hardly look back, cementing his place in the Essex squad and receiving his county cap in 1970 – the same year he made his highest-ever first-class score of 121 against Somerset at Taunton.

The all-rounder's finest year came in 1974, when he was handed the Cricket Society Wetherall Award for the 'Leading All-Rounder in English First-Class Cricket' after a splendid summer during which he plundered 963 runs and took 73 wickets at a miserly 18.12 apiece.

After taking 81 first-class wickets in 1976, 77 in 1977 – including a career-best 6 for 26 against Northamptonshire at Northampton in May – and 48 in 1978, Turner was again in top form during 1979 – a season that also encompassed his Benefit year.

The graft of workhorse Turner made him popular with the crowd. He may not have been the most spectacular player in the side, but his commitment connected with the fans.

'He was one of the meanest bowlers,' said Francis Ponder. 'Every ball was on the spot. Six overs of Stuart Turner calmed the opposition down quickly and he was perfect for the one-day game. He was a bit more than dibbly dob. You could see the pressure building up.'

STUART TURNER: 'People used to say that the Essex wicket used to seam around a bit, which it did, but you still had to use those conditions. They used to say that Norbert [Philip] and John [Lever] were the thoroughbreds and I was the donkey. I was the guy that would come on and would peg away at one end while they were having a rest, pick up two or three wickets, then they would come back and clean up.

'I just loved to bowl. Tonker used to say that if you didn't bowl you didn't get wickets and he was right. I bowled whether I was tired or not. I remember one game against Sussex at Hove in 1974 when I bowled about 40 overs straight. For some reason, probably injuries, Robin Hobbs was captain and I just bowled for virtually the whole day. If someone threw me the ball I bowled. Nine times out of ten it was uphill into the wind, but that was what I did. There was one season that I used to open the bowling a lot because of the injuries and I used to relish taking the new ball too.

'I feel a bit irked when people used to say "Stuart Turner the one-day cricketer" because I played 361 first-class matches and took 800-and-something-odd wickets and scored nearly 10,000 runs. I certainly wasn't a one-trick pony. I did love the one-day game and it was good to me. I was the only guy that did the double in the John Player League of taking 300 wickets and scoring 3,000 runs. No one else did that. John Lever was the first bowler to take 300 wickets in that competition, Derek Underwood was second and I was third. The competition was good to me.

'I look back and always think I was one of the best all-rounders who never played a one-day international. I thought I was very unlucky. When I looked at some of the blokes who got picked, they weren't fit to lace my boots as all-rounders. Again, that was a result of the Test squad and one-day squad being the same group of 15 players. If I'd just pulled the Three Lions on once it would have made me so happy. It would have made my father so proud. I came close on a few occasions and was often talked about in the papers. I nearly went to Australia in 1976 when we got thumped by Lillee and Thompson.'

Backing up the all-round ability of Turner was Keith Pont. An active member of Essex's squad during the 1979 successes in the Benson and Hedges Cup and County Championship, Pont could do damage with both bat and ball.

Born in Wanstead in January 1953, Keith was the second of three cricket-playing brothers, two of whom would all go on to represent Essex. Ian, born in 1961, was a fast-medium bowler who took 65 wickets during four seasons at Chelmsford between 1985 and 1988. The eldest, Kelvin, who was born in 1949, would play second eleven cricket for Essex but never make a first-class appearance. Keith and Ian are one of seven sets of siblings to pull on an Essex sweater. A talented all-rounder, Keith was arguably stronger with the willow than the leather, but still possessed the skills to make an impact in both disciplines. At the age of 26, he was also a more than useful fielder and grabbed 14 catches during that successful summer.

During the 1979 season, Pont's abilities were especially useful in one-day cricket. It said much for Pont's importance to the cause that on the 22 occasions on which he was called upon to bowl, he would finish the match wicketless only six times.

With the bat, Pont's late middle-order aggression was often just what the doctor ordered. Aside from a half-century in the final John Player League fixture of the season against Glamorgan at Chelmsford, he would pass 30 on six other occasions.

Undoubtedly the most important of those batting cameos came in the Benson and Hedges Cup semi-final against Yorkshire at the County Ground. With Essex chasing 174 for victory, Arnie Sidebottom and Graham Stevenson appeared to have the hosts in all kinds of trouble at 99 for four – the moment when Pont strode to the middle – 112 for five and 139 for six.

A short time later, Pont had made a vital 36 and Essex were on the brink of victory when he fell to Howard Cooper with the score on 169. Although the bowling of John Lever, Norbert Phillip and Ray East, who each took two wickets to restrict Yorkshire, and the batting of Graham Gooch, who made 49, had been important, Pont's heroics were just as crucial in carrying Essex to a Lord's showdown with Surrey.

In the championship, Pont would be picked in eleven of Essex's 21 matches (the other was abandoned). In those games, his return totalled eight wickets – a tally perhaps more due to the fact that he was under-utilised than any lack of skill – and 286 runs – his lowest total since 1974.

KEITH PONT: 'I would have liked to have bowled more. I swung the ball a lot when I first started bowling. As a young cricketer I hadn't played much one-day cricket and then when I started to I had to learn to bowl straighter instead of swinging it from wide of the crease. I ended up being someone who was straight up and down, and the art of swing went out of my repertoire fairly early in my career. I was a second change bowler and could come on and do well when needed. In one-day cricket I became the fifth bowler, but then Gooch would come on and bowl what I saw as crap, but that is my opinion. I didn't mind the idea of sitting back but it would get frustrating when you knew you could make a contribution.'

Among those 286 runs, however, was the important knock of 77 made at Chelmsford in the innings and 40 run victory over Derbyshire in mid-June. Pont would also make a defiant 59 against Middlesex at Colchester's Castle Park six weeks later, but it would not be enough to stop the champions-elect from succumbing to a crushing ten-wicket defeat.

KEITH PONT: 'I got to a point where I was wondering where my career was going. I was trying to do well and get in. The opportunity to move to another county in those days was far less than it is these days. I never wanted to play for anyone else, though. There were nods and winks for the potential for moving but you want to be with the county you grew up with. I took the easy option by staying with what I knew. Whether I was afraid to go to another county I don't know.'

Following his retirement from the first-class game in 1986, Pont took on the role as the ECB's director of development. However, his career might have taken such a different path, had his sense of humour been taken the wrong way.

KEITH PONT: 'I realise now what could have happened to my career. I could have been banned for life! It was at Burton-on-Trent during the time when Brian Taylor was captain, with nine people watching. There was this guy who was about 6ft 7ins and had this bike with the saddle up really high. He was sitting watching and I'd been going from third man to third man [at the end of every over]. I asked if there was any chance I could go to mid-on, and he said I had to carry on. I asked this guy if I could borrow his bike and he looked at me in disbelief and said yes. The over finished and off I went on the bike. I went around the pitch and I was just off the square when I was spotted. My studs got stuck in the chain and I went straight over the top of the handlebars. I rushed the bike back and it was mayhem on the field. I didn't get into trouble, though.

'We saw benefit matches as the chance to have some fun. When David Acfield bowled, I'd go and field outside the boundary. Then I'd move further back out of the ground, and, at Basildon one time, I went and fielded on the roundabout before climbing up a tree and waiting for a catch there.'

A talented gloveman, Neil Smith served his wicket-keeping apprenticeship with his home county of Yorkshire for four seasons, during which time he was a mainstay in the second eleven. Many Yorkshire members believed Smith would be the natural successor to Jimmy Binks, the former England Test player who kept wicket for the White Rose county for a decade and a half between 1955 and 1969. The 1970 season saw Smith given his big chance to emerge from Binks' shadow, but a shaky start saw him dropped from the Yorkshire side in favour of the 18-year-old David Bairstow. The latter established himself in the team and left Smith to seek his fortune – and a regular first eleven place – elsewhere. He chose Essex, making the move south in 1973 at the age of 24.

Ossett-born Smith replaced another county stalwart, Brian Taylor, at Chelmsford, quickly settling into life in the Essex dressing room. A larger-than-life character in more ways than one, the wicket-keeper quickly established himself as a reliable presence behind the stumps.

After recording 67 dismissals in his first two seasons with Essex, Smith was awarded his county cap in 1975 and celebrated with his most successful campaign with the gloves and the bat, taking 61 catches and five stumpings and hitting 695 runs at 26.73 in 22 first-class matches.

While his batting was never his strong point, powerful right-hander Smith was still a useful lower-order player who could hit the ball a long distance on occasion. As such, the wicket-keeper was sometimes promoted to the top of the order, particularly in one-day cricket. A career return of 4,187 runs at an average of 15.68 was a perfect illustration of Smith's somewhat hit-and-miss approach with the willow.

Moving on to the championship-winning season of 1979, Smith was his old consistent self with the gloves, completing a more than competent 59 dismissals in first-class cricket and a further 15 in the one-day game. While he was a consistent presence in the championship, Smith also had the pleasure of twice catching the great opening batsman Sunil Gavaskar during the visit of the touring Indians.

With the bat, one of the few high points of Smith's season came in the 99-run County Championship victory over Leicestershire at Chelmsford in mid-June. Batting at number eight, the wicket-keeper arrested a middle-order collapse by making an unbeaten 90 – passing 2,500 career first-class runs when he reached 23.

That innings would be one of three half-centuries he made that wonderful summer, the others coming against the Indians (65) and in a late-season championship fixture against Northamptonshire (63), both also coming at the County Ground.

Unfortunately for Smith, his time at the top of English cricket would not last as long as many of his team-mates'. A loss of form saw the Yorkshireman lose his place to David East in 1981. After captaining the second eleven for a season, he returned to his home county to go into business. Sadly, like his Essex career, Smith's life was also cut short. Cancer claimed the popular wicket-keeper's life at the age of 53 on 3 March 2003.

KEITH FLETCHER: 'He was a good keeper. In this day and age, he wouldn't get in, though, as he wasn't a good enough batter. These days you have to be a good number seven. He didn't play for us for that long. Unfortunately he lost his nerve. I didn't think you could get the yips keeping wicket but he did. When the ball came past the bat he blinked and if you are doing that too often you are going to drop the thing and he retired himself. He said "I can't do it". However, he took a fine catch, diving down the leg-side in the [Benson and Hedges Cup] final. It helped us win the game.'

Smith will be remembered as one of the 'Clouting Louts' as they were known. The group included himself, Norbert Phillip and Turner – batters lower down the order who knew how to hit a long ball.

STUART TURNER: 'It was a fair assessment. It was something that was started back then and someone would say "Send in the Clouting Louts". Our game was to get on with it. In fact, for two seasons I opened the batting in the John Player League to get us off to a flier. I was a pinch-hitter but I couldn't have been that bad a player because I got four first-class hundreds. I got them in a manner that probably wasn't for the purist but that was the way I played. I could defend if I had to but I liked to attack.

'I remember one game one year [in 1982] against Hampshire in the Benson and Hedges Cup when we couldn't qualify. We'd bowled them out for 130 and thought it would be a doddle. We were 14 for 6 when I went to the wicket and we won it. I got 55 not out and Ponty and David East helped. Malcolm Marshall was playing for them and we were expecting to get rolled over for 20-odd but we did it. I could bat, but did it in a slightly unorthodox manner.'

Essex's bowling line-up in 1979 was nothing short of formidable and it should come, in hindsight, as no surprise they were top of the pile come the end of the season. Essex were covered, in more than ample measures, both in seam bowling and spin. Depending on the weather and situation, the side was able to change to suit the need of the team, without weakening its strength.

Having two high-quality spinners is a feature few sides are lucky to possess in the modern era. India and other nations on the sub-continent are renowned for producing spinners, but in England it is increasingly rare to see two spinners bowl in tandem.

KEITH FLETCHER: 'We were fortunate we had two very good spinners. Easty, I think, was unlucky he never played international cricket. Derek Underwood was around [at Kent] at the time, Norman Gifford was around [at Worcestershire]. East was as good as Gifford and different to Underwood. David Acfield was very under-rated. He was a good bowler and you can tell they could bowl by the amount of wickets they took in their careers. Ackers was one of the best off-spinners around at the time. There were quite a few. Most sides had two spinners so there were quite a few good ones. When I had to choose between them I chose Easty because he could bat and he could field. He was a good catcher close to the wicket and was useful coming in at number eight or nine. The majority of batters were right handed, so he was always leaving the bat when he bowled. He was going to give you a little bit more. He was very amusing. He was funny and has a quick wit. He would blow hot and cold like all those sort of people. He didn't mind the odd bit of rain so he could sit and do nothing!

'East made [Lancashire's] Ken Shuttleworth laugh at Ilford once. He was a con-merchant and conned Ken. He walked past him when batting and told him to pitch it up and he would get him out no problem, and Ken pitched the first two up and Easty stroked them both through the covers for four. You can imagine Ken – steam was coming out of his ears. There was a lot of dust on the pitch and Easty knew what was coming next. He knew he was going to get a bouncer and he dived forwards into all this crap which was on the wicket and when he got up he was covered in dirt all over him. It was completely pre-meditated and Christ knows what would have happened if Ken had picked up on what Easty was going to do. The Lancashire players collapsed laughing and it was the only time I saw Ken laugh on the field.'

JOHN LEVER: 'What was interesting was Ray and David Acfield were totally different characters. They came from totally different backgrounds. The only thing they had in common was they bowled spin. Ackers was in and out of the side quite a bit. Fletch would choose one spinner so Ackers was left out. They roomed together all of their careers. Sometimes Ackers was slightly morose and quite rightly upset about being left out of the side. Him and Easty would argue. They would argue off the field and on it – about the fields they would have, one would have three around the bat, the other would have a man out and yet they would then have a couple of drinks afterwards and be off to bed together. They shared a room all the way through the time I played. There were those two spin bowlers going up the stairs having a ruck but still consoling each other about the plight of spin bowlers in England, the pitches, the captains, the people who don't understand them, the seamers who get it all their own way, and the umpires' decisions which always go against them. It was a really weird set-up.'

Educated at Brentwood School and Cambridge University, an Olympic fencer in Mexico City in 1968 and Munich in 1972, and a Commonwealth Games gold medallist at Edinburgh in 1970, David Acfield's talents were many and varied. Among them was the ability to spin a cricket ball, a capability he used to good effect during a 20-year career with Essex.

Born in Chelmsford in July 1947, Acfield joined the county of his birth while still an undergraduate at Cambridge. His debuts for both his university, where he earned Blues for both cricket and fencing, and Essex came in 1966. The off-spinner would play for Cambridge until the term ended before heading back down to Essex for the remainder of the season.

Following his graduation, Acfield was awarded his county cap in 1970, celebrating by taking five for 14 in a John Player League match at Northampton in July of that year. The continued presence of Robin Hobbs in the Essex side restricted the youngster's opportunities, but he would still produce consistent, probing bowling performances when called upon.

Hobbs' departure for Glamorgan in 1975 allowed Acfield to stake his claim for a regular position in the first eleven, and he did his cause no harm by taking eleven wickets in a championship match against Surrey at the Oval the following summer.

By the time the title-winning season of 1979 had come around, Ray East had replaced Hobbs as Acfield's main rival for a place in Keith Fletcher's side. Again, the former British sabre champion's chances were limited by a rival, but Acfield was a true clubman, never complaining about his lot.

It was therefore no surprise that, when called upon, Acfield often produced the goods. When Lancashire visited Valentine's Park, Ilford, in early June, he did not bowl a single ball in the first innings as the Red Rose county were skittled out for just 84. Lancashire were asked to follow-on and, from 75 for two, were reduced to 123 all out in the main by Acfield's four for eleven.

At Colchester in the final week of July, Acfield was at it again. Having taken 2 for 4 as Gloucestershire succumbed for just 92 in their first innings, the off-spinner ripped out the visitors' middle-order second time round, taking 6 for 56 in a mammoth 40-over spell as Essex sneaked home by four wickets.

Aside from the accurate bowling that saw him take 855 first-class wickets for his county, a seldom-appreciated part of Acfield's game was his dogged batting. Although he would record a top-score of just 38 in his long career, many of the regular number eleven's innings formed part of important last-wicket partnerships.

The 1979 season was no different. A second innings stand of 42 with Stuart Turner against Nottinghamshire at Southend in mid-July set Essex up to complete a 46-run victory, with Acfield taking 5 for 28. The following match, an innings and 33 runs thrashing of Hampshire at Bournemouth, Acfield would add 40 with centurion Brian Hardie before taking another five second innings wickets.

DAVID ACFIELD: 'In terms of my fencing career I probably went on too long. For the sake of my cricket career, I probably should have stopped after the 1968 Olympics. I played three games that season and then in 1972 I played half the season and then packed up and went to the Olympics in Munich. It wasn't really ideal for being a professional cricketer, and you have to remember that I wasn't a professional anyway. I was an amateur [to enable me to fence at the Olympics] and was getting married in 1972 and I needed to be able to pay my mortgage. So I needed to go professional and there was never a doubt that I would turn to cricket eventually.

'I don't really know why I continued to fence but I'm pleased that I did because in 1968 I had never won the British [sabre] championship. I then won it in 1969, 1970, 1971 and 1972, and that's probably what kept me going. Nobody had ever won it four times on the trot. By the time I had got to the Olympics in 1972, though, I wasn't enjoying it as much. I had just gone on too long so there was never a choice. It was always going to be cricket before too long.

'In 1973 we [Acfield and East] both took 40-odd wickets and we were tipped to go to the West Indies but, in my case, they picked [Leicestershire's] Jack Burkinshaw and [Surrey's] Pat Pocock. The next year, 1974, I hardly played a game because Robin Hobbs was there and Keith said we couldn't play three spinners. So I hardly played in 1974 and 1975. I had just got married and got a mortgage and had been capped and suddenly I was left out of the side. It was hard work, very hard work. I stuck at it. Nowadays I'd probably have left but in those days we didn't think about leaving.'

Acfield's spin partner in 1979, Ray East, was considered one of the most popular characters in county cricket. Many humorous stories have been gathered over the years of East's japes around the Essex camp, often getting up to mischief during the hours of play and even, at times, while bowling himself. On a day when skipper Keith Fletcher had preferred to use his seamers rather than East's spin, he was finally called upon to bowl and yelled his name to the scorers, as if they didn't know, like in club cricket. He is also, to this day, an effective impersonator of well-known players.

RAY EAST: 'The Essex crowd either loved or hated me. I'd like to think the majority loved me. It would go wrong being the joker as they expected me to do things. Occasionally you'd get it wrong – you'd get out or drop a catch, not that I dropped many. Sometimes they would say "That bloody idiot East". Some thought I didn't play for England because I messed about. I don't agree with that. It was the only way I could play the game.'

JOHN LEVER: 'The car backfiring at Ilford when he fell down was my favourite Ray East moment. He got into his delivery stride and a car went down Cranbrook Road and backfired and he just went down in a heap. There was a deathly hush around the ground. It seemed like a long time but was only a second or two, and then everyone couldn't stop laughing and started clapping. The batsmen and umpires didn't have a clue what was going on.'

There was more to East than his wit, though, and his slow left-arm bowling brought more than 1,000 wickets for the Essex-born joker. His early years were spent playing village cricket for Brantham, where it was recommended to him that he try and forge a career in the game. After time spent in the second eleven, his first-team debut arrived in 1965. During the following season he began to impress enough to have a sustained role in both the championship and John Player League. Against Worcestershire in 1968 he recorded fantastic match figures of 15 for 115. During the next summer, the New Zealanders were on the wrong end of East's spinning mastery when he took 8 for 68 at Westcliff. It was during this season that he produced two of his best one-day performances, taking 5 for 18 against Worcestershire at Harlow and 6 for 18 against Yorkshire at Hull, both in the John Player League.

In 1972 he also made a mark with the bat, scoring 89 not out against Worcestershire at Leyton. He made it into the record books in 1982 when putting on a record tenth-wicket partnership of 81 with Stuart Turner in the NatWest Trophy. His one and only first-class century arrived in 1976 when he scored 113 against Hampshire at Chelmsford.

East's best ever season came in 1978 when he took 92 wickets in what was his benefit year. 1979 was not so prolific for East, who took 43 wickets in first-class games – two more than Acfield, but at an average of 30 with only one five-wicket haul.

Essex's success may have been built around the prowess of their seam bowlers, but the spin duo of Acfield and East were a steadying influence, and the latter was able to assert himself more than his rival and room-mate in the one-day game, taking 24 wickets at 15 apiece. A hat-trick in a Test trial was the closest he came to earning England honours, despite being instrumental in Essex's rise to glory.

RAY EAST: 'I believe I didn't play because of Derek Underwood. He was a fantastic bowler. If he hadn't have been around I'm sure I would have played for England, not being big headed. Then there was Norman Gifford and other left-arm spinners, who I felt I was as good as. Maybe they looked at me and said "That idiot, he doesn't concentrate and he might do this and he might do that". Apparently I'm in *Wisden*'s top 50 players never to play for England.

'Lever should have played more. If he had another half a yard or yard more pace he would have played triple the amount of games. Essex were overlooked a bit. If you played for Middlesex you played for England. There were some extraordinary players who played for Middlesex and went on to play for England because they played at Lord's.' East later went on to captain the Essex second eleven before moving into teaching at Ipswich School.

John Kenneth 'JK' Lever was one of the best bowlers ever to pull on an Essex sweater. In his 23 years with the county, Lever took an almost unfathomable 1,462 first-class wickets at a miserly average of just 23.49 apiece. A left-arm fast-medium exponent with a smooth, almost casual approach to the crease, the Stepney-born seamer was equally effective in both first-class and one-day cricket.

After making his Essex debut as an 18-year-old in 1967, Lever was awarded his county cap three years later. It would not be long afterwards that he would start showing the form that would earn him 21 Test caps for England and lead Essex to their first County Championship in 1979.

A super-fit, ever-willing team player who was eager to bowl in any conditions, Lever stated his intentions by taking 5 for 8 to bowl Middlesex out for just 41 in a Gillette Cup second round fixture in 1972. That same summer, he recorded figures of 5 for 18 against Warwickshire at Edgbaston in the John Player League. Those two performances were the shape of things to come.

Lever was a prolific wicket-taker in one, three and, for England, five-day cricket. In 1975, he would take 85 first-class wickets, followed by another 70 the following season. That form earned him a Test debut against India in Delhi the week before Christmas 1976. Lever's impact would be both immediate and spectacular.

While fellow debutant Graham Barber, the Middlesex batsman, was dismissed for a fifth-ball duck, Lever removed all six of the Indian top-order en route to figures of 7 for 46. That return was the best ever recorded by an Englishman playing in his Test debut. Lever's record stood until Derbyshire's Dominic Cork took 7 for 43 against the West Indies at Lord's in June 1995. Accusations, denied, by the Indians that Lever used Vaseline to aid the shine on the ball have done nothing to diminish his reputation as a swing bowler of the highest order. For good measure, Lever would take 3 for 24 in the second innings to complete what turned out to be career-best Test match figures of 10 for 70. His efforts helped England to victory by an innings and 25 runs. Lever would finish the series with 26 wickets at just 14.61. In total Lever would go on to take 73 Test wickets at a very respectable 26.72 apiece. He would also play 22 one-day internationals, taking a further 24 wickets at just under 30.

Back at Chelmsford, the 1977 season would bring a further 58 first-class wickets, but it was 1978 when Lever's left arm went into overdrive. That summer brought 106 wickets at an astonishing average of just 15.18. The achievement made Lever the first Essex bowler to take 100 first-class wickets in a season since Brian Edmeades 12 years earlier, and also saw him named as one of *Wisden*'s five Cricketers of the Year.

DAVID ACFIELD: 'If we played on a flat wicket, JK swung it. I remember one year at Gloucester that no one had got any wickets for two days but suddenly one evening he swung it and if he could swing it they couldn't play it. Left-arm over is always a wonderful thing to have if you can swing the ball because right-handed batsmen would always plant their feet. If you can swing it in, most batsmen have a trigger movement forward in English conditions and they plant their feet in front of middle-and-off and he'd trap them LBW.'

STUART TURNER: 'He [Lever] was an athlete and a fine bowler. I don't think there have been many better left-armers with a greater variety. Possibly, he should have played more for England. There was the unfortunate moment when he was accused of cheating in India and he came back from that and whenever we played Northampton he'd come up against Bishen Bedi. Bishen was one of them who accused him of using Vaseline, and it was wrong of him to say that. He was a very genuine number eleven and whenever he came to the wicket when John was bowling no prisoners were taken. It really upset John because he was a man of integrity and it just wasn't him. It was sad that it all came out.'

Into the title-winning summer of 1979 and the irrepressible paceman, now past his 30th birthday, was showing no signs of slowing down. A further 106 first-class wickets followed – each costing a miserly 17.30 – as Lever led from the front yet again.

In successive championship matches – against Leicestershire at Chelmsford and Warwickshire at Edgbaston in mid-June – Lever took 13 wickets in each. On two other occasions – in the visit of Lancashire to Ilford in early June and the trip to Bournemouth to take on Hampshire in late July – he would take seven wickets in a single innings.

That glorious year also saw Lever in scintillating form in one-day cricket. A further 43 wickets were taken at 14.34 apiece as Essex lifted the Benson and Hedges Cup. It was therefore fitting that it was Lever who claimed the wicket, bowling Surrey number eleven Peter Wilson, to clinch the trophy at Lord's on 21 July.

On Lever's retirement at the end of the 1989 season, the man who selected him for that unforgettable Test debut – the former Surrey and England seamer Sir Alec Bedser – paid him a fitting tribute in the *Colchester Evening Gazette*, a newspaper in which Lever wrote an entertaining weekly column.

'John was a 100 per cent performer, a fine fellow and a real trier. He wasn't the quickest of pacemen, but he had all the main attributes to be a good bowler. His attitude was exemplary, similar to mine. An attitude I regard as more on the old-fashioned lines, willing to do anything, not afraid of hard work. He was always amenable, a good team man, who was ever willing to offer advice and help to those around him. And as an England tourist he was second to none. I never ever heard him complain and he was a real pleasure to be with – a truly fine fellow.'

The expectation was there in the stands whenever Lever had the ball in his hand, according to Francis Ponder.

'The expectancy level, like with Gooch and McEwan scoring runs, was there when Lever was bowling. Whenever Gooch went to the crease we in the crowd thought he was going to get a ton. Likewise, when Lever had the ball in his hand, he was the strike bowler and we thought he was going to be among the wickets. Nine times out of ten he was. He was great to watch because he had such a lovely rhythmic action. His whole action, from the start of his run-up to his delivery was just right for a fast bowler. It slotted into place perfectly. He spoiled us as fans.

'I'm not sure he struck fear into the hearts of the opposition batsmen in the way Sylvester Clarke [of Surrey] did. There were players like him who you could see terrified them. Lever wasn't a bowler who trundled in and did the same thing. He varied his pace and while he didn't have a fearsome bouncer, the line was always right. I never saw him all over the place.'

Lever comprised one half of an opening bowling attack that would give opening batsmen sleepless nights, the other half being Norbert Phillip. Expectations were not the highest when Phillip came in, according to Francis Ponder. Spoilt by the brilliance of fellow West Indian Keith Boyce, Essex fans wondered what they could expect from Phillip.

'Who was Norbert Phillip when he came in?' said Ponder. 'He was just a West Indies all-rounder who wasn't particularly quick but became another typically good Essex signing. We had been used to seeing Essex open the bowling with John Lever and Stuart Turner, but it had become John Lever and Norbert Phillip with Stuart Turner coming on first change. Lever must have been good for him as he was so accurate and a left-armer as well. It must have got him a few wickets.'

West Indian Phillip's arrival at Chelmsford owed much to the Test and County Cricket Board's decision to turn down Essex's bid to sign New Zealand star Richard Hadlee for the second half of the 1977 season. The TCCB insisted that for the Kiwi all-rounder to join Essex, the county would have to offer him a three-year contract – an option the club turned down.

With Essex's plans to recruit Hadlee scuppered, Phillip himself expressed a tentative interest in joining as an alternative. While he was clearly not in the same class as the New Zealander, taking 28 Test wickets to Hadlee's 431, the Dominica-born player was still a more than handy performer with both bat and ball.

Despite his impressive displays for both the Windward Islands and Combined Islands over the preceding decade, Phillip would arrive at Essex in 1978 as a virtual unknown.

Had fellow West Indian Keith Boyce not been forced to retire from injury in 1977, Phillip may never have pulled on an Essex sweater. But while Boyce was much-loved by Essex fans after numerous explosive performances, which made him one of the most exciting cricketers in the country during the 1970s, Phillip filled the void with gusto. He quickly won over his team-mates and the county's members, however, scoring 645 runs and taking 71 wickets in first-class cricket during his first summer in England. Among his most notable performances that season was a brutal innings of 134 against Gloucestershire containing seven sixes and 12 fours.

1978 also saw Phillip make his Test debut for the West Indies, taking six wickets as an opening bowler in a thrilling three-wicket defeat to Australia in Georgetown, Guyana. He would go on to play nine Tests for his country, taking 28 wickets and scoring 297 runs with a highest score of 47 against India in Calcutta in December of the same year.

Into 1979 and Phillip returned to Essex in decent all-round form. He would take a further 70 first class and 27 one-day wickets with the ball, while adding 521 runs in all forms of the game with the bat. The all-rounder's finest performances of that unforgettable season occurred against Derbyshire. In the first meeting between the two sides, Phillip took 5 for 23 as Essex's opponents were thrashed by an innings and 171 runs at Chesterfield. Then, in mid-June, he returned four wickets in each innings as the visitors were routed by an innings and 40 runs at Chelmsford.

Phillip also took eight wickets in the match as Sussex were defeated by ten wickets at Southend in early July. With the bat, his highest first-class score of the summer came with 66 against Surrey at Chelmsford on 25 August.

Of all of the 15 players to line up for Essex during their inaugural championship-winning season, Gary Sainsbury was the least heralded and the least used. Sainsbury, a left-arm medium pacer and right-handed lower-order batsman, turned 21 in January 1979. The Ilford-born bowler had made his second eleven championship debut against Sussex at the little-known Hoffman's Sports and Social Club Ground in August 1977. The following year, he would make a further six second eleven championship appearances, returning figures of 5 for 43 against Sussex at Hove in his final innings of the summer.

In 1979 Sainsbury found himself behind fellow left-armer Lever, overseas star Phillip, and all-rounders Stuart Turner and Keith Pont in the queue of seam bowlers at captain Fletcher's disposal. Indeed, even the gentle swing of Graham Gooch would be chosen ahead of young Sainsbury.

As such, it came as no surprise that first eleven opportunities hardly added up to much for the Bath University statistics graduate. By the end of the season, he had totted up just one first-class appearance and, even then, Essex had already wrapped up the title by the time Sainsbury was handed his solitary chance to impress.

That opportunity came with the visit of Northamptonshire to Chelmsford on the final three days of August. On his first-class debut, Sainsbury delivered 12 wicketless overs in the first innings as Wayne Larkins and Allan Lamb made hay in the late summer sunshine at the County Ground. The young bowler at least had the catch of Robert Carter off the bowling of Acfield to celebrate.

Essex declared before number eleven Sainsbury had the chance to bat and so it came to Northamptonshire's second innings for the former Beal High School pupil to stake his claim. It took him just a handful of deliveries to take his first championship wicket, trapping Geoff Cook LBW with the score on just five. The visitors subsided to 137 all out and Essex went on to win by five wickets, but Sainsbury's chance had come and gone in the space of three days.

During the same season, Sainsbury took 41 wickets in just eleven second eleven championship matches at a miserly average of 20.07 apiece. The following summer, 1980, Sainsbury would again play just one championship match and this time he fared rather better. However, a return of 4 for 80 in the first innings against Surrey at The Oval could not stop Essex slumping to a ten-wicket defeat. It would be his last first-class appearance in the county's colours.

Sainsbury had to make do with Second eleven and Under-25s cricket in 1981 and 1982 before leaving Chelmsford for pastures new. He would join Gloucestershire in 1983 and ended his first-class career in 1987.

Keith Fletcher (centre) discusses field placings with Stuart Turner and Ray East

Chapter Three

April 1979

The big names were in place, but the faces had to fit in the dressing room. Thankfully, they did just that, with the camaraderie making cricket a joy, not a chore for the players.

DAVID ACFIELD: 'We did have a great team spirit and great fun. I just cannot believe some of the stuff we got away with – things like JK bowling an orange at [Yorkshire's] Brian Close with the first ball after lunch. It was just absolutely crazy. Ray Illingworth said that we'd never win anything and that we were mad, but through the madness we were also quite good. It was fun and the team are all still great friends. We get together and just sit in the corner and talk about cricket. We have dinner parties and the wives sit at one end of the table and we sit at the other. They know we're going to talk about cricket and we don't want to talk about shopping so it's fine.

'We grew up together at the end of the 1960s. Keith, myself, JK, Ray and Stuart were all there then and then "Lager" [Brian Hardie] and Neil Smith came in during the 1970s. The nucleus of the side grew up together in the 1960s when we only had 12 players on the staff. I think that forged the team spirit. We lost a few players along the way, like Robin Hobbs, who was a real character and the ringleader in many respects, and Brian Edmeades, but people came in to replace them. Norbert Phillip came in to replace Keith Boyce and Ken McEwan came in and fitted in perfectly. A lot of us were Essex people and we had grown up and played together. That was it. You can't make team spirit. We were happy all the time. Somehow we just gelled.'

BRIAN HARDIE: 'They had all come through under Brian Taylor and were known as Tonker's Tigers at the time. It was in the John Player League that they had made their mark. They were all local and all good cricketers. Myself and Neil Smith, who had come down from Yorkshire, fitted in well in the dressing room. I fitted in quite easily. There wasn't any coldness towards the outsiders at all. I stayed down in Essex when I finished playing. I could have gone back to Scotland but I chose not to. Stuart Turner and I lived close to one another and these were the days before sponsored cars, so we drove the kit van. We used to stop at transport cafes and got on very well together, as we still do now.'

RAY EAST: 'Ray Illingworth was captain at Leicestershire in 1979 and he was overheard saying we had too many idiots and would never win the championship. I don't know who he was referring to – it might have been me. We were all characters. I got the blame for all sorts of things – like riding the bike, which wasn't me [it was Keith Pont]. On the radio and in the media it was me who had done something. We had great camaraderie in the dressing room and on the pitch. We were second to none. Every team was envious of what we had. They had cliques but we didn't. You went out in the evening and didn't know who you would go out with – it was whoever wanted to go. We had great players but when they are all pulling together and you enjoy each other's company it has to be an asset.'

KEITH FLETCHER: 'We had a great team spirit. It is easier to have a great team spirit when you are winning than when you lose. We would all meet in the bar on a Tuesday night if we were playing Wednesday, Thursday, Friday at, say, Edgbaston and just drink together. It wasn't pre-arranged, everyone would just meet up and have a few drinks.

'Half a dozen would go for an Indian, a few others would go for a Chinese. It was magnificent. We were all great friends. I find it strange these days that the players turn up in tracksuits at some ungodly hour, practice, play the game, shower and go home. They never mix with the opposition. However tough the game was, I would always be down in the bar and would say to the opposition captain I would see him in there so both sides would end up in there and spend 45 minutes chatting and enjoying each other's company.

'There was good-hearted banter on the pitch. I played against [Yorkshire and England fast bowler] Fred Trueman in my early days and he was never nasty, not what he said to you. There was no nastiness in 1979. What you hear from the wicketkeepers these days would have driven me barmy. If Smithy was doing that I would have soon told him to shut up because he would have been getting on my nerves and I don't think it is right. When we were around the bat and the spinners were bowling I was close to the bat and we were always saying things but not nasty things. It was just chat. The batsman would say he was going to hit the ball at me and I'd say it doesn't matter if he does because he doesn't hit it hard enough.'

JOHN LEVER: 'There was always that humour. The humour in the side, with certain people like Easty, who quite rightly was given the name of being a real card, but there was so much in there. Ponty, Ackers, they were all bloody funny people and you do need that because it is a tough ask.'

GRAHAM GOOCH: 'There was a retired judge called Maurice Barclay and his wife Elaine who used to take all the players out but there was a pecking order. There was a middle crew that I was in. The judge used to follow us around and stay in all the posh hotels and he'd invite Fletch, Ackers and Kenny out. They loved Kenny. He could do no wrong. There was a middle group of myself and Neil Smith and then the "Louts" of Easty, Ponty, Stuart Turner and Brian Hardie. They would have a few pints and a burger and chips!'

It is interesting to note that five of the players from the 1979 squad have gone on to become teachers. Their knowledge and appreciation of the game has been passed on to youngsters around the county.

STUART TURNER: 'I don't know why we've all got into teaching. I've been lucky that throughout my working life I've done things that I enjoy and get paid for it. I got the job at Forest in 1986 and I've been there 23 years now. I just fell on my feet. Initially it was as the head of cricket but Forest wanted to integrate me into the whole school life, meaning I took football and hockey in the winter and taught PE. I did that and I've had an absolute ball. John followed me and went to Bancroft's, then Brian at Brentwood and Easty is now involved at Ipswich School, as is Mike McEvoy at Colchester Royal Grammar. The games we have against each other are always good for banter. We used to have the better of Bancroft's but it's evened itself out now. It's certainly funny how it's all worked out.'

With cricketer's pay not covering their living expenses all through the year in the 1970s, they were forced to find jobs in the winter to pay the bills. Essex's future heroes were no different.

BRIAN HARDIE: 'I did various things. I went back up to Scotland for a couple of winters and did a labouring job, then I managed to get myself a job with a credit card company in London. Then I did what a lot of cricketers do and I went overseas and played in New Zealand for two winters. At that time, my benefit year was coming round so I stopped that for a year, then after that had finished I went back out to play in New Zealand for a couple more years. Being a county pro was a job whereby you had to work in the winters. You didn't earn enough during the season to last all year, but that wasn't a bad thing. I think we all enjoyed our experiences in the winters. I was fairly naturally fit myself and it wasn't until my last six or so years that I needed to work to get myself ready for the start of the season. Having said that, some people were fit to play cricket and some weren't. People talk about you needing to be physically fit to be mentally fit but I think, collectively, we were mentally strong.

'In my first season with Essex, I was playing against Kent and Colin Cowdrey was coming towards the end of his career. I'd always thought he was a fairly large gentleman but he seemed to be quite alert at the end of the day, whereas I was flagging because I wasn't used to fielding for six hours. He had been doing it for his whole career. He was match-fit and was able to last.'

RAY EAST: 'We had to work. Now there are opportunities to coach and play cricket all over the world but we had to find numerous jobs – some of them strange and you had to take what you could get. Lever and I had a winter of driving cars around for a firm. It was quite an experience watching Lever pass me on the road. We had to go to Edinburgh once and I had a brand new Rover, which in those days was a smart car, and Lever had a 1300 Avenger. He kept passing me. I looked at my speedometer and I'd be doing 70mph and he would be flying past. We were running these new cars in doing I don't know what speeds.

'I worked for a chap called Eddie Gray in Ilford and that was gluing parts on to table tops and I had been there two weeks when someone said I must wear my gloves at all times as the glue will wipe out your fingers. I thought that's a good occupation for a spinner to have!'

KEITH FLETCHER: 'I worked selling fuel to farmers and different places. I did it for 20 years. Even if I went on tour and got back in February I'd still go and do it for a month. The mortgage had to be paid so I had to work.'

JOHN LEVER: 'The money was pretty horrendous. If you had a family and didn't work in the winter you would struggle. We could not really get people back before the end of March but if they were away playing cricket that was fine.'

DAVID ACFIELD: 'I was a teacher. I taught every winter. My first job when I left Cambridge was as an insurance broker in the West End but that was because my boss was at the top of British fencing. I then became a teacher for two terms every year and got sacked every April and reinstated in September! I had an understanding headteacher at Rainsford School in Chelmsford.'

STUART TURNER: 'I had to work during the winters and I did all sorts. I was a milkman, a postman and all kinds of other things. Fletch was working for an oil company. One winter I was on the dole and didn't have a job. It was always difficult, particularly when I was bringing up a young family. In the winter 1975-76 I went to South Africa for the first of two winters as I'd got a coaching job and that was fantastic. They were hard times, but most of us wanted to play so badly we did whatever we could. Things improved in 1978 and then in 1979 when we started winning things and the support was coming in. With my benefit year and the improved salaries I did ok.'

The first team squad reported for training with Ray East the only playing member missing because of an injury picked up, of all things, playing football!

RAY EAST: 'I played football in the winter for Woods in the Essex and Suffolk Border League. I liked my football and was injured taking a free-kick. I changed my mind – I was going to chip it into the box and saw the goalkeeper off his line and tried to drive the ball in and pulled a muscle in my quads.'

The players showed their appetite for a good season as they made sure their fitness levels were high. While the predictable pre-season rains stopped them training outdoors for a period, the squad sought the indoor facilities to ensure techniques were honed and eyes were well and truly on the ball.

JOHN LEVER: 'I was in charge of training in those days and I was always keen on fitness and running, as was Goochie, and I took the ideas we had from the England set-up and brought them back to Essex. I was not the most popular guy at times but I thought it was important. It certainly helped me play as long as I did. We had a normal pre-season. We have always been lucky enough to have top, top groundsmen down there [at Chelmsford] who keep the ends of the square dry so we could have our pre-season there and bowl lots of overs on pitches you are going to start off on at the start of the season. I did worry about going overseas and playing on hard bouncy wickets and then coming back and finding your first game is, say, Northampton, where it is not going to bounce shin high. You get frustrated. Then the nets we bowl in, the batsman is on top most of the time and you get used to bowling a good line and a good length.

'Pre-season in those days saw us go for a sandwich in the local pub and the committee would pop in and Doug Insole would put his head around the door and say "Good luck" and give encouraging words like "If it means winning the game or walking off if you have nicked it, we as a committee would rather you walked off," which is pretty strong stuff really. He wouldn't stand there and say "Why the **** did you edge it?" They didn't make you feel under pressure. They were very much for playing the game in the right way and producing England players. Tom Pearce would also come in and make a flippant remark and walk through to the Gents and he was a lovely man who everyone respected. We weren't happy with the money we were getting but the answer from their side was if you win things you will earn money, which was part of the incentive as well.'

RAY EAST: 'Being the fittest, John Lever got the job as our trainer. There were always three of us at the back – myself, Neil Smith and Ackers. They didn't like it and I wasn't a fan of it. One of Ackers' famous statements was if someone hits the ball three miles we were the first team to get it back. When Neil Foster joined us after 1979 he would be at the front whenever we went on a run and with about half a mile to go JK would say "find your way back in your own time and push it". Foster was miles in front and showing off. Ackers would be moaning about the young pup showing him up, saying it's about bowling the ball and not being able to run three miles. When we get back someone says "Where's Foster?" and he was in with the physio, which was more ammunition for Ackers!'

DAVID ACFIELD: 'I couldn't see the point in it. I hated running. I never broke down and was just naturally fit anyway. I was fencing for Britain and was doing seven-days-a-week anyway. I didn't want to go running anywhere. I hated running and I still do. I don't believe in it. What annoyed me most was all these superstars who could run up and down and then, the minute they got on the cricket field, they were injured. Get out and play was my philosophy.

'I think you have to have a mental block to be able to run. You need to be able to switch off and I can't switch off. I think you've got to be fit for cricket but what annoys me about the modern-day players is that they are not getting fit for the game. They are always injured. That always annoyed me when I was chairman of Essex and continues to annoy me as a member of the committee and chairman of cricket. I would always sit in the committee room and they would say this player is injured and they'd look at me and I'd say "Don't wind me up again. I'm sure he can run three miles but he can't bowl two overs". I get very annoyed with it. I lost interest in running. They used to go running in Central Park [in Chelmsford] but I soon got fed up with that.

'We used to run halfway around Writtle or something and then have a net, but there was never any doubt that we'd be going down to the Orange Tree for a couple of pints. I'm not anti-fitness but it's not for me. If I wanted to get fit, I'd do it by bowling. I really believe that you can't get fit for bowling by doing anything other than bowling. People forget that when I was at Cambridge I used to bowl 52 overs on the trot. It's the mental thing that matters – concentration. I don't believe that fitness enables you to keep your concentration at all, it's a mental thing. The number of times I have talked to young bowlers and they say "I was trying this or trying that" and I say to them "Just bowl and keep the batsman under pressure". I wasn't very good but I could bowl straight and that was it. That's what you have to do. Concentration is crucial but I don't think people concentrate on the mental side of the game. It's all about repeating the action.'

STUART TURNER: 'We used to do lots of shuttle runs and sprints and finish off with five-a-side football. We were told to take it easy so nobody got injured but I can tell you that it used to get fairly heated. Everyone got stuck in.'

Alcohol was not the evil it is today in professional sport. Players would frequently have a social drink among themselves and with supporters, chatting about the day's play without the press seeking a sensational 'boozing' story.

BRIAN HARDIE: 'Myself and Stuart were always the first ones to arrive at the ground. We were two of the guys who were naturally fit but we liked to warm-up longer than anyone. If there was a thought that someone had enjoyed themselves too much, Fletch would tell you and you would go and prove him wrong. We all pulled for each other and had respect for one another. We had to be there to do the donkey work for the thoroughbreds in the team like Lever and Phillip.'

JOHN LEVER: 'We certainly picked our times for enjoying ourselves. If we had a good day in the field and bowled a side out then the bowlers tended to have a few beers. God knows what they'd think about it now. The bottom line was, if you were fit to do your job the next day then that was fine. Turning up at the ground and wanting to be there was a big part of it. The opposition see you turn up and we were all joking and laughing – most of the time, not all of the time – and there was that sort of happy feeling. It was David Lloyd who said we turn up, laugh and joke and enjoy the game and next thing you know we have gone away with 24 points. A lot of sides thought we were a bit too much of a clown side. At the end of the day we had a balanced side that could bowl a side out on any wicket. That was the name of the game.'

While drinking was part of the culture of county cricket in the late 1970s, some of Essex's more refined playing members also enjoyed the finer things in life. Acfield, Denness and captain Fletcher earned a reputation for seeking out the finest restaurant in whichever town or city Essex were playing. The others, meanwhile, would be happy to make do with a takeaway.

and then put down a mark. He came in with this high knee lift, which helped him adjust his stride so he got to the crease at the right place. He swung it yards, with a low arm. I used to get slightly annoyed with him because he used to undercut the ball a bit so it would land on the shiny side but he still swung it. I'd be working hard on the ball at one end, and Fletch would be too, and there is Norbert hitting the shiny side and he got wickets. He was fit, he was not really a drinker. He'd go to bed fairly early.

'We have always been lucky with our overseas players but he was probably one of the few who did not really mix in with all the other Essex players. We had Keith Boyce, who was very much part of the whole set-up and I think that was one very poignant moment, that when we won something, Boycie wasn't there. He was Essex through and through, and a lot of players felt that. But in the end, injury took him out of the game.'

The John Player League campaign got off on the right foot, although the first hour of the match would have suggested otherwise. Essex, who preferred Lilley at the top of the order ahead of Denness to face Warwickshire, were in a slight pickle at 87 for 4 by the end of the 25th over. Gooch made 33, but it was left to Hardie and Pont to help post a respectable total. Hardie finished on 48, passing 2,000 runs in one-day cricket in the process, while Pont hit 29, in a partnership of 69 in ten overs. Hardie's score turned out to be the highest of the match. Dennis Amiss and David Smith put on 47 for the first wicket but they had been slow in compiling their runs, notching only 17 in the first ten overs. East broke the stand and showed fine accuracy and control to take 3 for 20. Pont also took three wickets to emerge with a fine all-round display, helping Essex to a 15-run victory. Warwickshire's lack of batting depth was left showing, as Lever finished with figures of 2 for 15 off 8 overs and Acfield also got in on the act.

The result provided great encouragement to Essex, particularly in comparison to the previous season when the weather had wrecked their chances in the competition during the opening few weeks.

Fletcher, in his weekly column in the *Essex Chronicle*, said he was always confident his side was going to win the match: 'Ironically, others suffered on Sunday, while we managed to get in a full afternoon's cricket. Conditions were not ideal; the wicket was slow and turning a bit. In the circumstances our batters got a reasonable score. Brian Hardie's form was especially pleasing and, with the ball, Keith Pont did as well as anybody. Certainly he conceded some runs when Warwickshire were chasing hard in the latter stages, but overall he did well. In fact, it was a most impressive all-round team performance.'

Fletcher believed team unity was required, together with players in the side who could pop up with a match-winning performance, even if others had missed out. He felt these qualities were present in the Essex squad, and seeing them on show against Warwickshire provided a morale booster. The Essex skipper was pleased with the effort shown during the run-up and beginning of the season, as they demonstrated they meant business. He expected competition for places to hot up in the coming weeks, when Phillip arrived from the West Indies to give extra penetration.

The new season saw former Essex leg-spinner Robin Hobbs begin his stint as skipper at Glamorgan. Hobbs had disappeared from the first-class scene a couple of years earlier and it was a surprise to many when he re-appeared as captain of the Welsh county.

Fletcher aired his own views on captaincy to the *Essex Chronicle*. 'Captaincy is something which needs some time to get used to, and I think that it took me two or three years before getting a real grip on the job. But the involvement is fascinating and of course, skippering a side is particularly enjoyable when you have a winning outfit.'

John Lever was a match-winner in all conditions, although the early-season weather caused him to wrap up warm against the elements

Chapter Four

May 1979

Essex began their Schweppes County Championship campaign against Kent on 2 May at Chelmsford. It was an opportunity to see which of last season's top two sides was likely to be challenging near the top this time around. It also gave Essex the chance to gain a psychological boost if they could beat the team which had pipped them eight months previously.

Phillip landed in England from the West Indies and, on reporting to the county at Chelmsford, declared himself fit and ready to play. Essex named a 14-man squad, including McEvoy, Lilley and East, who would subsequently miss out. The champions were without Pakistan World Cup captain Asif Iqbal.

In freezing conditions, Essex won the toss and decided to bat before making slow progress. Showers restricted the day's play to 49 overs, during which Denness made 37, Gooch 13, and McEwan 20. The players pulled out their woolly sweaters to brace themselves against the biting wind, as Essex finished the day, brought to a close early by rain, on 128 for 3.

However, the second day started disastrously for Essex. Fletcher (41) and Hardie (13) departed after adding just one run to the overnight total. Hardie went in the morning's third over when a flier from Richard Hills caught the edge of his bat and gave Chris Tavare a catch in the slips. It was the same combination which ended Fletcher's innings, leaving Essex on the brink at 129 for 5. From here, Essex could either have crumpled, or produced a fight-back of the kind performed by sides which become champions.

It was Turner they had to thank for getting them out of the sticky situation. He smashed a brilliant hundred before lunch to lead the recovery, aided by Phillip and Pont. Kent's hopes of running through the remaining batsmen were shattered when Pont and Turner went on the offensive. Pont lived dangerously against the wily Underwood, but was able to bring up the first boundary of the day. Then Turner marked his intentions, hitting Hills for a straight six. Pont followed suit, lifting Underwood over long-on, the ball landing a couple of feet short of the fence. Underwood had been hit out of the attack, and the introduction of Kevin Jarvis, rather than slowing Essex down, only made the scoring rate accelerate. Turner took 16 off Jarvis's first over, including two fours and another six. The 50-partnership arrived within 40 minutes.

West Indian John Shepherd replaced Hills and the runs continued to flow freely. Pont hit him to the leg boundary and Turner then hit Jarvis for two more fours, bringing up the 200 in the 69th over. The stand was worth 75 in 50 minutes when Pont was caught at slip by Bob Woolmer when trying to drive Shepherd, for a valuable 33.

KEITH PONT: 'I saw myself as the glue. There were these world-class players but it is the mortar which holds the bricks together. I had to go in at the end of innings and do my bit but I was never the focus of attention.

'I would say that being regarded as a six-and-out player is very harsh. The bottom line is we played in an era when it was 100 overs and I would be going in with only nine overs to go and it isn't exactly conducive to getting your eye in. Therefore the players five, six, seven onwards would find themselves looking to try to move the thing on. The only other time you got in was when the ball was moving around or turning all over the place and nobody could score a run. People would say "Well, now you have your chance," and I'd be "Well hang on a minute".

'I'd like to think of myself as a player who, when it was there to hit, I didn't mess about. I played some decent innings over the years. I could hit the ball a long way, but we all struck the ball. In one year I hit 45 sixes and was leading the table in the country. Gooch struck the ball beautifully and hit very measured and cultured sixes. It depended on the situation. Lilley was another big striker of the ball. It was like a jigsaw. Once you could see the picture you could keep putting the pieces in and in every match Fletcher had the unique ability to say "The picture I am going to build is this, and these are the pieces I am going to use to make it fit". At no stage did he have to cut the piece to make it fit. My hitting was never coached out of me. I'm well built, while someone like Ken McEwan was no slouch but was a beautiful timer of the ball.'

Phillip came to the crease for his first innings of the season. He was soon off the mark, while Turner carried on throwing the bat. He inflicted more heavy punishment on Jarvis, bringing his 50 up with an aerial boundary.

Turner had been at the wicket for just an hour. He soon picked up his third six, as Kent made further bowling changes without significant effect. Johnson was driven over long-on for six and Phillip gained similar reward, with the half-century stand brought up in nine overs. Johnson's next over featured two sixes before Underwood was brought back on to stem the flow of runs. Nothing could stop Turner, though. He reached the fourth century of his career by hitting Shepherd over mid-wicket.

STUART TURNER: 'That was bizarre. It had rained and the wicket started to do a few things and we lost early wickets. I went out there and thought the only way to play was to attack. I hit five sixes and lots of fours so I didn't have to run too far. It didn't only get our season off to a good start but it also got my benefit year off to a good start!'

Turner's ton had taken 110 minutes and included five sixes and eight fours. His blitz ended on 102 when he was caught at long-on by Shepherd. Fletcher then declared at 305 for 7.

KEITH FLETCHER: 'I had been learning about captaincy for yonks. When Brian Taylor was made captain I was vice-captain so I had a say and could chip in then. I learned captaincy from a young age and I kept learning. I was certainly ready captain-wise to captain England, but as a batter I was too old. I got the best out of people by treating everyone differently. People are not the same. Some need a kick up the arse and some don't. Some need an arm around them and need encouraging.

'Goochie and McEwan, if they got four low scores they'd think they couldn't play. They amazed me. It was my job to build them up and tell them they were good players and say just because you got three bad scores it hasn't made you a bad player. I was an agony aunt and needed to give them their confidence back and thankfully I was able to do that. If a bowler was going through a rough time I would look after him a bit. If there was a bit of stick going around I might not bowl him so much and bowl someone else and bring him back at the right time so he'd get a wicket and off he'd go again.

'We used to target sides. I'd look at the fixtures at the start of the season and I would target sides I knew we could beat. There were Notts and Kent who were good sides and we'd think we would have to play bloody well to win. And they would have to play well if they were going to beat us. We were confident of steamrollering some sides. We crucified teams if we were given a half-decent wicket to bowl on. We knew it and luckily they knew it as well. You wouldn't let them get off the ground. Sides were scared of our team, certainly of our batting line-up. They knew they were up against it and if we played well we were going to beat them. They knew we were going out there to win. We may have had a laugh and a joke and be sociable but when it came down to the nitty gritty it was us against them and that was it.'

It was an exhilarating day's cricket, the kind expected in the three-day format, as opposed to today's four-day structure. Turner's hundred would be the fourth fastest of the summer, behind India's Kapil Dev, Gloucestershire's Mike Procter, and team-mate McEwan. In 38 overs, Essex scored 176 runs, as the game became almost like a John Player League encounter. As well as giving his benefit a boost, Turner's fireworks also bolstered Essex's collection of cricket balls.

The club were faced with the prospect of having to replace four balls, costing £21 each, which disappeared out of the ground after meeting with Turner's bat. A search party was sent out to find them, and instead of finding the missing four, they came back with five!

Turner's innings was deemed by many as one of the best the County Ground at Chelmsford had seen and he later told the press that he was acting on orders from skipper Fletcher to 'Give it a go'. It was the way Turner preferred to play, rather than putting up the shutters when trying to save a match. He was delighted to be told to go out and give it a whack and said he would have settled for a quick innings of 40. But to go past three figures in such a fashion meant it was his best century to date, particularly as it was scored against the reigning champions.

Kent began their innings slowly and reached 150 for 2 by the end of the second day. Charles Rowe was 64 not out at the close, and when he went out to bat on the third afternoon, after a rain-delayed start, a new Prime Minister was in place. Margaret Thatcher was now leader of the country. Phillip and Pont had taken a wicket each, but Kent were not in any hurry. They used up all of their 110 overs to post 250 for 8, with Rowe carrying his bat for 108.

The Essex bowlers had kept it tight, although Lever and Turner had produced 52 wicket-less overs between them. Pont took 3 for 44, while Phillip managed to beat off the cold weather to take 3 for 37 from 24 economical overs. It would be the first of many impressive performances in conditions he was far from used to.

STUART TURNER: 'Norbert kept himself to himself. He found it quite hard coming from a little island in the West Indies into the mix of the Essex dressing room but, make no mistake, he was a fine cricketer. We played at Southport once against Lancashire when they had Clive Lloyd, David Lloyd and Harry Pilling playing. We got 300-odd and had about 40 minutes before stumps to bowl at them. It started to get a bit dull but Clive Lloyd had told them that Norbert wasn't very quick. He wasn't slow, though, and after his first ball, all the slips took four-or-five paces back. He was really motoring and he knocked the first three of them over very quickly. Little Harry was at the non-striker's end watching the mayhem unfold and he walked past me and said "I'm not coming back tomorrow". It had got Norbert's goat and his pace took one or two of them by surprise, especially Clive!'

Essex did what they could in giving away few runs and stopping Kent from taking a lead. It was no use for gaining victory, though. Time was ebbing away.

A draw seemed inevitable, but another remarkable passage of play saw Essex nearly throw the game away. Denness and McEwan were both out for ducks and Essex found themselves in the startling position of 19 for 6. Gooch made it to 11 when he was LBW to Underwood, which meant a long run would be taken as punishment.

GRAHAM GOOCH: 'In 1978 I realised that I had to change my game, not only technically, but I had to be fitter, stronger and have more stamina. That's when I really started running and going to West Ham to train with the players. There was no organised structure with regards to fitness training back then. You basically did your own thing. The fitter and stronger you are, the better player you can become. I've never seen a fitter player become a worse player. I used to do a lot of running. There was one period in the early 1980s when I was banned from playing for England when I would run from home in Gidea Park to Valentine's Park in Ilford and play all day. That was a bit over the top, to be honest, but I was into the running then. I used to run down the side of the A12 about eight or nine miles.'

Essex continued to slide desperately towards an embarrassing total. Thankfully, at 28 for 8, Lever and Phillip calmed the situation and Essex closed on 43 for 9, a total nobody would like to be associated with, and the match was drawn, leaving Essex with six points and Kent five.

The championship was to be put on the back-burner as the one-day competitions took priority in the fixture list. Essex were hoping to put the demons of their second innings debacle behind them when they went to Northampton to face Northamptonshire in the first Group 'C' game of the Benson and Hedges Cup.

Skipper Fletcher had to decide whether to change the side from the one which drew with Kent. Lilley for Denness was the only alteration, as Fletcher went for youth over experience in the shorter form of the game.

THE GLORY RUN BEGINS

A bright, clear, bitterly cold morning saw Essex put into bat on a slow and easy pitch. It was a choice Northants would probably have regretted at the halfway stage. Lilley and Gooch put on 67 for the first wicket. Lilley went first, LBW to Peter Willey trying to pull a ball that didn't get up as high as he expected.

McEwan didn't last long, caught off the occasional bowling of Wayne Larkins for 3. His dismissal saw Fletcher join Gooch and it was these two who put Essex in the driving seat. Their partnership of 96 lasted 23 overs, and once Gooch was out for 83, Hardie added a quick 35 to take Essex to 230 off their 55 overs. Fletcher was not out until the final over of the innings, as he built his stay at the crease sensibly, seeing his side through before being bowled by Sarfraz Nawaz for 65.

Cook and Larkins gave Northants a rousing start. That was until Acfield was tossed the ball and showed that Essex could prosper without the injured East. Acfield threatened to slow the scoring rate so Cook took it upon himself to try and attack the spinner.

However, Cook's aggression led to his downfall, as Gooch was lurking in the outfield to take the catch, and soon after, Larkins did the same. Willey and Allan Lamb – one of England's brightest prospects – were at the crease with Northants 88 for 2 and in a position to win. Willey struggled, though, and was bowled by Pont for 8. Lamb pressed on with Jim Yardley, adding 79 until Phillip bowled Yardley. The game moved into its final stage with Northants requiring 34 to win off the last four overs, with five wickets in hand. It could go either way and provided an exciting finale for the spectators.

Essex were handed the advantage when Lamb was caught on the boundary off Lever, trying to launch a third six. From here on Northants were going to struggle as the tail-enders were left facing Lever and Phillip, who shared four wickets.

Sarfraz was at the crease with six needed from the final two balls, but he couldn't cope, leaving his side three runs short. The Essex attack was too strong, together with the astute captaincy of Fletcher, which brought him the gold award for both his batting and leadership. The game showed the ever-growing nerve Essex were developing. In the most important part of the game – at the death – they stayed calm and saw the game out, with Fletcher displaying the kind of thoughtfulness which would bring him the captaincy of England. After the game, Fletcher told the *Essex Chronicle* he felt Northants didn't have much chance of topping Essex's total.

'They batted really well and in the end it was a close call. Runs saved and tight control won it for us in the end. Mind you, not many sides would fancy their chances needing 10 off the final over with John Lever bowling. Our ability to contain sides and to show the necessary enterprise in the field seems to be improving – and Keith Pont is bowling as well as anybody.'

Essex's 100 per cent record in the John Player League stayed intact on 6 May at Chelmsford when Derbyshire were the visitors. It was Essex at their crushing best on a day when their batsmen and bowlers were firing on all cylinders. Essex were unchanged and Derbyshire's decision to bat first looked far from wise when last man out Mike Hendrick walked back into the pavilion. The scoreboard showed 114 from 40 overs. Earlier, at 72 for 2, Essex had expected to chase a reasonable total. But Pont bowled wonderfully as the visitors suffered a severe collapse. They were never allowed to score freely and it all went downhill from the moment the partnership between Tony Borrington (33) and South African Peter Kirsten (23) was broken.

Pont broke the stand by having Kirsten caught in the gully by Turner. The timing of Turner's catch could not have been better. The voice of Essex president Tom Pearce over the tannoy had barely finished giving an appeal to support Turner's benefit year when the ball stuck in the all-rounder's hands. His superb piece of work earned him £300 in the collection boxes.

STUART TURNER: 'I couldn't have wished for a better benefit year. It helped fill the coffers, if you like. It was hard work running a benefit, even though I had a terrific committee, and playing as well. It's a very social year. You are out at pubs and at various functions trying to whip up support, but I always had terrific support from our members. They have always been like that with the players. A benefit was an important part of a cricketer's pension, to some extent. Possibly that's not the case so much now because the salaries are a bit special. We had a game at Shenfield and that illustrated the fantastic support you got from your team-mates. They knew how important your benefit year was to you and nine times out of ten you'd get the full team out. Sometimes it was a bit onerous as you'd just played a three-day championship game but they were always light-hearted affairs so you'd happily turn out.

'It was difficult to fit the games in. You'd look at the fixture list during the preceding winter and try and slot them in. The clubs were fantastic at supporting you as well. It doesn't work like that now. You used to have ten games or so, but it's much more corporate now.'

Acfield took a fine catch at mid-on to end Borrington's effort. It was the start of a spell of cricket which saw nine Derbyshire wickets tumble for just

42 runs. Pont returned his best figures in the competition – 4 for 24 – and he was indebted to some smart fielding. It was not only left to him. Phillip and Lever were at their most accurate.

JOHN LEVER: 'What we took a certain amount of pride in was our fielding. Because we were a young side, we were not up to the standards of today, but we were quite an athletic fielding side. The people that came into the side when we had injuries, although we were fairly lucky with that situation, were the Lilleys of this world – brilliant fielders and really part of our one-day side. Ponty was a good all-rounder and had a good arm, and we had some catchers in Gooch, McEwan and Fletcher, who were second to none.

'There was this confidence in the balance of the side, with left-arm over, right-arm, two spinners if we needed them, back-up seamers and the final part of that jigsaw was if we scored our runs we scored them quickly because Goochie didn't mess around and Kenny didn't mess around. We had what we called the "Clouting Louts" down the order, who would go in and give it a real woof if you needed it, especially on wickets which did a little more then and turned quite a bit. If you were going to play up and down the line you were going to get out. There would be people around the bat and the batsmen would go in and have a go.'

The pressure was off as Gooch and Lilley began Essex's reply. Lilley didn't last long, though, caught off Tunnicliffe for 3, which brought McEwan and Gooch together. They laid the foundations for Essex to go on and win the game handsomely. Initially, they were happy to survive and see off England bowler Mike Hendrick. Once he was out of the attack, the pair upped the tempo and took the score to 53 and, when McEwan was out for 22, Essex were almost at the halfway stage and had plenty of wickets in hand.

Fletcher's experience and Gooch's class meant victory was never in doubt, Gooch finished on 68 not out, hitting two sixes and five fours in a fantastic exhibition of driving. One of his sixes was a mighty blow off England spinner Geoff Miller, who later became chairman of selectors, which landed outside the ground. Gooch was in fine fettle, passing 50 twice in his first three one-day innings for Essex and, although McEwan had yet to really spark, it would not be long before he showed his class.

Essex's performances during the opening few weeks of the season had provided hope for the coming months. Apart from the second innings against Kent, they had the edge over their opponents, and the bowling in particular looked like it would not let them down. Fletcher put much of the side's form down to the improved fitness of the players. In an age when sport science was years away and the idea of rigorous fitness plans was seen as detrimental, Essex were making sure they were in shape, not to get through the season, but to end it at the top.

Terms like 'match fitness' and 'pre-match training camps' with players staying in hotels as a team to focus on the next game were laughable. As long as the players were fit enough to perform, their ability would do the rest. Fletcher, in the *Essex Chronicle*, talked of his side's physical health:

'It is much too early to start predicting things, but we have made a satisfactory opening and much of that must be down to fitness. We have seen a greater emphasis placed upon this aspect of the game in recent years and with so much more limited-overs cricket, fitness is essential. Last year Derbyshire got to the Benson and Hedges Cup final and an awful lot of that was due to the exceptional level of fitness they showed in those opening weeks. It would be good if we could follow that example.'

Fletcher felt his side's pre-season had been as gruelling as he had known. Despite a few of the side, such as Denness and himself, getting on it years, they felt sharp. Extra zest was found when they saw the likes of youngsters Lilley and McEvoy charging around the field. And with this extra yard, Essex could make the difference between a close defeat and a tight victory, like in the first Benson and Hedges clash with Northamptonshire.

Fletcher told *Chronicle* readers he felt for team-mate McEwan, for whom Lady Luck was being unkind. 'Fortunately, quite a few of us are getting runs as well. Kenny McEwan is the exception so far, but he has suffered some desperate moments of ill-fortune. Against Kent, for example, we were beating the bat maybe twice an over without too much obvious reward. Yet the first decent delivery he faced got him out. In the second innings, he tried to get his bat out of the way of a lifting ball but it nicked the glove and he was caught. Against Northamptonshire he was caught by Jim Watts at an unusual backward square cover position after striking the ball really firmly. That is how it goes sometimes, and others have been enjoying better luck.'

Fletcher picked out Gooch for words of praise. He said the opener had a 'new edge to his game' and was keen to stay in the England reckoning, which meant scoring heavily. Hardie was also praised for his early-season form, which had produced a few valuable knocks. Fletcher was delighted to have the situation where Lilley displaced Denness for the one-day games and then the former Kent man was the chosen one for the championship, with McEvoy also knocking on the door.

The demands of the game were beginning to change, with the youngsters required to do the legwork in the field. Despite the improved fitness of the senior players, the three one-day competitions – Benson and Hedges Cup, Gillette Cup and John Player League – saw games come thick and fast, with plenty of travelling up and down the country.

There was no chance of Essex running dry in the summer of 1979. Sponsors and backers of Essex cricket, William Teacher and Sons Ltd, offered an Essex player-of-the-month award – the thirst-quenching prize being a gallon of Scotch whisky. Teachers, who were also backing Turner's benefit year, had already handed a gallon to Gooch as a special man-of-the-match award when Essex defeated Derbyshire in the John Player League. Essex were also named as Benson and Hedges team-of-the-week by former player Trevor Bailey for their win over Northamptonshire.

A trip to Lord's in north-west London was next up for Essex. Known as the Home of Cricket and its spiritual headquarters, it is regarded as the single most important cricketing temple in the world. Named after its founder, Thomas Lord, the ground is the home of Marylebone Cricket Club (MCC), as well as Middlesex. The pitch had a significant slope from one side to the other, which left many bowlers leaving the ground down in the dumps rather than joyous at having performed there. The eight-foot slope affected bowlers' run-ups and rhythm and, while some were able to overcome the effects, others could not and were made to look significantly less threatening than at other grounds.

Pont was left out of the Essex team to accommodate East. The all-rounder could understand his inconsistent selection, but it did not mean he liked it:

KEITH PONT: 'You always knew you were going to have to play very well to just be in the 12 or 13 and it was a decision that was then made or prompted by injury, or it may have been prompted by the conditions of the pitch. Also, how well you were playing. I don't think there were nine players assured of their place. Maybe six or seven were, in terms of selection.

'They were always given the opportunity to continue or get into a good vein of form, unlike the rest of us who had to do it immediately. I may be one of the only players who scored a hundred and got dropped the following day on two occasions. I was pretty world-class in that respect. But that was the side we dealt with. I took it on the chin because I wanted to be part of the side. There was immense frustration, especially if I was doing well and was then left out of the side. It was always a challenge.'

Unfortunately, the game came to a soggy end, with only two innings possible. Middlesex won the toss and chose to bat, and openers Mike Brearley and Mike Smith put on an opening stand of 76 on a wicket which looked full of runs. Lever's first ball of the day left Smith's heart in his mouth as a huge LBW appeal was turned down, and, other than a few other anxious moments, Essex were left frustrated. Brearley played and missed three times to Lever in one over but he was quickly onto anything dropped short.

The 50 partnership arrived in the 14th over as neither Lever, Phillip nor Turner made a breakthrough. It was the introduction of East, not fully fit, that gave Essex their first wicket when he had Smith stumped by his namesake Neil for 33. Middlesex continued to cruise along, with Brearley caught by Gooch off Lever for 73 and Graham Barlow scoring 45. It wasn't until Phil Edmonds and John Emburey came in that any aggression was displayed. Edmonds reached 40 and Emburey 33 when captain Brearley, in the manner which has him perceived as England's greatest ever captain, called his side off five balls short of completing 100 overs. The reason was to prevent Essex from taking one more wicket, and thus earning another bowling point.

Brearley's gamesmanship appeared to have worked, when Essex lost openers Gooch and Denness cheaply to the pace attack of Mike Selvey and West Indian thunderbolt Wayne Daniel. This left McEwan and nightwatchman Ray East to repair the damage at 45 for 2 overnight. East showed he was more than useful coming in higher up the order, sharing in a third-wicket partnership worth 50.

RAY EAST: 'I didn't mind being nightwatchman. At the end of my career there were a lot of fast bowlers. I'd never been hit on the head in all my career and, going in as nightwatchman with no helmet on, I never thought I would get hit. The West Indians were coming into the game. I always got the feeling Malcolm Marshall wanted to tickle you on the head and hit you. He was a very fine bowler. I did enjoy it. I managed to get my only century as nightwatchman and Fletch and McEwan weren't happy as they didn't get in! Whoever said I was too good to go in at number nine was right! I thought I could bat and fancied myself to get a few runs. No batsman fancies playing quick bowling. If they tell you that, they are lying. When I was younger I didn't mind it. I could get out of the way of it. Because I was a spin bowler it was recognised I played spin bowling quite well. Sometimes I was promoted in the order if the spinners were on.'

McEwan looked to be coming into form and went past 10,000 career first-class runs, although he was dropped behind the wicket by Ian Gould off the bowling of Selvey when on 22. East's resistance ended when he tried to hook Jones and succeeded only in looping the ball to square leg. Fletcher (32) and Hardie (40 not out) stuck around after McEwan was bowled by Selvey for 66 as Essex made their way to 224 for 7 when rain arrived. It didn't go away either, washing out the final day's play and preventing Essex from having any chance of notching up their first championship win. The umpires looked at the saturated pitch and deemed no cricket would be played.

WHEN WILL EAST BE FIT?
To make matters worse, there were serious concerns about the fitness of East. He hurt his hip while batting with McEwan and went to see a specialist for a diagnosis. There were reports he would miss as many as the next six matches, but skipper Fletcher played it down in the *Evening Echo*:

'It is far too early to rule out Ray for that long. With daily treatment he could be back in action for our next championship match against Derbyshire in five days' time.'

East had already missed three games because of a groin injury, as his season started painfully. Fletcher said it appeared the groin problem had spread to his hip, but he was hopeful it was not serious and should not prevent him from playing for too long. Should he miss a fortnight of cricket, it would mean Essex trying to qualify for the quarter-final of the Benson and Hedges Cup, with zonal games against Surrey, Combined Universities and Sussex, without him. East would also miss games against Hampshire and Nottinghamshire in the John Player League.

Fletcher was keen to have the bowler, who had taken 92 wickets in the previous season, in his side, as they had no bowler of his type to replace him, although Acfield would provide a reliable spin option.

KEITH FLETCHER: 'Acfield was one of my big mates. I used to eat with him most nights. Friendship never came into my decisions over who played. I picked the players who I felt would win us the game. If it was Easty or Ackers who got left out, then it was them who got left out. If it was Pont then it was him. It was always going to be between two or three for the last position. I had my bankers, nine of them, then picking the last two was the hardest bit.'

Without East, Essex lacked part of their relaxation therapy, although Pont was more than adept at providing the humour.

KEN McEWAN: 'Fortunately, I was warned by many people about the Essex humour. I can honestly say that I had at least one good laugh a day, every day during my time at Essex, thanks mainly to Raymond East. However, everyone contributed to the humour in their different ways.

'There were so many funny moments, but one in particular comes to mind. We were playing Surrey at Chelmsford for a place in the final and were chasing a reasonable total when we lost a few wickets, but were still cruising. Out of nowhere, Ray East ran a couple of us out and we lost by one run. Needless to say the dressing room was full of doom and gloom and was silent for quite some time when the phone rang. The person on the other end was asking to speak to Ray, who had a pub in East Bergholt at that time. We thought something had gone wrong at the pub because he never said a word and when he eventually put the phone down, he took his bag and left, saying nothing. At our next game, three days later, he told us about this call he had in the dressing room – he thought that it was a supporter who was extremely upset about losing the game. To make it worse, when he got back to the pub this same bloke with a cockney accent phoned him again and let him have it. This went on for the next few days. When Ray was not about Keith Pont told us it was him, so we all knew, except Ray! This went on for a couple of seasons, because every time Ray made a mistake, he would say "I suppose that bloke will phone me again" and sure enough, he would receive a call. That was the kind of banter that would go on.'

KEITH PONT: 'Ray was the overt humorist. My humour was very much behind the scenes. Fletcher said to me at 11.30am to get loose in one match. He was rolling his arms, gesturing. At 6pm he was still doing it and saying the same thing. I shouted '**** off!' He put the ball on the ground and said "Really, you are on". I marked my run up and ran up. When I was four paces short of the wicket I went all floppy and did some sort of silly action and it bounced three times before it reached the batsman. The ball stopped at the wicketkeeper's feet!

'They moved my marker once. As I ran in, my strides were getting longer and I shouted expletives at Gooch, who was the guilty man. Then, after tea, Gooch and McEwan had magazines stuffed down the back of their trousers and, as I came in to bowl, I was a yard from the strip when they pulled out the magazines while fielding in the slips and started reading them. I bowled the ball and it went through. I shouted at the captain "How the hell am I meant to bowl if they are going to do that?" Gooch shouted back "You're not going to get an edge anyway!"

'I used to mimic the walks and stances of the opposition players. We had that all the time. We used to have a lot of schoolboy humour in the dressing room. When Mike Denness joined, I remember him asking where his boots were and I'd hung them up on the rafters. He asked if I'd get his drink for him and I'd tell him "Get it yourself, you're not playing for England now!" We did a This Is Your Life down at Mike's house and I played Colin Cowdrey with bits of cotton wool in my mouth, which makes you gag. We had some laughs and an atmosphere that was extraordinary.

'I remember going out with Ray East and we were at a restaurant. You had to get money for the overnight stay and Fletch, [official club scorer] Clem Driver and Ackers were having a meal in a different, nice restaurant and we found them and Ray was at the window with his lips stuck to the glass, creating mayhem with the people inside.'

RAY EAST: 'Keith Pont was a character, a real funny bloke. In one of his first games he scored a century at Edgbaston and was dropped five or six times before reaching 100. Their skipper said he would like to go out with Ponty that evening because if there were a couple of bottles of wine he would turn it into 500 with the luck he had – he must be related to God. He was quite a mimic. He would do anyone around us, like the scorer, Clem Driver.

'The humour was my way of dealing with the long days and sometimes pressure. It would relax everybody else. When the next ball was about to be bowled I was ready and it was instantaneous. It wasn't practiced. They tried to pair me with Derek Randall and he was a funny boy but he had rehearsed it all. When the car backfired at Ilford I just fell to the ground as though I'd been shot. There were Irish connections at the time. It wasn't something I'd thought about doing. I couldn't play now. It looks to me that if you smile it's the wrong thing to do. We were entertainers.

'I was a great lover of John Arlott. He was a wonderful reporter and commentator. He was doing television for the John Player League and we were playing down at Glamorgan. Ebbw Vale it was – a small ground. There were big grass hills around it with sheep. We were fielding and someone hit the ball to me. My favourite trick was to clap my hands and throw the ball up in the air as if a wicket had been taken. There was John on the television saying "A really marvellous catch by Ray East, he's plucked that out of the sky". The ball had gone 100 yards over there, hit a sheep on the hill and John's left saying "Oh dear, he's fooled me again …' He came in and saw me afterwards, telling me I'd stuffed him out of sight.'

KEITH FLETCHER: 'Keith Pont was a lot funnier than Easty. He had a great sense of humour. He was bits and pieces – bat at six and bowl a bit. He'd pick up useful wickets as he swung it out. He did a job. The idea was to get 350 and declare at 5.50pm so you needed people to come in down the order and play for the side.'

Essex had claimed ten points from their opening two championship matches, which was enough to leave them in fourth place, with very few results possible around the country.

The weekend of 12-13 May would be one of the worst in the whole season for Essex. Suddenly, they looked anything but prospective one-day champions. Essex travelled to The Oval to face Surrey in Group 'C' of the Benson and Hedges Cup. They had won their opening game in the competition and were unbeaten in the John Player League, so spirits were high. Surrey, though, had never been beaten by Essex in the competition in six attempts, and that record would remain intact. Surrey chose to bat and progressed to 133 for 2 when the players took lunch after 38 overs.

Geoff Howarth and Roger Knight, two players who would feature heavily against Essex later in the competition, put on 105 in 19 overs for the third wicket. Graham Roope kept the momentum going with 26 not out, despite being fortunate on two occasions. First, he was caught on the boundary by Turner, only for the luckless fielder to step over the line, and then, the same fate met Gooch, who was also unable to stay within the playing field. Surrey looked set for a high total in the region of 220 until Lever came back into the attack. Lever removed Knight for 52 and then went on to hit the stumps three times to finish with 4 for 29 from his 11 overs.

Essex's reply started badly when Gooch went for 2 and McEwan for 6. With their two best batsmen back in the pavilion, the chances of Essex winning were sliding by the minute. Lilley and Fletcher went about trying to take Essex to a position from which they could at least have a go at winning the game. Lilley was bowled by Sylvester Clarke for 33 and, after Hardie was out for a duck, Fletcher and Pont put on 90 in 22 overs. Pont was bowled by Peter Wilson and when Turner came and went in the space of one ball, Essex were left with too much to do. Fletcher tried to hold the innings together until he was bowled for 62. It left the tail-enders with an impossible task and Essex fell seven runs short.

Had Pont, Turner and Fletcher not been out in the space of three overs it may have marked the end of the side's terrible run against Surrey. As it was, it showed why Essex had not been successful in the past, failing to make the most of a run-chase not beyond the talent they possessed.

When the sun came up and stayed out for the next day, Essex had the opportunity to make up for their disappointment as their John Player League match at Southampton against Hampshire was being screened live on television. East was again missing, as the same side was chosen as the one beaten by Surrey. This time, Essex were asked to bat first, but their performance was no better. They failed to make the sort of start required to build the basis of a big total. Gooch, Lilley, McEwan and Hardie were all back in the pavilion by the 22nd over, with only 67 on the board. Gooch made 25 but McEwan failed again.

McEwan's first five innings of the season in one-day cricket had raised a mere 47 runs and Lilley (11) was also struggling to make an impact, having been preferred to Denness. The skipper was doing his job and making sure the side at least made it through their overs. A hard-hitting fifth-wicket stand between Fletcher and Pont produced 61 in 10 overs. Pont was the chief aggressor, striking three massive sixes before being run out for 38 when dashing for a leg bye. Fletcher was four short of his half-century when he was bowled by Tim Tremlett. It was left to Turner and Phillip to try and give Essex any chance of winning the game by adding late runs. They put on an unbroken stand of 30 by running a large number of singles and choosing to utilise shots not found in the coaching manual to leave Essex 172 for 6 from their 40 overs.

When Lever bowled John Rice for a duck it gave the false impression that Essex may be a match for Hampshire. A second-wicket partnership between West Indian Gordon Greenidge and David Turner made sure they suffered their first defeat of the season in the competition and their second in the space of two days. Greenidge and Turner put on 135 in 31 overs to see Hampshire through to an easy victory. The pair batted with an ease and fluency that made Essex look an average outfit. As the partnership grew, they treated the bowling with contempt, piercing the field with flowing strokes, which entertained the sun-drenched crowd and those watching on television.

Poor Lever could not be faulted. He had given his all and yorked Greenidge when he had scored 75 from 97 deliveries. His next over saw him remove Turner for 60, but it was too late for Essex to even come close to triumphing. The home side had 11 balls to spare when Trevor Jesty and Nigel Pocock saw them to victory. Pont was dealt with severely, going for 48 off seven overs, while Phillip, Acfield and Turner were all wicket-less. Lever was beginning to come into form and his figures in one-day games were already impressive. At this point, in the John Player League, he had sent down 24 overs and conceded 51 runs, taking seven wickets.

Fletcher explained in the *Essex Chronicle* that the weekend's results had done little for his side's morale or ambitions. He felt they would simply have to pick themselves up and start all over again as plenty of time remained to make a mark in all four competitions. The captain tried to see the recent defeats as a reason for the players to strengthen their will to win. However, there were areas of the side he knew needed to improve.

'What we need is for our batting to knit together a bit more. One or two players are still searching for their touch, and, in truth, that cost us in the Benson and Hedges match against Surrey. The runs were there for the taking.'

He backed McEwan to end his one-day run drought and felt, knowing the South African to be a confidence player, that he just needed to feel the ball on the middle of the bat a few times and he would be back in business.

No major *post mortem* took place, but the defeats showed what Essex were missing when East was absent. The bowling attack lacked variety without his slow-left arm and he would be absent again when Essex went to Chesterfield to face Derbyshire in the championship.

Fletcher confirmed East had gone to Southend Hospital for X-rays and tests which the club hoped would throw more light on the problem. One specialist thought East was suffering from a hip injury, while another thought otherwise, leaving Essex, and East, wondering. The player himself believed the injury stemmed from the previous winter when he pulled a muscle taking a free-kick in a football match and claimed he had not been properly fit since. Fletcher rated East as one of the top-three spinners in the country and the side missed his character, as well as his wickets.

On a lighter note, Essex found they would scoop a large sum of money should they lift the Benson and Hedges Cup. Insurance brokers Jardine Matheson placed a bet of £1,500 at odds of 7-1 with Ladbrokes. The company's 150-strong Essex-mad Chelmsford-based workforce was full of cricket fans all dreaming of a trip to Lord's. Little did they know their dreams would come true.

FLETCHER ENDS CENTURY DROUGHT

Essex kept faith with their line-up at Derbyshire, with the usual change of Denness replacing Lilley at the top of the order. Young South African Reuben Herbert was brought into the 12 but was overlooked. Although Denness soon went for 10, it was a day when Essex could finally enjoy scoring runs in the sun. It took some time for them to get going. Gooch went about his business at pedestrian pace, scoring 10 in the first 19 overs. He witnessed McEwan hole out to a long-hop for 21, which brought Fletcher to the crease. They batted beautifully, albeit with slight fortune when Fletcher was dropped at slip when on 5.

The unusually inhibited Gooch took an age to reach his half-century – nearly three hours. When he did it was in style, pulling the ball over mid-wicket for six. Gooch's second 50 was a complete contrast. He was forceful and aggressive, taking just over an hour to reach his ton. When on 109, his stay ended as he aimed leg-spinner Kim Barnett through the covers and missed. Gooch's mastery was overshadowed, though, by that of Fletcher.

Fletcher's unbeaten 140 was the skipper's first century for two years, after his efforts the previous season had seen him return to the pavilion 35 times in first-class cricket without a three-figure score to his name. He came close, scoring ten half-centuries, but couldn't quite make it to the magic figure. This was his day, though. He flashed past 100 and carried on, hitting 18 fours and a six before the 100 overs were up, with Essex 335 for 4. The total meant they had earned full batting points and Derbyshire gained only one bowling point, as they were well and truly put to the sword.

There were two overs left in the day's play when Derbyshire came out to bat. They were left wishing it was already over when Lever castled Kiwi John Wright for a duck. Overnight rain freshened the wicket a little, allowing the seamers to run through the Derbyshire batters before lunch. It was a devastating spell of bowling and helped Essex regain the belief, after the blip in the one-day games, that they were a real force.

Phillip was the main engineer of a thrilling morning, taking 5 for 23. Derbyshire slumped to 43 for 4 when rain halted proceedings. Phillip, by that time, had taken the wickets of opener Tony Borrington and nightwatchman Phil Russell. The slip-fielders' hands were being kept warm, so regularly was the ball taking the edge of the bat. McEwan held on to remove Kirsten, and then Turner had Geoff Miller caught behind for 2. Derby crumbled woefully, losing five wickets for five runs and it got worse. The slip cordon grew and Turner gave Phillip his fifth wicket, clinging on when Colin Tunnicliffe edged.

Lever, swinging the ball prodigiously, finished the innings off, this time Gooch snaffling the ball behind the stumps to remove Bob Taylor. It was a fine example of how to use the conditions to your advantage, as Fletcher applied the pressure and was paid handsome dividends.

Unsurprisingly, the Essex skipper asked Derbyshire to follow-on, given the conditions, and they made it to 14 without loss when the rain returned. No further play was possible as rain and sometimes even sleet covered the ground until the next morning.

When the final day arrived, the pitch remained firm, but the atmospheric conditions were none the better for batting. The Essex seamers tore into the batsmen and, although they made it to 32 for 1, Derbyshire soon fell apart for a second time. Lever took the first three wickets to fall and Turner was soon in on the act. Sixteen of the Derbyshire wickets that fell were catches, with eight being held in each innings. There was only going to be one winner in this match, provided the rain stayed away.

At lunch, all eyes were on a huge black cloud which was floating ominously nearer. Essex wasted no time in cleaning up before the rain did likewise. Derby stumbled to 101 all out, Lever taking 6 for 52 from 24 overs, Turner 3 for 20 from 11 and Phillip the other wicket to fall. Acfield was left to bowl just four overs in the match as the moist conditions suited the seamers perfectly, while Pont was not required at all because of the relentless penetration of the others. Turner's six wickets in the match cost 32 as Essex took a full 20 points to take them joint top of the championship table with Somerset.

KEITH FLETCHER: 'Stuart was a fine performer and a great foil for JK and Nobby. He would bowl all day for you which is ideal for a captain. He would drag himself off the pitch after bowling 25 overs if he had to. He swung it both ways, and was aggressive, which suited his character. If he didn't have that aggression he wouldn't have been as good a bowler. He could have played one-day cricket for England. He was a good enough bowler and would have come in to bat around number eight. At the time they were looking in other directions. [Lancashire's] Barry Wood played quite a few times in one-dayers and he was up the order but Stuart would have been a far better bowler if you compare the two.'

RECORD BREAKERS
It was back to the Benson and Hedges Cup on 19 May, when Combined Universities took a break from their studies to visit Chelmsford. On paper, Essex could expect a comfortable victory. They came up against one of their own in the form of Derek Pringle for the second time in a month. However, not even he could slow the Essex charge on a record-breaking day.

Essex would go on and break three competition records as the poor Universities bowling attack was made to suffer. Gooch and Lilley's opening stand of 223 was the first to be broken. Gooch gave the impression very quickly that he was in the mood for a feast of runs when he began to attack the bowling right from the off. His 50 came from the first 72 runs scored and his 100 took only 96 deliveries.

Lilley, meanwhile, was passing his previous highest one-day score and reached his first one-day century. If Gooch, who went on to win the gold award, fancied a big lunch, he was out at the right time, caught in the deep for 133 to the final ball of the opening session. McEwan came in and kept the run-rate high, combining with Lilley to add 82. Lilley was out in the 52nd over for 119, including one six and 12 fours. Pringle sent McEwan back for 44 to give him some bragging rights, and his day would get a little better later on.

Essex's total of 350 for 3 was another record high. The University side could only hope for a respectable total in reply. Aziz Mubarak and Pringle made 88 between them to give some respectability, but the rest of the team was dismissed without fuss. Lever did most of the damage, earning 4 for 18 from 11 overs. Turner continued his form from the championship win over Derbyshire, taking 3 for 33, while Acfield was finally able to remove the sweater and take a couple of wickets.

All out for 136, the victory margin of 214 runs was the third and final record in a one-sided encounter. Essex had to try to take the wickets as quickly as possible because, in the event of a tie on points, the surviving team would be the one which took the most wickets per overs bowled. Essex were sitting at the top alongside Surrey, Sussex and Northamptonshire. All four had gained six points and had one match each remaining. The top two qualified.

Fletcher kept things in perspective when facing the press and praised the students for their efforts, but admitted it had not been like playing a county side. His views on Gooch were printed in the *Essex Chronicle*:

'Since he re-established himself in the England side, there has been a whole new edge to Graham's attitude. He has worked tremendously hard to make himself a better player, and temperamentally he has got things just right. The rewards for being a Test regular these days are such that anybody who earns a place will be especially keen to stay there; and such things apart, Graham is of course a very ambitious and forward-looking cricketer who simply wants to get to the top of his profession.'

The weather was the winner when Essex went to Trent Bridge to face Nottinghamshire in the John Player League on 20 May. The game was abandoned without a ball being bowled. It would have marked Ray East's return, but he would have to wait a few more days to pull on his whites again.

Gifted all-rounder Imran Khan and his Sussex team-mates stood in the way of Essex making it through to the quarter-finals of the Benson and Hedges Cup. The Pakistani, who went on to become one of the game's all-time greats, possessed the talent to turn the tide of a match in an instant, both with bat and ball. Essex were given a warning as he demonstrated his abilities against Surrey the previous weekend, when he won the gold award and kept Sussex's cup hopes alive. A potent swinger of the ball, Imran could also give it a fearsome clout with the bat. Essex, though, had no reason to fear the opposition any more than they should be feared themselves.

Gooch went into the game on the back of two centuries, while Fletcher was also scoring well, averaging 80 so far in the competition, with two gold awards safely tucked away at his home. Against Sussex's Imran, Essex had the wickets of Lever to rely upon. Fletcher had to think long and hard about the make-up of his team. East was considered fit enough and had acted as 12th man in the University game. He wasn't to make it, though, as Fletcher kept faith with Acfield as his spin option.

Overnight rain and showers delayed the start until 12.15pm. The sun was out when the two teams arrived in the morning, only for a torrential downpour to leave the ground covered with tarpaulins. Head groundsman Eddie Neath and his staff were quickly into action, mopping the water up when the rains stopped. The sun eventually flitted in and out and the wicket was unharmed. Until there was any definite decision on when play would begin, the two skippers delayed naming their teams to the public.

Sussex had to decide between picking Kepler Wessels, the South African strokemaker, or Pakistan's weaver of magic, Javed Miandad. Imran Khan was the first-choice overseas player and only two could play at a time. Miandad got the nod and was soon in to bat after Sussex won the toss.

The Essex bowling and out-cricket was at its best. Lever was used in short spells from either end to give Essex an attacking outlet throughout the innings.

He started well, having John Barclay caught behind by Smith for 19. Sussex crawled along during their early stages. Miandad countered Essex's pace attack by running singles and this helped him reach 47 when Acfield caught him off Turner, who had lured the Karachi-born batsman into playing a rash stroke.

Imran came to the wicket with plenty expected of him. He compiled just 20 before Phillip dismissed him, a dolly catch taken by Fletcher accounting for the star man. Sussex laboured for too long. Turner went for only 16 from his 11 overs. Pont was the only bowler to cost more than four runs an over, while Lever's 3 for 33 showed he was a man intent on keeping his place in the England team. It was a superb containing exercise by Essex, keeping Sussex to a manageable 188 for 8 from their 55 overs.

When Gooch and Lilley went out to bat, the Essex crowd hoped to see a repeat of their emphatic display against Combined Universities. While that was unlikely to happen against the Gillette Cup holders, the pair raced off and made sure that an Essex victory, and a place in the quarter-finals, was never in doubt. The pair were in ruthless form, adding 108 in 25 overs when Gooch was caught at mid-wicket for 66. Bernard Webber, reporting for the *Essex Chronicle*, wrote that he had never seen Gooch on such a smooth, confident run. It was a breathtaking catch which brought an end to his stay, but the crowd had been thrilled by three fours in one over off Chris Phillipson and eight other boundaries.

Twenty-year-old Lilley was given a standing ovation for his near faultless 70, spanning 38 overs. His eye for big-hitting brought him three sixes, one of which was a seemingly effortless strike off Barclay which had the crowd in the new River End stand cowering for cover. Inevitably, he won the gold award for taking Essex to within touching distance of victory.

McEwan eased his way to 44 and, attempting to reach his 50 with a six, he holed out. It was Lilley who took the plaudits, though, being singled out as the county's best batting prospect since Gooch arrived on the scene half-a-decade previously. Lilley's natural aggression was perfectly suited to the one-day game. The decision to prefer him to the experience of Denness seemed like a gamble at the start of the season. Now, though, it looked like inspired captaincy. Lilley was pressing hard down the neck of Denness for a place in the championship side. The experienced Scot had scored just 66 runs in four innings.

Essex were voted team-of-the-week, carrying with it a prize of £360. Former captain Trevor Bailey nominated them for their record-breaking achievements against Combined Universities. Fletcher also received further acclaim. He picked up a crate of champagne after winning a national newspaper's cricketer-of-the-week accolade. He earned it following his undefeated 140 at Chesterfield, the knock which paved the way for Essex's victory by a margin of an innings and 171 runs.

There was controversy elsewhere in the final round of group matches in the Benson and Hedges Cup. The build-up to the quarter-final draw was overshadowed by events in the West Country. Somerset captain Brian Rose declared only 20 minutes into his side's clash with Worcestershire, which affected Glamorgan's chances of being knocked out through the complicated rules regarding run-rates. Keith Fletcher told the press it was a 'disgrace' as no consideration had been given to the paying spectators.

With so many days' play being interrupted by rain, the Essex players had plenty of spare time on their hands. Scorer Driver had been teaching them the virtues of the game of bridge to pass the time.

The quarter-final draw was made at Lord's on Friday, 25 May. Group winners were pitted against group runners-up, and Essex were given a boost. They were paired with Warwickshire, with the tie originally set to be played at Ilford, although it would later be moved to Chelmsford. Essex would face England Test bowler Bob Willis, who was less effective in one-day cricket, and another former Test bowler in David Brown. Dennis Amiss and Alvin Kallicharran provided the bulk of the Midlands side's runs. Warwickshire had reached the semi-final of the competition in 1978, bowing out to Derbyshire.

THE COST OF RAIN

The May Bank Holiday weekend arrived amid grey clouds and heavy rain. It was not just Essex who suffered, as the whole country groaned under the leaden blanket which ruined the sporting spectacle.

Essex were supposed to be playing Surrey at The Oval in the championship, but not a ball was bowled across the three days. It was hoped the game would be decided on a one-innings basis, the winners collecting 12 points. But following an inspection early on the final day, umpires David Halfyard and David Evans ruled out any possibility of action. Torrential rain had left the ground wet through and Surrey officials estimated the lack of cricket cost them £6,000 in gate receipts. Neither side scored any points.

It summed up what had been a sad start to the summer for county cricket. Essex were not alone in having spent as much time in the pavilion as on the pitch. So far, 10 of their 12 days of championship cricket had been affected by rain, four of them being washed out completely.

Spectators thought they were finally going to be entertained when the two teams made it onto the pitch for the John Player League fixture. But Essex's luck was out, as was the whole Surrey line-up inside 38 overs, during which Essex never let up. There was a gut feeling that Essex would never lift the John Player League Trophy. To play so well and not be rewarded was cruel. They had finished runners-up so many times and, going into the game, knew a victory would take them joint top of the table.

That appeared to be a formality when Phillip reduced the home team to 8 for 3, before they struggled on to 27 for 5 and eventually 88 all out. Phillip took 4 for 26, while Lever and Turner took two wickets each. Surrey had no answer to the Essex bowlers. When seamers Phillip, Lever and Turner were not bowling, Surrey were only able to score at less than two runs an over off Acfield and Pont.

Essex lost Gooch early, but were 25 for 1 off 9.4 overs when the game ended. When rain fell, Surrey skipper Roger Knight was asked if he wanted to continue. Essex had a faster scoring rate but the match needed to last ten overs for there to be a result. Knight led his team off, with Essex two balls short of claiming all four points. Both teams earned two. Ironically, Surrey actually bowled 10.1 overs, if wides were taken into account, which they were not.

Disgruntled spectators, and the Essex players, felt the final two balls could have been bowled, despite the rain. Ever the diplomat, skipper Fletcher remained philosophical. He told the *Evening Echo*:

'I'm not angry – just bitterly disappointed. We thrashed them out of sight and still didn't win. It was raining pretty hard when the umpires brought us off. Apparently Surrey captain Roger Knight was given the option of coming off or continuing, and he chose to come off. And I have to be honest and admit I'd have done the same in his position.'

It was Essex's turn to start counting the cost of the weather when the final few days of the month provided little respite from the wretched rains, which ruined so much of the opening to the cricket season. Summer was supposed to be in full swing, but instead, spectators were forced to carry their umbrellas around, for the darkened skies were proving as unrelenting as the Essex bowling attack.

ILFORD FESTIVAL

Cricket came to Valentine's Park, Ilford for what was supposed to be one of Essex's enjoyable festival periods – the first of the season. It was the same depressing sight when play was due to get underway in the championship clash with Glamorgan. The moisture in the air suggested another fruitless day. Little did Essex know they would be leaving east London with broad smiles across their faces.

RAY EAST: 'I always thought we should take the cricket around the county. Chelmsford is a nice place to play but it wasn't always the best for us spinners because it's such a small ground. The ball frequently went in the river as I always bowled from the bottom end. The fire brigade used to sound the sirens when I came on to bowl to warn the public and people rowing on the river – "Watch out, East is bowling, there could be a missile projected your way." Ilford and places like that were alright on a nice day with all the marquees around. But when it was miserable and raining, and at Southend when you are having your lunch in a marquee and you're being hit on the top of the head by water coming through the roof, it's a bit miserable.'

There was no rain when the players reported to the ground, but an overnight downpour had left the surface unplayable. Umpires Cecil Cook and Arthur Jepson decided to have another look in the afternoon, and when the players started their fielding practice, rain threatened again. It duly arrived, and the players were back in the dry, where they stayed for the next day as well.

General manager Peter Edwards was left counting the cost. He predicted it would leave the club thousands of pounds out of pocket if play did not get underway at all. The Ilford festival had been a big money-spinner in the past, and to lose a week of cricket would set the books back by £6,000. On the first day, only £120 was taken at the gate – enough to cover the cost of the players' food for the day. During the week, Essex also needed to find around £2,000 to cover additional expenses, so they were staring down the barrel of a financial disaster.

They were more fortunate than other counties. Home teams collected the gate revenue and Essex had played predominantly away from home up to that point, so they were not quite counting the pennies in the way some of the other counties were. However, they were short of around £10,000 at that stage, according to Edwards.

Such was the concern surrounding the ground and the weather that Essex decided to switch their upcoming Benson and Hedges Cup quarter-final from Ilford to Chelmsford. Edwards said there was a higher chance of the game going ahead, and finishing, if it was moved, as Chelmsford was able to recover quicker from rain.

The sun finally shone on the final day at Ilford and the teams settled for a single-innings match. Glamorgan, led by former Essex spinner Robin Hobbs, batted first on the premise that the wicket would take spin once it dried. They found the going tough: it took two hours to pass 50, during which time Turner had taken a magnificent one-handed catch in the gully off Lever to remove John Hopkins. But generally it was hardly the excitement the crowd wanted, after waiting so long to see action.

Glamorgan reached just 58 from the 44 overs possible before lunch and they continued in this vein until 3pm. Fletcher had tried his twin spin-attack of East and Acfield with no luck for 33 overs. It was East's first game for three weeks and his inclusion meant Pont was left out. Lever kept probing, taking his second wicket when bowling opener Alan Jones, but Glamorgan showed no signs of accelerating. So, it was left to Fletcher to take matters into his own hands. He brought on himself and Hardie, who had never bowled at this level. They took five wickets between them and, despite conceding seven runs an over, the objective had been achieved as Glamorgan declared on 188 for 8.

Essex were left with just 105 minutes to chase the runs and, fuelled by the frustration of seeing their opponents grind along, set about scoring at the five-and-a-half runs an over needed. The Essex batsmen dispelled any fears about the state of the wicket, the same one on which Glamorgan were unable to move faster than a snail's pace until the declaration bowlers came on.

Denness was out for 14 when the score was 44 and Gooch and McEwan gave the spectators what they had been waiting for. They were in superlative form as their display of controlled hitting took Essex to the 12 points in 27.3 overs. They had five overs to spare, which proved how well they controlled the scoring rate. Gooch ended seven runs short of his century and McEwan was 67 not out. The pair were masters of the run-chase, and showed the type of temperament and skill required to win in tight situations, and, more importantly, to win trophies.

BRIAN HARDIE: 'People used to like me to get out so that Ken and Goochie could bat together. When you had them in together, Goochie would hit the ball with immense power and Ken used to hit it just as hard but with half the effort. They were both a joy to watch but when they batted together they could be unbelievable. We had a very short chase at Ilford and they knocked off the total in no time at all. They were both tremendous to watch in different ways.'

The result took Essex to the top of the championship. They had a lead of ten points and would take some knocking off their newly-found perch.

The whole team celebrates as Keith Pont takes a wicket

Essex supporters celebrate the Benson and Hedges Cup final victory over Surrey at Lord's

Graham Gooch hits out
during his gold award-winning
innings of 120 against Surrey in
the Benson and Hedges Cup final

All-rounder Keith Pont
attracted a cult following in the
Tom Pearce Stand at
Chelmsford in the 1979 season

Overseas players Norbert Phillip and Ken McEwan proved very popular with Essex fans

Spinner David Acfield proved to be
a very reliable performer for Essex

Left-arm slow bowler Ray East was a real character who never shied away
from having a laugh at his own expense

Grim Reaper John Lever's superb seam bowling meant dozens of opposition batsmen heard the dreaded 'death rattle' during the 1979 season

West Indian Norbert Phillip was an aggressive competitor with both bat and ball

All-rounder Norbert Phillip watches the ball carefully

Left-arm slow bowler Ray East
was a match-winner with the
ball during the 1979 season

Former Kent and England skipper
Mike Denness added much-needed
experience and plenty of runs at
the top of the batting order

South African batsman Ken
McEwan was a joy to behold
whenever he was at the wicket

Chapter Five

June 1979

Essex fans were able to feast on more than just their county stars during June. The month was dominated by the Prudential World Cup and the England selectors were ready to name their squad on 3 June. Essex's three-day game with Lancashire was in progress when news filtered through of their choices. Two of Essex's players were in contention.

Gooch was seen as a certainty following his recent form and established position within the England set-up. Lever, meanwhile, was bowling as well as he had ever done and was regarded across the country as one of the best in all forms of cricket. However, he was the unlucky man and was omitted from the 14 announced by the selectors. The surprise inclusions were Middlesex batsman Mike Gatting and Northamptonshire opener Wayne Larkins.

For Gatting, it was a second bite at the cherry and a chance to redeem himself after the tour of Pakistan in 1977, when he played one Test and made just 5 and 6 with the bat. His occasional seam bowling was thought to have given him the edge over Lever, who was deemed a luxury despite a decent tour of Australia in the winter. The squad already contained Chris Old, Bob Willis, Mike Hendrick and Ian Botham to bowl.

Fletcher was surprised to see Lever's name missing from the squad, and while he was pleased to keep hold of his opening bowler, he could not understand why the selectors had not gone with more specialist one-day players for the tournament. Gooch's selection meant he would be absent from county cricket once the competition began, so reserves Lilley and McEvoy were pressing to replace him.

KEITH FLETCHER: '[England captain Mike] Brearley didn't rate JK for some reason. I haven't got a clue why. He was a fine bowler by 1979. He had developed and reached his pomp from about 1978 and was still a fine bowler when he retired. He was an athlete. So was Norbert Phillip when he got moving, but he didn't get moving that often! JK was a bit like Stuart Turner in that he would bowl until he dropped. You couldn't get the ball out their hands. That helps. He was a top performer.'

It was a remarkable month for Lever, who went on to produce some of the most extraordinary bowling figures ever seen. He found the perfect way to get back at the selectors, who had overlooked him and, in the process, made the whole country question his omission.

JOHN LEVER: 'With Fletch's cricket knowledge, I still think he is by far and away the best captain I ever played under. Summing up batsmen, summing up how they played, setting fields accordingly, in fact made me a very lazy bowler. It wasn't until I played for England that I realised how lazy I was. I just let him do things.'

For Essex, though, June did not get off to the best of starts when their championship game with Lancashire was interspersed by a John Player League match.

JOHN LEVER: 'The JPL used to pack grounds out and the gates had to be shut. There was a good chirp when we played a JPL game. At the public beer tent end, where you didn't want to be near, the Ilford ground was a bit bumpy. Ponty was fielding down there in front of the stand. He went down to stop the ball which was travelling quite quickly. He went down and at the last minute he thought it was going to pop up. It hasn't and he hasn't got down to it so it's gone straight through and hit the boundary board. A bloke in the crowd shouts out "Oi Pont! I can do that, give us your job!" Pont came off and was laughing and we told him to stay down there with the pissed up public and it was nice chirps. They were all quite funny on the boundary.'

Gooch was left wishing Fletcher had either chosen to field first or lost the toss. He was out for a duck. The wicket was not the best seen at Ilford and the sky was overcast. McEwan and Lilley did not last much longer and it was left to Fletcher and Hardie to repair the damage, reaching 66 in the 22nd over when the Essex captain was out for 27. Hardie stuck around with the tail once Pont and Turner had gone cheaply and Smith contributed a breezy 23 not out. The rare sight of Acfield in pads and gloves with bat in hand was necessitated as Essex stuttered to 120 for 8 when Hardie's innings ended. It was the second time Acfield had batted so far in the season, which said a lot for Essex's batting line-up. They closed on 127 for 9.

Lancashire's reply began no more convincingly. They lost Andrew Kennedy and Barry Wood by the time the score reached 16 in the ninth over. Essex fans lived in hope when they saw Lever scatter Wood's stumps. David Lloyd and Frank Hayes rallied and kept the scoring rate similar to Essex's, trailing by two when the 30th over arrived. Acfield brought about the end of Lloyd, and Turner took the wicket of Hayes, but Lancashire stood at 88 for 4 and West Indian Clive Lloyd was at the crease. He helped his side coast home, along with Bernard Reidy, who struck three sixes – two off Acfield and one off Lever to finish the match.

The defeat left Essex shy of the league leaders and they had proved in front of a television audience that they still possessed the ability to go from brilliant winners to second-rate losers. They had already played one day of the championship match, during which their batting had shown no signs of what was the follow in the John Player League.

That first day's play was delayed until 12.10pm. Denness and Gooch made up for lost time by posting a 50-opening partnership, after Fletcher had won the toss. Both openers went soon after, but McEwan was at his imperious best. In a little under two hours he exploited his array of shots, driving back over the bowler's head and through the covers, to score 88. The South African dominated in conjunction with Hardie, until he inexplicably shouldered arms to a straight delivery. It was a rare misjudgement which robbed him of a deserved ton. Hardie was joined in useful stands by Turner (25) and Smith (30 not out). Hardie came to the crease in the 36nd over, and by the time the 92nd came around, he was raising his bat to the crowd and Fletcher was calling him and Smith off the pitch, with 339 for 6 on the scoreboard. Essex were given three overs to try and oust the Lancashire openers before the close of play.

LEVER CRANKS IT UP

By the time Essex came back on the pitch on Monday, following their Sunday League defeat, there was widespread sympathy for Lever following his omission for the World Cup.

The atmosphere was close and the wicket green. It was as though someone high up above was looking down on him and felt he needed a dose of fortune. While the conditions may have been in his favour, he needed no added skill for what he was about to produce. In a wonderful spell of seam and swing bowling, Lever taught Lancashire a lesson. He was devastating in the morning session, taking all of the first five wickets to fall. The ring of fielders behind the wicket continued to expand, after Smith and Gooch were the grateful recipients of edges. There was no answer to his menacing swing, except to be dismissed and trudge back to the pavilion, beaten by a man performing at the top of his game. Lever ended with 7 for 27 from 14 overs. Lancashire were all out for 84.

Lancashire were forced to follow on, 255 in arrears. They never looked like succeeding, and fared no better when the slaughter began for a second time. Lever added two more wickets to finish the match with 9 for 47, as Essex sped to victory and tightened their grip on the championship. The visitors managed to rally their way to 120 for 5. Then it was Acfield's turn to join in the fun. He took the final four wickets in the space of 11 balls, without conceding a run. Lever probably would have finished with more wickets to his name, had bad light not led Fletcher to resist bringing him back in case the umpires chose to bring the players off.

RAY EAST: 'It was an extraordinary year for John. He just kept bowling everyone out. Seam seemed to predominate. He was such a phenomenon. He was so fit. He had a long run as well and didn't get injured. He needed the long run to get his rhythm. He just bowled and bowled and bowled, it was unbelievable. If you needed a wicket you'd throw him the ball, but he could bowl for two hours. On the first morning of a match if it was swinging around a bit he would stay on and keep bowling. Me and Ackers were the sweater carriers but I never got fed up watching John bowling as he was winning matches.'

Essex left Ilford with a 26-point lead at the top of the table and an extra day of rest was theirs because of the early finish. They would be refreshed and ready for their biggest game of the season up to that point – the Benson and Hedges Cup quarter-final against Warwickshire.

It was a happy camp, with Fletcher pleased with the way his players were performing. Apart from one or two days when they hadn't reached anywhere near their potential, their cricket was of a high enough standard to stand above the rest of the country.

The skipper expected teams to raise their game against Essex from here on, as they were the team of the moment, the big guns who needed knocking off their perch. He felt some teams would develop an inferiority complex which they would find difficult to escape, working in Essex's favour. It was a case of that in the win over Lancashire. Once Essex had them on the floor, there was no way they were going to get back up again.

Prior to 1979 Essex were perceived as more of a one-day than a three-day side, but the balance was beginning to shift towards equilibrium. The challenge for Fletcher was to keep his side going in pursuit of every trophy, while they were still up for grabs.

Only one game remained, however, before Gooch joined up with the England squad for the World Cup, but Fletcher, disappointed to lose his prolific opener, believed his deputy, whether it be Lilley or McEvoy, capable of standing in. For the loss of Gooch, Essex could at least console themselves with the gain – or retention – of Lever.

Fletcher voiced his surprise to the press at Lever's omission. He felt England could have done with more specialist players, such as Lever, Yorkshire wicket-keeper David Bairstow and Leicestershire's Roger Tolchard.

Fletcher named a party of 12, waiting to see the state of the Chelmsford pitch before naming his team. Lilley was in for Denness, which was no surprise. The youngster had scored nearly 200 runs in his last two Benson and Hedges Cup matches. Fletcher would have to decide whether to play two spinners or play an extra all-rounder in Pont. It was he who got the nod over the unfortunate Acfield, who had produced his late cameo in the Lancashire game a couple of days earlier.

Essex won the toss and elected to bat as they went in search of a coveted place in the semi-finals. They had an inauspicious start when Lilley was dismissed for a duck. Only four overs had gone when, with the score on two, the youngster was caught in the slips off the bowling of Anton Ferreira.

A crowd of 4,000 was basking in the sunshine when McEwan arrived at the crease. Ferreira and fellow opener Bob Willis both got the new ball to move sufficiently to disturb the Essex batsmen and Lilley was unable to counter the lateral movement. However, McEwan dispatched an early boundary to show it was not going to be easy for the Warwickshire bowlers, despite Gooch taking eight overs to get off the mark. Willis's accuracy was such that he conceded a mere single in his first six overs and during this opening spell Essex were under the cosh. It would not remain that way for long.

Gooch gradually put his foot on the accelerator and slipped into top gear as the Warwickshire attack felt the full force of his blade. McEwan played with grace and style to score 50 and put on 105 in 25 overs with Gooch. Fletcher kept the scoreboard ticking over, trying to give Gooch the strike, but adding 43 himself in a partnership of 90 spanning 20 overs.

The final ten overs saw Gooch really open his shoulders. Essex hammered 97 and Gooch overshadowed the contributions of his team-mates, striking 19 fours and a six while on his way to 138 – an innings which earned him the gold award. He was eventually trapped LBW by Willis in the final over, but the damage inflicted by the 25-year-old had been done. His power always needed augmenting by a temperament which kept him at the crease, and this was an emphatic example of the two working in harness.

Pont added an unbeaten 22 to take Essex to an imposing total of 271 for 5 from 55 overs. Ferreira's last three overs cost 45 runs. Warwickshire needed a quick start if they were going to threaten the winning score, but it never materialised. Although openers David Smith and Amiss saw off the opening spells of Lever and Phillip, Turner came on to ruin Warwickshire's dreams of lifting the cup. He had Amiss caught behind and the same combination then removed dangerman Kallicharran.

Smith and Philip Oliver carried the scoring rate along but, after the tea interval, East dismissed both batsmen in the space of three overs and wickets continued to fall regularly to see Essex reach the semi-finals. It was a convincing 44-run victory as Essex marched into the last four for only the second time – the first being in 1973 when they were beaten by Kent at Canterbury.

A home tie with Yorkshire stood in the way of a place in the Benson and Hedges Cup final. Essex were now considered favourites to lift the trophy and Fletcher believed the first obstacle could be cleared. He felt the home draw meant his side possessed the advantage and, with the way his side were playing, nobody should be feared.

SEMI-FINAL EXCITEMENT

In the wake of the quarter-final triumph, the club anticipated its biggest ever crowd for the semi-final on 4 July. The match was bound to be a sell-out, as cup fever began to grip the county. Essex considered the possibility of erecting extra seating, but whatever they did, they knew they would not be able to house everyone. The winners of the clash at Chelmsford would meet the victors of Derbyshire versus Surrey at Lord's.

Fresh from his super century, Gooch now turned his attention to the World Cup. He would not be available for Essex again until 27 June. Prior to going into battle with Australia at Lord's, he was praised highly by his county skipper Fletcher in the *Evening Echo*:

'There is no doubt in my mind that he's a much better batsman than 12 months ago. He's learned a lot since then and has returned from the winter

tour of Australia with a burning ambition to succeed. I feel it is this determination rather than any change in technique that has made him a better player.
He's been a joy to watch over the opening weeks of the season and has been
playing with enormous confidence. I just hope everything continues to go his
way during the next few days.'

Gooch went into the World Cup averaging well over 50 for the season. He
was coming in lower down the order for England, rather than his usual position of opening for Essex. Brearley opened with Geoff Boycott against
Australia, allowing Gooch to show his power once the new ball had lost its
shine.

Australia were out to lick their wounds after their thrashing in the Ashes
the previous winter. A dull, grey day didn't prevent a special atmosphere. A
crowd of 25,000 saw England win by six wickets and Gooch was in top form
again, scoring 53 in a partnership of 108 for the third wicket with skipper
Brearley. He was man-of the-match again.

A surprise was sprung on 9 June at Chelmsford when McEvoy was chosen
ahead of Lilley to partner Denness at the top of the order for the championship game against Leicestershire. It was set to be a personal battle between
Denness and Lilley, 16 years separating them, to underline their claims to be
Gooch's opening partner when he returned from World Cup duty. Gold
awards in the Benson and Hedges Cup strengthened Lilley's claim and many
thought he was unlucky not have ousted Denness, who had yet to pass 50 in
the season. It was an intriguing poser for Fletcher, and the competition for
places would help bring the best out of his players.

But McEvoy it was who strode out to the middle with Denness on the first
morning at Chelmsford, and he didn't come back until the score was 63, when
he was bowled by Ken Higgs for 21. It showed Essex could not just survive
without Gooch at the top of the line-up, they could prosper with his replacement in the team.

However, after the promising start, Essex subsided badly. McEwan and
Fletcher were dismissed in quick succession. Denness and Hardie doubled the
score from 78 for 3 to 156 before the younger of the two Scots was dismissed
for 30. Turner and Phillip suffered the ignominy of not scoring, which left
Essex in trouble at 157 for 6. Full batting points looked a long way off.

Smith had troubled the scorers twice in the championship so far, before he
joined Denness in the middle. Now was the time he was needed. Far from clas-
sical in his approach, it suited what Essex required – runs, no matter how they
came. He put on 92 with Denness when the opener finally fell to Shuttleworth
for 122. Perseverance with Denness had paid off. He may not have possessed
the brute aggression of Lilley, may not have come up through the Essex ranks
like Lilley, but he was a wise professional who knew what he was doing.
Leicestershire might have succeeded in getting him out, but they didn't get
Smith out. He took the score past 300 and was left 90 not out when the overs

ran out. He was at the crease for 100 minutes and hit one six and nine fours, the last of which earned Essex a valuable batting point.

It left Leicestershire with a tricky 40-minute spell to negotiate before the close. Bad light prevented Essex from making inroads. Rain meant a delayed start on Monday, and Leicestershire, thanks to Barry Dudleston and Brian Davison, were in a healthy position at 178 for 3. Enter Lever. His month of months was already underway. Nine wickets against Lancashire announced as much. This time, he announced it to the rest of the world. He took the wickets of Davison, Roger Tolchard, Chris Balderstone and Nick Cook in the space of four overs to help Essex to a lead of 71. The trusty hands of Turner swallowed four catches in the slips, including one diving effort, as Lever finished with 6 for 76 from 23 overs. East chipped in with two wickets.

The second innings began woefully for Essex. They were 10 for 3, as Denness as unable to repeat his form in the first innings, McEvoy tasted a duck, and Fletcher went without scoring. For McEvoy, it was the start of a wretched run of form, which he was unable to shake off.

MIKE McEVOY: 'I was on a roll with the side doing well but I wasn't having a great season. I seemed to get a lot of starts throughout my career – getting into the 20s and seeing off the opening bowlers. Whether it was a mental thing that I couldn't kick on and get runs, I was conscious of getting into the 20s and 30s and tensing up. I thought I'd have to move on and go from 50 to 100, which caused more tension. It wasn't until later in my career that I got it out of me and I went on to score a century for Worcestershire. I was putting too much pressure on myself.

'There was a big jump between second-team cricket and first team. There were many world class opening bowlers around at that time. It wasn't easy going in and playing against these guys but it was exciting. It was the medium pacers which tended to get me out. As a young player, when I'd seen off the openers, I was wondering what my role was. I was very conscious of Fletcher and McEwan still to come in. Did the side need me to push on rather than leaving these guys in the pavilion? Now I look at it and think why was I thinking that? It was my job to carry on going, but the thoughts entered my mind and the bottom line is I didn't do as well as I wanted to. I did like to bat all day. I think I had the technique and ability to go out and play. It was kicking on and getting big runs that was my problem. I was out LBW a lot as well. We didn't have the technology to see what I was doing wrong and it meant you had to work things out yourself, which I happen to think is a good thing.'

McEwan and Hardie helped Essex to 48 for 3 when the day ended. A draw was not much use. They decided to play positively and go all-out for victory on the final day. Hardie dropped anchor and provided support for those around him, who would play their shots.

There was an early setback when McEwan's off-stump was knocked back by Leslie Taylor for 39. Essex were searching for a lead of around 250. The wicket was showing signs of life so Essex fancied their chances of bowling Leicestershire out before the end of the day. Turner helped them to score at a run a minute, hitting 46, while Hardie made 40 and Phillip 27. The tail failed to wag as quick runs were sought and Essex found themselves all out at lunch for 181, a lead of 253.

Leicestershire were left 165 minutes and 20 overs in which to chase the total. Phillip and Lever reduced them to 33 for 3, but Davison, who scored an attacking 72 in the first innings, showed his ability in the second as well. He received a massive stroke of luck when on 16. Turner bowled him, but the umpire called a no ball. An unplayable delivery from Phillip finally sent him on his way for 67.

Lever was in full flow when play entered its final stages. He had already forced Leicestershire to 66 for 7 when he again proved simply unstoppable. The game was completed with 16 overs still due to play. Lever had taken 7 for 41, Tolchard, Paddy Clift and Cook were all out in one over, and Leicestershire were all out for 153. Lever walked away from the ground with a career-best match record of 13 for 117.

STUART TURNER: 'People would wonder why the ball would swing so much but John just had a talent. We worked on the ball, of course we did. Fletch used to tell us to keep the shine on the ball for as long as we could for everybody. I started off as a seam bowler who would try and hit the seam. I wasn't quick but I was brisk. As I got older I started to swing it both ways and it was a skill I learned. I used to bowl back of a length and if there was any bounce I'd take advantage of it.'

Nearest rivals Hampshire and Northamptonshire drew, while Essex were claiming full points, taking them 40 points clear at the top of the table. No other side had won more than one match:

Fletcher told the *Essex Chronicle* he thought Essex were always in control, except when Davison was at the crease. Davison's positive attitude left Essex wondering if they were going to be denied maximum points on the final afternoon. The skipper was pleased Denness had answered his critics, following the suggestions that youth should be given its chance over experience.

The Benson and Hedges Cup semi-final was already uppermost in everyone's minds. Fletcher said his side would give their all on what promised to be a terrific occasion. He requested the supporters play their part – three weeks before the game was played: 'Our support so far this year has been very good, although, like everybody else, we have been affected by the weather. Come rain or shine, though, I expect 4 July to go down as one of the most memorable occasions that has occurred in the time that any of us have been with the county. Yorkshire will be battling away just as hard as we will, so nothing can be taken for granted. While it is fair to say that hardly anybody in and around Essex is contemplating defeat, no Yorkshire man worth his salt will be thinking in terms of anything other than victory.'

Such fighting talk showed the enormity of what was looming in the coming weeks. Belief was building that this was Essex's year. This would be the season when they would not mess up and would be able to bring silverware back to Chelmsford for the first time. For the first time in their history, they were the team to beat, the team who other counties did not want to face.

Essex officials were preparing for record gate receipts from the game on 4 July. It was made into an all-ticket affair – believed to be for the first time in the club's history – as a deluge of mail swamped the offices. Edwards had never known anything like it. It reached the stage where the GPO made a special journey just to deliver the mail to the club. Hundreds of letters were coming through, many of them enclosed with cash, in just a matter of days.

By making the match all-ticket, the club would save thousands of fans a wasted journey. Arrangements were put in place to transport four portable stands to the New Writtle Street ground. This would enable a further 2,000 spectators to enter and ensure a full house of around 9,000.

Arrangements were also being made for additional parking in the vicinity. However, judging by the demand, Edwards was sure the ground could have been filled twice over. It was impossible to satisfy everyone and many were left disappointed at the decision to make it all-ticket. But Essex were keen to look after the interests of their 5,500 members first of all. They were given first choice of tickets at the Chelmsford office up to 25 June, when the rest would go on general sale.

A limited number of reserved seats were available for £4.50, while the rest were priced at £3 for adults and £2 for senior citizens and under-16s. The expected record gate receipts of £20,000 would not go into the Essex coffers, however. After deducting a small percentage for match expenses, the remainder went to the Test and County Cricket Board.

Nowadays, it is hard to imagine such a clamour to see a game of county cricket. Chelmsford sits mostly empty for the majority of the summer. The only time it is filled is when the Twenty20 competition gets going. But in 1979, cricket was an entertaining day out. Runs, wickets and results were what the fans wanted to see. And more often that not, that is what they got.

Francis Ponder watched Essex all around the county and said the experience kept him coming back for more. 'An hour of Gooch meant 60 to 100 runs on the board and when going for victory that is what you need. I watched the county play all around at the out grounds. They were the nomads of cricket, taking the cricket around the county and the county came out in force to watch them. They came across some pretty crap wickets. It wasn't like it is now, having your headquarters at Chelmsford and knowing the ball will come through evenly all day.

'They were a good county to watch. The players were approachable. Professionalism has since taken over and the players are aware of the media. It is high profile and it puts them on their guard. I look at Nasser Hussain now.

He and Derek Pringle were a headache when we were trying to interview them and now both are in the media themselves. They were a pain in the bum and are now doing the job which they made so difficult for the likes of us! Pringle would give one syllable answers if he could. It would be "Yes" or "No". In 1979, though, the guys chatted away to spectators on the boundary and signed autographs.

'The festival cricket was good wherever it was played. There always seemed to be something in the wicket. Colchester was one of the better grounds and it was great to watch there. You never quite knew what you were going to get at Ilford or Southend – especially when the tide came in. It definitely had an effect on the ball swinging about. Essex were playing the game the right way and you always knew you were going to see some action. There were two championship games in a week and a John Player League game on the Sunday so you would see three different teams in a week sometimes which was brilliant. It must have been great for the batsmen as well, as they had the chance of up to five innings in a week.

'Four-day cricket was brought in to help players build an innings and it was going to be the reintroduction of spin bowling. People just took longer, though. Geoff Boycott may have loved it, but for brighter cricket it didn't work. The three-day game invariably meant one of the teams needed to declare to make a game of it. The drawback was for the purist, who couldn't stomach the 15 to 20 overs of filth bowled up on the last day – to get a result, the non-bowlers would chuck up some rubbish. But after that you would get 60 overs of quality cricket to watch. Invariably, Acfield and East coming on to bowl on the third day at an out ground like Colchester meant they were going to be in the wickets.

'I enjoyed the three-day game and the Sunday game format. That kind of cricket week was a cracker. If you go now you don't know if the game is going to last into the fourth day if you'd planned on attending that day, or you may have to watch one team bat for nearly two days because that is how they have chosen to pace it. I can understand the players saying it [three-day cricket] burned them out, but for the spectator it was great to watch. You knew you were going to see the possibility of your side batting again quite soon. It was cracking cricket played in the right way. When they [Essex] succeeded they succeeded well and when they failed they failed well.'

Meanwhile, Gooch and England were waiting to see how dry the pitch would be up in Lancashire. Monsoon-like rain fell in the previous month, prior to the World Cup clash with Canada at Old Trafford. Lancashire had taken the precaution of having the pitch patrolled and guarded for 48 hours before play started to make sure nothing stopped the game going ahead. When it did, the crowd were hardly given value for money. Canada were bowled out for 45 and England polished off the runs in 13 overs. Gooch played his part, scoring 21 not out.

McEwan's Mastery

There was no let up for Essex, who went straight into another championship game at Edgbaston. Warwickshire were far from full-strength because of the World Cup, and it showed. Essex, and in particular Lever, were rubbing their hands at the prospect of continuing their excellent form. Lever went into the match on the back of 22 wickets in his last two games.

An unchanged team was chosen by Fletcher, and Warwickshire chose to bat under a sky which was producing rain across the rest of the country. It was a day Lever would not forget in a hurry. The humidity meant he was primed to bowl a vast number of deliveries deemed unplayable. With the efficiency of a machine, Lever bounded into the wicket and put the ball on a length encouraging batsmen to play. When they did connect, it would be the edge of the bat, not the middle. And when they missed, the clang of death would be quickly ringing in their ears.

David Smith was trapped LBW, to be the first to go. Captain John Whitehouse was next, getting it all wrong to a ball differing slightly from the one which got Smith. Where was the next one going? Andy Lloyd was dropped twice by Turner off Phillip, who showed his catching fallibility after his display against Leicestershire. He made up for the spillages by having the same man caught by McEvoy at slip. At 87 for 4, Warwickshire's hopes were not completely faded. Soon after lunch they were gone. Lever bowled a spell of 5 for 16 in 15 overs to wipe Warwickshire out. An annoying stand of 45 between David Hopkins and Richard Savage for the last wicket led them to 185 all out.

Lever finished with 8 for 49 from 30 overs. It was a monumental effort from a man enjoying the best spell of bowling in his career. The figures beat his previous best of 8 for 127 in 1976.

McEvoy fell in Stephen Perryman's first over, leaving East to come in as nightwatchman. If Warwickshire thought they might be able to get him out early the next morning, they were in for a surprise. East proved hard to dislodge, hitting seven fours in his 49 and putting on 85 for the second wicket with Denness (34). Warwickshire's struggles worsened when Perryman was taken to hospital for an X-ray on his ankle.

It was not a game merely centring on the mastery of Lever. There was another Essex player doing his utmost to strike fear into any team. McEwan was joined by Keith Fletcher and the runs began to pour. McEwan gave only one chance, when on 22.

When Essex declared on 394 for 7, McEwan was still there, 208 not out, surpassing Percy Perrin's 74-year-old record for the highest individual score against Warwickshire. His main support came from Fletcher, the pair adding 219 for the fourth wicket.

KEN McEWAN: 'From the day I arrived at my digs, Mrs Queenie Saville's home in Balgonie Road, Chingford, to the day I left my own home in

Chelmsford, I felt totally at home in Essex – one big happy family with players, supporters and sponsors all closely knit. My main aim was to score as many runs as quickly as I could for whoever I played for – the only frustration was that I could not do it all the time. Fortunately for me, that was the way Essex played their cricket, and I was allowed to express myself freely. I was fortunate to have attended Queens College in South Africa where the facilities were fantastic and I had a very good grounding allowing me to play the way I played.'

Not a bludgeoner of the ball, McEwan relied more on precision and timing. It didn't mean he was shy when it came to clearing the boundary. In this innings, he did so five times, including two successive blows off Christopher Clifford, which were deposited over long-off without any fuss.

JOHN LEVER: 'Kenny was such a good player, who was so under-rated, certainly in South Africa. They didn't rate him as highly as everyone who played against him. He needed to bat every day as he thrived on it. He didn't thrive on the South African situation of playing once a week, then two weeks later playing another game. He was a top fielder and a good batter with a great technique, a decent tennis player who beat us all. He beat us one day and was taking the piss – he had the racket in his left hand.

'He is not a typical South African. He is fairly quiet, unassuming, not the Graeme Smith type. He used to sit in the corner and giggle. I will always remember the seasons he played and you would catch him sometimes when Alan Lilley would come out with something and Kenny would just be dumbfounded. The arguments later on between Pringle and Neil Foster were monumental and Kenny would just be sitting there giggling.'

By lunch on the final day, Warwickshire had reached 97 for 2 and there appeared to be no problems for their batsmen. Their control of the match was wrenched from their grasp by that man Lever, and East, who produced his first significant contribution of the season with the ball.

Lever completed another milestone in his scintillating month of wickets, finishing with match figures of 13 for 87. He took 5 for 38 to bowl Warwickshire out, with more than a little help from East's 4 for 34, for the lowly total of 134. It gave Essex victory by an innings and 75 runs. That made it 23 wickets in five days for Lever.

JOHN LEVER: 'I turned on the TV and the weather man said "The same sort of weather that John Lever seems to be enjoying is going to continue". It was slightly humid and sunny and it swung quite a bit, but to get a mention on national TV, I was thinking "Bloody hell".

'It just happened. It wasn't a reaction to being omitted from England's World Cup squad. My England career, I feel, I should have played a bit more. Everyone is going to feel the same way. The proof of the pudding is the wickets you get. I got quite a few for Essex and also got 70 odd in 20 Tests which is not a bad return so I do feel I should have played more.

'It's always a problem when you start off like a house on fire and it dries up a bit. You become a one-minute wonder, or have been found out, or aren't quite quick enough, which is a criticism I would have accepted. It is because I was left-arm. I think any left-armer has to rely on swing. There are two left-armers playing for Australia at the moment and they don't swing it. They won't get a top number of wickets. At that time Goochie gave me the nickname "Stanley". There was an advert on TV – how do you do it Stanley? – it stuck a little bit. Confidence was huge. I just expected to get wickets as soon as the first ball goes down and it swings a lot. I think my character – feeling as though I was fit, had done lots of running, had strong legs – kept me bowling and any number of times Fletch would say have you had enough and I would say just one more and then if I got a wicket I would carry on. I bowled long spells.

'Ackers, at the beginning of the season, along with Ray East, would not bowl for a long time. Through April and May the wickets were soft and a bit green so the ball would nip around a bit and Ray East would stand there at mid-off saying "I don't really feel part of this, I'm a fast bowler's sweater carrier", as he took the sweaters to the umpire and back again.'

Essex now led the championship by 60 points after Somerset and Kent suffered in the rain. It was a huge gap at that stage of the season and one which Essex would do supremely well – or badly, as the case may be – to relinquish. Having played so well up to that point, they would need to lose form spectacularly to be caught.

While Essex were about to go into their third back-to-back championship match against Somerset at Bath, Gooch was top-scoring for England in their six-wicket win over Pakistan at Leeds. In an extraordinary match dominated by the bowlers, Gooch was involved in an important stand of 47 with Boycott. It took a marvellous catch to remove him for 33 – the second highest score in the match. The result saw England through to the semi-finals, where they would meet New Zealand. Despite the clamour for Lever's inclusion in the squad, it was difficult to argue with the impressive performances of the England bowlers up to this stage.

Essex were spared facing two of the world's greatest players in Ian Botham and Viv Richards when their five-match winning run in the championship came to an end. Even without Botham and Richards, Somerset provided Essex with their sternest test for more than a month.

Summer arrived, even though the wicket was wet and slow. Somerset chose to bat. Lever found the going somewhat tougher than during the past two weeks, and, come mid-afternoon, he had just the one wicket to his name – his 50th first-class dismissal of the season.

Lever and his fellow bowlers toiled until 6.15pm, when Somerset declared on 277 for 9. It was painstaking stuff, as Lever went for two runs an over, and Turner, who took two wickets, and Acfield, who took three, being hit at a rate little more than two. Essex were left to negotiate their way through 45 minutes of cricket before the end of the day's play. They didn't make it. McEvoy made it five runs in his last three innings when he was stumped off the bowling of Keith Jennings. Not a wise piece of cricket in the circumstances.

MIKE MCEVOY: 'I remember it – it wasn't me charging down the wicket. I toppled over and was stumped down the leg side. I thought my front foot had come back in and wasn't out! It was quite hard going in at the end of the day and facing the last 20 overs or so. It was a case of survival but you had the target to aim for.'

East was back in his familiar role as nightwatchman, and when play started on the second day, he was worthy of more than such a tag. He batted confidently, adding 82 with Denness (39) and 63 with McEwan, who was enjoying his finest spell of the season. Two sixes in successive balls suggested the South African was on his way to another century, but he was bowled by Dennis Breakwell for 71, scored in 82 minutes. Hardie's 54 helped obtain full batting points, as Essex ended on 302 for 8.

STUART TURNER: 'Ray was a very talented bowler and he could bat too. He used to con bowlers as our nightwatchman. The poor guy who was next in after Ray used to be sat on the edge of his seat because Ray didn't obey the rules of a nightwatchman. He used to play his shots. I remember an incident when Tom Cartwright was bowling, and he was a fine bowler who could pitch it on a beer mat and do all-sorts. Ray went out and swept the first three balls he faced for four. He had a terrific talent for doing things like that.'

By the end of play, Somerset stood at 55 for 4 and in need of a minor miracle to save the game on the final day. Lever, Phillip and Turner had all bowled hostile spells, which could have been even more fruitful had four catches not been dropped.

Seeking to strengthen their position at the top of the table, Essex found it tough going on the final day. Just 15 runs were added in the first half an hour, but hopes were lifted when Lever dismissed Mervyn Kitchen. Nightwatchman Colin Dredge was surviving one LBW appeal after another, but from 63 for 5, rather than it being a formality for Essex, Somerset mounted a courageous recovery. Vic Marks counter-attacked, scoring 20 in his first four overs at the crease. He added 43 in ten overs with Dredge, who was on the receiving end of a number of bouncers.

Fletcher rang the bowling changes to try and gain a breakthrough, though none was immediately forthcoming. East eventually took the wicket of both Dredge, for 55, and Marks for 93. It was not Essex's turn to bat yet. Breakwell was given time, much to the annoyance of Fletcher and the Essex team, to score 54 not out when Somerset were finally called off by skipper Brian Rose.

It left Essex with 260 to win in 142 minutes, a task later criticised by Fletcher. Hallam Moseley posed problems for the Essex batsmen and Denness and McEvoy were out in the first few overs. Moseley was only playing because the giant Joel Garner was with the West Indies side playing in the World Cup.

He certainly took his chance, recording 5 for 18 as Essex hung on for a draw, finishing on 87 for 7.

The result saw Essex's lead cut to 56 points and Fletcher vented his anger at Somerset's tactics in his *Essex Chronicle* column. 'Inevitably we are going to lose somewhere, sometime, although I must say I was pleased that we did not get beaten in the three-day game against Somerset. You might think there is little difference losing and drawing such a match, but when opposition captains give one as little chance as did Brian Rose on the last day at Bath, they don't deserve to win matches. He really left us with no chance whatsoever on the final afternoon, and, although the wicket was doing a fair bit by that late stage, Somerset were unable to press home the initiative. Had they left themselves a bit more time and offered Essex some kind of challenge, they may well have also bought themselves an opportunity to finish the job.'

For Fletcher, it went down as a game Essex could have won. Catches were dropped at important times but he could not have any complaints about the way his players had been performing. There was no respite, as the John Player League was back in full flow and the championship match against Derbyshire was due to start the day after the draw with Somerset.

Wedged in the middle of the three-day match at Bath was the John Player League fixture. It was heavy going on a wet pitch after Essex chose to bat first. Lilley came in for McEvoy, while East was replaced by Pont. Denness and Lilley went cheaply and only Fletcher looked comfortable, staying to the end to score 51 not out. McEwan (14) was the only other batsman to make double figures in what was one of their poorest displays of the season. A score of 120 was not going to trouble Somerset, whatever the state of the pitch and they cruised to victory by nine wickets, with seven overs remaining. To cap what was a sad day, the Essex Supporters' Club coach broke down, delaying their return home.

Meanwhile, the nation was gripped by England's escapades in the World Cup. An appeal was broadcast by both team's managers before the match at Old Trafford, asking for spectators to behave following trouble during the match between England and Pakistan at Headingley the previous weekend. A capacity crowd of 22,000 saw New Zealand cover themselves with glory but just fail to book a place at Lord's for the final. In 60 overs, England made 221 for 8, with Gooch, in typical fashion, establishing the innings in the middle order. He put on 47 with Botham, including a six over the sightscreen, before he played on to his stumps for 71 – an innings which would once again earn him the man-of-the-match award. Gooch bowled three overs costing eight runs as England went on to victory by just nine runs.

Gooch and England would face the West Indies in the final, after the latter's 43-run win over Pakistan at The Oval.

A century in a second eleven match with Middlesex earned Lilley a place in the three-day side for the championship clash against Derbyshire at

Chelmsford. It was his first game of the summer in the longer format and his inclusion saw McEvoy unsurprisingly dropped. Also recalled was Pont in place of Acfield. The visitors won the toss and elected to bat on a good-looking wicket. They were in trouble when Phillip took two wickets in his first two overs and Lever made a further breakthrough in his fourth. Worse was to follow for Derbyshire when Hill was beaten for pace by Lever when playing back and was adjudged LBW.

Much would depend on the class of South African Peter Kirsten. He didn't have much time to show the contents of his batting locker, as he was bowled by Lever for 11. Essex had reduced Derbyshire to 53 for 6. Then Fred Swarbrook, John Walters and Tunnicliffe all hit half-centuries to put Essex on the back foot.

Derbyshire's fightback led some to wonder whether Essex were letting their grasp on the championship slip. They had not dominated the last few days of cricket in the way they had the early part of the season. The draw and defeat at Somerset could have been easily wiped from the memory, had Essex continued to dismiss the Derbyshire middle order and tail.

However, even great teams sometimes fall from their pedestal. It was not as if Essex were not trying. Their luck had run out. The three half-century makers were consistently beaten without finding the edge. It took a gallant effort from Lever and Phillip to bowl Derbyshire out for 258 in 97 overs. Lever took 5 for 72 and Phillip 4 for 59, as Fletcher stuck with his seamers on a wicket looking a little green. Before the close of play, Lilley failed to grasp his opportunity, gone for a duck, which again brought East to the middle as nightwatchman.

If proof was needed that Essex's title charge was not to be derailed, McEwan provided it on the second day. East began sensibly, scoring 19 before he was out. This brought the South African and Denness together. What happened next was pure class from McEwan. He raced to three figures in only 85 minutes, helped by 14 fours and two sixes. He so dominated the partnership with Denness that out of the 131 runs it produced, he had smashed 109.

It was the fastest century of the summer so far, beating the previous fastest ton scored by team-mate Turner, who took 113 minutes to blast Kent all over the park in May. Having resumed the day 250 runs behind Derbyshire, Essex were soon overtaking them. Scorching drives were the order of the day, as McEwan latched on to anything full, smacking up to three boundaries an over.

The cover boundary was being peppered by McEwan's off-side strokes, as Derbyshire captain David Steele juggled his bowlers to try and put a brake on the run flow. Steele even brought on his own slow left-armers and was greeted by the ball disappearing back over his head for six. McEwan's first 50 took 43 minutes and came up with a maximum off the opposition skipper.

Denness was content to take root at the other end. When the stand reached 100, McEwan had scored 83 of them. The partnership was finally broken in its 36th over when the score was 170. Denness was caught at slip for 35. His departure did nothing to halt McEwan. His thirst for runs saw him plunder 185 out of 239 scored during his 47 over stay at the crease.

GRAHAM GOOCH: 'Kenny McEwan would have been a fantastic Test player. He was one of those players you just loved to watch. You have players who get runs but they are not particularly eye-catching and pleasing to watch. Mark Waugh and David Gower were fantastic players and they were great to watch and that's the sort of player Kenny was. He was a great player, a prolific scorer and would have been a success in Test cricket.

'Ken would come in and caress the ball around. He was a stroke-maker, an artiste as a batsman. He played for us for eleven or 12 seasons before Allan Border came in 1986. He packed up and went back to his farm in South Africa, but he's a lovely fella.'

KEN McEWAN: 'I suppose I was naive enough to think South Africa would change and that we would be allowed to play again eventually, and, fortunately, things did change and we are playing international sport again. It just took longer than we all hoped for.'

McEwan's innings allowed the next Essex batsmen coming in to play without the pressure of keeping up the scoring rate. It also proved Essex could turn on the style at any moment, and any talk of them losing their touch was rammed right back down their critics' throats.

Pont and Turner refused to slow things down, instead ploughing on to help Essex to their highest score of the season. Pont gave one spectator even more to smile about when he launched a six into the tea bar. The fan dutifully plucked the ball out of the air one-handed and casually lobbed it back. It was an innings of authority from Pont, who had point to prove. In and out of the side, he was a durable cricketer. An extra seamer and scorer of quick runs when needed, he gave his captain plenty to think about when selecting the team.

Essex declared on 435 for 9, a phenomenal effort, from McEwan especially. The championship leaders had enough time to take a Derbyshire wicket before the close of play. Lever was charging in, even though the opportunity to put his feet up was fast approaching. He trapped Iain Anderson in front of the wicket to leave Derbyshire 1 for 1 overnight.

A fifth-wicket stand delayed Essex's march to another innings victory. The visitors resumed needing 176 to avoid that embarrassment and, with nine wickets in hand, there seemed no reason why they shouldn't force Essex to bat again. Fletcher was forced to remove Lever and Phillip from the attack when a breakthrough did not seem to be coming.

Turner came on at one end and Phillip switched ends, which did the trick. Steele, the one batsman capable of playing a long innings and denying Essex the win their batting display deserved, was snapped up at forward short leg by Hardie. The Scot was an expert in this position, fearless and quick to snap up any chance that came his way. Denness clung on to a catch in the gully off Turner to oust Kirsten, making the score 28 for 3.

The pitch was on the lively side. Overnight rain freshened it and the fizz remained well into the morning session. Derbyshire found it difficult to hit anything past the Essex field. Lever returned to take the fourth wicket, ending the resistance of opener Alan Hill (19) with the score on 36. Borrington and Barnett provided some resistance, holding up the inevitable. The pair's stubbornness saw the scoreboard barely move and spectators wishing they would either hurry up and score runs or simply get out. Borrington added three in his first half an hour. Barnett was no quicker, taking 20 minutes to get off the mark. Eventually, they put on 50 for the fifth wicket and, predictably, once Lever and East ended the partnership, Derbyshire had nothing left in the tank.

Lever, who passed 900 first-class wickets when taking his third in the innings, and Phillip took four wickets each to guide Essex to victory by an innings and 40 runs.

The final of the Prudential World Cup somewhat overshadowed Essex extending their championship lead to 69 points. They now travelled immediately to Tunbridge Wells, Kent to take on the defending champions.

ALL EYES ON GOOCH AT LORD'S
There were no empty seats at Lord's for the biggest match in the world in 1979. The moniker of world champions was up for grabs. The West Indies were out to retain it from their 1975 triumph and came to London with a line-up chock full of star names. The majority had either played, or would later play in English county cricket, lighting up grounds all over the country with their destructive, free-spirited batting and pace bowling which made batsmen reach for an extra arm and chest guard.

Brearley sent the West Indies in to bat. Much had been made of England's lack of a fifth specialist bowler. Essex fans would note that Lever was taking wickets for fun in county cricket and ask 'Why is this man not playing for our country?' Brearley and the England selectors preferred Boycott, Larkins and Gooch – a triumvirate of part-timers as fifth bowler. Gooch's medium pace was useful, though he could never be considered as a front-line international bowler, and the absence of Bob Willis made the West Indies' task easier.

England landed the first blow when Derek Randall, a whippet in the field, ran out Gordon Greenidge. Chris Old dismissed Haynes and the West Indies were 36 for 2. Then came the partnership which ultimately won the match. Collis King joined Richards at 99 for 4. The Barbadian not only helped himself to 86 out of a stand of 139, he took charge and outshone the player regarded as the King of West Indian cricket. It was a merciless display of cricket, with King facing just 66 balls and sending England's part-time bowlers relentlessly to the boundary. The threesome conceded 86 from 12 overs, with King striking three sixes and ten fours in a show of power.

Richards ruled the roost thereafter, reaching his century and going on to win the man of the match award for his 138 not out. The West Indies set England a target of 286. Gooch was going to have to produce something special if the hosts were to lift the trophy in front of their own fans.

The better batting conditions were England's as the sun came out and Boycott and Brearley stayed together for more than two hours, adding 129 for the first wicket. Boycott took 17 overs to reach double figures as the West Indies' pace bowlers did their job. Randall and Gooch led a brief assault but Gooch was bowled by the 6ft 8ins Garner. Whenever Garner came on to bowl, batsmen felt he would continue down the wicket and trample on them. His mixture of bounce from short of a length and yorkers made him one of the most testing propositions in world cricket. England were whitewashed before MCC members had time to get from the Long Room to their seats in front of the pavilion. Garner claimed five wickets for four runs in 11 balls and was twice on a hat-trick as England were bowled out for 191. West Indies had played a style of cricket which would be remembered for years to come.

GRAHAM GOOCH: 'That season was the start of my modern career. I had batted in the middle-order for Essex and a couple of times for England and done ok, and had my moments in one-day internationals in 1976. In 1978 I opened the batting after Fletch swapped myself and Brian [Hardie] around, which was the making of me and helped him as well. It helped my game and I got back into the England side. I went to Australia in the winter of 1978 and didn't do that well, but in 1979 I changed my stance and it was the start of the player that people saw over the next decade and a half, really. It helped me to drive the ball straight down the ground and changed me and made me a much better player.

'You have confidence in yourself but you work at your game and you evolve your game. That was the start of me evolving into the player I would be over the next decade or so. It was a change in technique, playing straighter, and all those things that I introduced worked for me and gave me a lot of success. I did well in the World Cup that year, and it all started to go right for me.

'I was very lucky. I had the two best captains that England have seen in recent times – Keith Fletcher and Mike Brearley. Brearley was a really great man-management captain and Fletch was a master tactician and a great innovator on the field. We were very lucky at Essex because he taught us the game, basically. He taught us how to react to different situations both as batsmen and in the field and passed on all of his knowledge. He was a very knowledgeable cricketer and we had the benefit of his knowledge down the years.'

Essex's Lever was given a great chance to stake a claim for an England Test place when he was called up by the MCC to play India at Lord's. Gooch was also named in the squad. A clutch of players were competing for a batting spot up for grabs. Gooch was sure to be in, but others, such as Larkins, needed to impress. Larkins endured a nightmare in the World Cup final. His bowling ran into the fire-storm batting of King and Richards, his fielding was nowhere near the required standard for Test cricket, and he was bowled first ball.

Kent were one of Essex's nearest challengers when the two sides began the three-day championship game at Tunbridge Wells on 23 June. It was the setting for one of the many great Ray East stories.

KEITH PONT: 'We got to just before tea against Kent at Tunbridge Wells one year and the umpire was Jackie Van Gelovan. He liked a drink or two, owned a pub, and had a really red face and was a wonderful laughing character. Ray came out to bat and he hit it straight down cover's throat. He's said to Jackie it was a bump ball. Jackie said it was out and tea would be taken. Ray argued all the way off. He never took his helmet off and was gesticulating all the way back to the pavilion. We went in for tea in this old pavilion and Ray sat in the corner with his green helmet and gloves on, eating his sandwiches through the grill on his helmet, shouting at Jackie across the room that it was a bump ball. He keeps repeating himself and Jackie tells him to shut up. They go back out after tea and there are two balls to be completed in the over. Ray has changed his helmet to a yellow one and walks out to bat. Jackie has had a few anyway and probably can't see the other end. He gives him guard and says play. Ray lifts up his helmet and says "Jackie, do you really think I was out?" At that point Jackie chased him off the field to the most extraordinary laughter. He ran off like a dog, stopping and looking back.'

The result of a match between teams at the top can often have a major bearing on where the title goes. In this instance, with the gap so huge, if Essex were to lose their lead would merely be cut. While defeat could set an alarm bell or two ringing in Essex heads, the sound wouldn't be heard too far away as the leaders were playing exciting, winning cricket and there was nothing to suggest it was going to change. Unless, of course, the trophy-less club could muster a way in which they would keep that unwanted tag. It would take some doing. But then, so does going 103 years without winning anything.

Fletcher lost the toss for the fourth time running in the championship, and Kent chose to bat. Gooch was playing in the World Cup final so Lilley kept his place, as did Pont at the expense of Acfield.

If Kent were to concede the title, they were not going to do so without a fight. This was clear from the opening day's play. It was a rare day of toil for the runaway leaders. For once, the Essex bowlers were not on top.

It began promisingly for Essex when Lever claimed his 51st wicket of the month by removing Charles Rowe with 13 on the board. When Turner struck to dismiss Bob Woolmer 25 runs later, Essex could afford thoughts thoughts of another rampaging success. However, Chris Tavare made sure this wasn't the case.

Tavare became known around the world as an immovable object. He would bat for hours and even days. He had the habit of walking halfway to square-leg after each delivery, forcing the bowler to wait for him to make his return to the wicket. His annoying style brought him 31 Test appearances and the Australians took a particular dislike to him. Despite his tendency to stick around longer than he was welcome, he could also play his shots. But it was rarely that they were seen.

Tavare came to the wicket in the seventh over and stayed until the 99th, when Kent declared. His time spent with Chris Cowdrey put a different complexion on an innings which had looked as though it may not last much past the lunch interval. Tavare was going through a lean spell, but showed why he was on the short list for the previous winter's tour to Australia. He underlined his trademark solid defence early on and then brought his strokes out to force Essex into a long spell in the field. Cowdrey, not so commanding, assisted in a stand of 113. He was Turner's second victim, caught by McEwan for 51.

East was given one of his longest spells of the season, bowling 32 overs, during which he took the wickets of Alan Ealham and John Shepherd before the total passed 200. Tavare batted on, ensuring Kent collected maximum batting points. They declared on 316.

By the close, Lilley had been pinned in front of the stumps from Underwood's first delivery. There was no shame in being one of Underwood's scalps. He was known as 'Deadly' Derek Underwood for a very good reason. His slow left-arm was more in the 'medium' bracket than 'slow'. When mixed with accuracy and turn, the outcome was a bowling technique and end product highly regarded on the world stage. Lilley did not allow himself long to work Underwood out. His opportunity to make a name for himself while Gooch was away had not been going to plan, so East kept Denness company until the close of play.

Torrential rain over the weekend flooded the ground and further overnight rain caused the match to be abandoned on the third morning. It gave the Essex bridge school time to master skills of a different type. Fletcher was not too disappointed by the early finish as he knew the weather had been kind to Essex during the opening summer months, compared to many less fortunate counties. He told the *Essex Chronicle*: 'It was simply a question of being philosophical when the rain interfered with our match against Kent, When there was uninterrupted cricket, the Essex bowlers did very well on a slow and unresponsive wicket, though there was mixed reaction at the prospect of watching Chris Tavare hit such a big score. He is a young man who has a bright future and must be considered unlucky to have missed selection for the tour to Australia last winter. In the good batting conditions which prevailed, he was able to get forward and play from there, and by the end of the afternoon we had all seen enough to convince ourselves of his potential. Let's just say it was a toss I would have liked to have won.'

Fletcher told readers the bridge came in handy when the rains came, and was a more popular diversion than watching the tennis from Wimbledon on television. The captain's focus was now on the Benson and Hedges semi-final which was looming large and he was keen for young players Lilley and McEvoy to score some runs.

'Things have gone pretty well for us so far but it would be nice if the youngsters, such as Alan Lilley and Michael McEvoy could get among the runs more. Both have so much ability and we have high hopes for them, but in recent innings they have too often been unfortunate enough to get in, and out again, at different times.'

Fletcher was unsure about ideas of Lever being recalled for the Test series against India. Despite Lever's tremendous form, Fletcher expected the selectors to stick with most of the bowling attack from the World Cup, meaning he would have his leading wicket taker available for the rest of the summer.

Although the weather had prevented Essex widening the gap over Kent, it had stopped their rivals making up ground. Nottinghamshire, lying second in the table, lost to Leicestershire, giving Essex some comfort going into their two-week break from championship cricket.

Gooch, one of England's major World Cup successes, was back in the Essex squad for the Gillette Cup first round clash with Lancashire on 27 June. His presence gave Essex a huge boost, as the club looked to put behind them the nightmare of the previous season's semi-final defeat to Somerset. Gooch's avalanche of runs dominated Essex's Benson and Hedges Cup progress and much was expected of him after his heroics in front of the television cameras and packed grounds at the World Cup.

The winners of the tie at Old Trafford would face an away match at Kent or Glamorgan. Lancashire and Kent both possessed extraordinary Gillette Cup records. Lancashire had won it four times and also been beaten finalists twice, while Kent were successful in two of their three trips to Lord's for the final.

GOOCH IS BACK

Lilley's sequence of just 21 runs in his last five innings led to Denness being preferred to partner Gooch. Lancashire won the toss and elected to bat on a pitch Essex would later report to Lord's for being 'unsatisfactory' for such an important match.

Barry Wood's involvement in the match was cut short when he felt the full force of a Phillip delivery which struck him below the belt.

RAY EAST: 'Barry Wood had been hit in the box by Norbert Phillip. He went down groaning and was on all fours. We asked him if he was alright and he groaned back "Water, water". When people get hit in the box, bugger it, everyone laughs. I shouted to the pavilion "He wants some water, *water*!" Out comes their 12th man with a glass of water and he runs on and I say "Give it to me, I'll take it on". He gave it to me and I said thank you very much and drank it. The 12th man said "he wanted the water". I said "No, I wanted a water, I don't know what he wants!" I saw Brian Taylor get hit in the box once and it was dreadful. He was a hard man, hard as nails. He couldn't walk. They had to carry him off.'

Alert fielding and tight bowling restricted Lancashire to 120 for 4 when the last 16 overs began. It was then, however, that 34-year-old Clive Lloyd and Jack Simmons changed the shape of the game. Lloyd stepped up a couple of gears and found a bludgeoning partner in Simmons. They thrilled the 8,000 crowd by adding 89 in 13 overs. The last ten overs yielded 102. Lever and Phillip came in for heavy punishment – Lever's 12 wicket-less overs costing 51 and Phillip's 70. Pont was the pick of the bowlers, with 2 for 25 off 12.

Set 248 to win, Essex's formidable batting line-up let them down, yet their start should have laid the foundation for victory. Denness and Gooch took the score to 52 in ten overs. The waywardness of Willie Hogg and Lee forced Frank Hayes to bring on his spinners – Simmons, Kim Hughes and David Lloyd. This brought a dramatic change to proceedings. Hughes picked up the prize wicket of Gooch when he held a simple return catch, and quickly followed it up with the scalps of Denness and Hardie. Sandwiched in the middle, McEwan was caught and bowled by Simmons. Essex suddenly found themselves in trouble at 80 for 4. A brief flourish from Fletcher (31) and Pont (27) hinted at a recovery. Yet it was not to be, Lancashire winning by 70 runs as Essex were all out inside 54 overs. The underdogs had conquered. Lancashire had only one championship victory in the bag and were out of the Benson and Hedges Cup, but the Gillette Cup was their competition yet again.

Fletcher admitted his side were well beaten and gave losing the toss as one of the key factors for Essex's exit. It left them with the Benson and Hedges Cup and county championship to focus on for the rest of the season. The John Player League was not in their sights.

June had been a memorable month for Lever, who took 53 first-class wickets, and McEwan, who played two of his best ever innings for the club. If someone had said to the players before the season begun they would be top of the championship and in the semi-final of the Benson and Hedges Cup come the end of June, they would have dismissed him as a fantasist.

Chapter Six

July 1979

PONTY'S BIG DAY

Essex began July having failed to win either of their previous two matches, having drawn with Kent at Tunbridge Wells in the championship and lost to Lancashire at Old Trafford in the Gillette Cup. As such, Keith Fletcher's men went into their John Player League fixture with Kent at Chelmsford on Sunday, 1 July without a victory since thrashing Derbyshire by an innings on the same ground on 22 June – their longest winless period of the season so far. Fletcher needn't have worried, however, as his players stormed back to winning ways with a nine-wicket victory over their near neighbours.

Ignoring the distraction of the Benson and Hedges Cup semi-final against Yorkshire three days hence, Essex reduced Kent to 77 for 7 before bowling them out for just 117. Gooch, with an unbeaten 48, Lilley and McEwan steered their side to victory with 14 overs to spare. It was a canter, and one that set Essex up superbly for their biggest match of the summer so far.

The build-up to the semi-final was tense, with players, commentators and newspaper reporters alike fully aware of the threat posed by John Hampshire's men. Yorkshire had lost just one of the 13 one-day matches they had contested in all competitions that summer. Crucially, perhaps, that one defeat had occurred on 1 July with a six-wicket John Player League defeat by Somerset at Scarborough. That day, only Bill Athey's unbeaten 50 had saved the White Rose county from total humiliation as they were skittled out for 128 by a Somerset team inspired by Ian Botham, who returned figures of 4 for 10.

As such, Yorkshire arrived at the County Ground fearing they might be beaten. In contrast, Essex were full of confidence. Rather than cowering under the pressure of battling for a place in their first-ever major one-day final, the players relished the challenge of upsetting the established order and booking their place at Lord's. Speaking to the *Evening Echo's* Alan Burkinshaw, John Lever exuded the optimism running through Fletcher's players.

'We are all looking forward to the match. The atmosphere should be tremendous and it will certainly help our lads to produce the better cricket. I am sure the match will be closely fought. Yorkshire never give up fighting and are a good side. But I feel we have the greater all-round strength. Obviously they have players who have the ability to win the game for them. We must respect Geoff Boycott, John Hampshire and Chris Old. They are great players but I feel we should also keep a watch on young Kevin Sharp. He is one of the country's most exciting young batsmen.'

The bookmakers shared Lever's optimism, installing Essex as 13-8 favourites. One factor surely swaying those odds was the fitness doubt over

Boycott. The England batsman had pulled a hamstring in making 130 in Yorkshire's championship draw with Somerset at Harrogate the previous week. The injury had prevented Boycott from batting in his county's second innings and, as Birkinshaw rightly pointed out 'his absence would greatly weaken Yorkshire's batting line-up and would improve Essex's chances of going to Lord's for the final on Saturday, 21 July'.

While Boycott was facing a race to be fit, Essex were at full-strength. Indeed, the only issue vexing Fletcher was his team selection. Acfield was pushing hard to be included at the expense of East, but the latter's superior batting and fielding made him a strong favourite to get the nod. Whatever decision the Essex captain would make, Birkinshaw himself was in no doubt that the home side would carry the day.

'I believe that the confidence gained from their great success in the County Championship this season, plus their great determination to prove to people outside Essex that they are capable of winning major trophies, will spur Fletcher's men to a memorable win.'

Come the big day, Saturday, 4 July, a capacity crowd of 8,000 spectators – 5,000 of whom arrived a full 90 minutes before the scheduled start – crammed into the County Ground. As expected, Acfield was left out in favour of East. More importantly, Boycott failed to recover from his hamstring injury, with Jim Love drafted in to deputise. Better news for Yorkshire came in the shape of a fit Chris Old, who shrugged off a rib injury caused by sneezing to take his place in the visiting side.

It was an event Francis Ponder wouldn't forget. The action, the perfect weather and the Chelmsford ground brimming made it the ideal sporting occasion to attend.

'It was a great day. They were one of those counties whose name was always up there as county champions, along with Lancashire. The perception was Essex would always do well to compete with the likes of them. Suddenly we were overtaking these teams. With Boycott and Bairstow in their ranks, it made it a big day without what was at stake. The crowd was ten deep in scorching sunshine. When you looked at the ground on a day when there wasn't any cricket on, it was hard to believe it was a county cricket ground before it was developed. Essex were still the poor relation of county cricket.'

Fletcher began the day well, winning the toss and inviting Yorkshire to bat. However, the decision appeared to have backfired as captain John Hampshire and Richard Lumb made a confident start. The latter square drove Lever for four off the third ball, sparking an opening stand that would muster 107 in just 27 overs, before Hampshire was caught by Turner off the bowling of East. At that stage, Fletcher later admitted 'I was glad to see the back of him, but still thought we would be left chasing a total in the region of 250'.

As it happened, the skipper need not have worried as his bowlers ripped into Yorkshire's middle order. The much-heralded Sharp was trapped leg before by Phillip without scoring, before East bowled Athey for just one. When Love was caught by McEwan off the bowling of Pont for two, Yorkshire were wobbling at 123 for 4. And still the wickets kept falling. Lumb was bowled by Phillip for 75 and the combined talents of Lever and Turner ensured the innings folded like a pack of cards. From a position of strength midway through their allotted 55 overs, Yorkshire crumbled to 173 for 9. Lever, Phillip and East finished with two wickets each, while Turner and Pont also took one apiece.

Chasing 174 to win in 55 overs to reach a first major final would prove no easy task, though, especially when Lilley was caught by wicket-keeper David Bairstow off the bowling of Graham Stevenson to leave Essex 2 for 1. When McEwan (18) and Fletcher (7) both perished, the hosts were 68 for 3, with only the imperious Gooch holding the innings together. In fact, the England man was doing more than that, caressing the ball around on his way to a fine 49. However, when he was dismissed by Arnie Sidebottom with the score on 99, alarm bells rang ever louder. What was needed was someone with a calm head and a sense for the big occasion. Enter Keith Pont.

A consistent contributor with the bat in one-day cricket already that season, Pont would be the man to steady the ship. An innings of 36 that spanned 25 overs was just what was needed to quell the nerves that had got the better of his more illustrious colleagues. Pont, who had failed to establish himself in the championship side, proved his worth when his team needed him most. Although he fell with five runs still needed for victory, there was no doubt as to the value of an innings played under severe pressure. Afterwards, the 26-year-old was understandably delighted with his own contribution.

'That was the most important knock I've ever played. There was no need to throw the bat and I made up my mind to go out and get my head down. If I did that, I was fairly confident the runs would come. And they did. I was annoyed at getting out when we were so close to winning but we're through to the final. That's all that matters.'

He was right. Essex had prevailed by three wickets and were on their way to Lord's. They were one victory away from the first silverware in the county's 103-year history and Fletcher, for one, was immensely pleased with Pont's match and gold award-winning display.

KEITH PONT: 'It was my opportunity to show it wasn't just about how hard you could hit it. It was about thinking and manipulating the play in such a way it would build. It was my chance to shine and I did. I felt very proud to receive the man-of-the-match and to be the person who achieved that to get us to the final. Nobody can ever take that away from me. I was a big hitter, but this was an example showing my 'six-and-out' tag was not warranted. As a player you develop and I became more of a man for this.'

Writing in *The Guardian*, Richard Yallop was equally impressed with Pont's calm in the eye of the gathering Yorkshire storm: 'Much credit must go to

Pont, so often a six-and-out man, who came in when Essex were showing signs of the shakes at 99 for four, curbed his natural inclination to swing the blade (noted by John Hampshire, who posted a long-on and long-off) and saw the crisis through with great responsibility. It was only when Essex needed four to win that he relaxed his guard, swinging and giving a catch to mid-off.'

All that remained was for Essex to discover who they would face in St John's Wood on 21 July. Surrey had travelled to Derby and, after losing the toss and being asked to bat first, had mustered just 166 for 8. Despite 70 from South African Peter Kirsten, the home side failed to overhaul their very reachable target and were bowled out six runs short with 16 balls remaining. Barbadian Sylvester Clarke and Hugh Wilson had been Surrey's heroes, taking three wickets apiece to lead Surrey to victory. On paper, Essex could not have hand-picked a worse opponent – in six previous Benson and Hedges Cup meetings, Surrey had won them all.

THE 'MAD STAMPEDE' BEGINS

Having watched their heroes reach their first major final, Essex's members reacted with understandable glee. In the *Evening Echo,* Alan Birkinshaw wrote excitedly of the 'mad stampede' for tickets. 'Cup final fever' was sweeping the county, but there was bad news on the horizon for the thousands upon thousands of supporters eager to book their place at Lord's.

The day after Essex's dramatic semi-final victory, general manager Peter Edwards revealed the county would receive just 4,000 tickets for the final. With 6,000 members and countless more fans desperate for a piece of the action, it became immediately apparent that not everybody was going to get in. Essex would request further tickets, but there were only two hopes. One was that opponents Surrey would fail to sell their own allocation of 4,000 – a long shot considering the county's close proximity to the final venue – while the other was that Essex would be offered tickets returned by counties who had failed to reach the final. Edwards was cautiously optimistic.

'Usually the counties do return some of their tickets and we are hoping that we may be able to obtain some for our fans. It seems as if everybody wants to go to Lord's. Sadly we will not be able to satisfy everybody. Naturally we have a duty to offer the tickets to our members first, and they will go on sale at Southend on Saturday [14 July]. We will also be selling them at Chelmsford, Ilford and Colchester. Then if there are any left we will be putting them on general sale from 16 July. Obviously we have had no experience of this sort of cup fever. But it is a nice problem to have and one we wouldn't mind having in the future.'

Tickets, Edwards announced, would be sold only to personal callers at the county's four grounds. Postal applications would not be accepted. If members wanted to be at Lord's, they would have to queue. Tickets would be priced from £4.75 upwards.

Birkinshaw himself correctly, if somewhat obviously, forecast that the final would attract a 'full-house' to Lord's. More controversially, the reporter suggested that Essex would enter the final as favourites: 'But they know they will have to lay low the Surrey bogy [sic] if they are to reward their supporters with the first major trophy in the club's 103-year history. Essex have played Surrey six times in the competition and lost on every occasion.'

Thankfully for Edwards and those members fearing they would have to watch the final live on television – the match was being screened by the BBC – their prayers were answered just 48 hours later with the announcement that 2,000 further tickets would be made available to Essex. Shockingly, however, the extra allocation came not from the eliminated counties but from Surrey! Edwards himself was astounded, but delighted to be able to cater for those who would otherwise have been left hugely disappointed.

'I was amazed by the offer of more tickets. With the match being played just a stone's throw from their Oval ground, I thought Surrey would have no difficulty in getting rid of their allocation. Still, I'm not complaining. The more available for our supporters the better. I'm not sure yet how many more tickets will be sent on to us, but I understand that we'll get in the region of 2,000. And I don't anticipate much trouble in selling them. The demand has really been fantastic.'

BACK TO THE DAY JOB

While Essex's supporters concerned themselves with securing their spot at the final, the county's players returned to action on Sunday, 9 July. A 7,000-strong crowd packed into Southend's Southchurch Park for the John Player League clash with Sussex. The game turned out to be a nerve-jangling affair as the masses were treated to a nip-and-tuck match that could have gone either way.

Batting first, the hosts made 199 for 5 from their 40 overs, with Gooch leading the way with a patient 77. The England opener hit just four boundaries in an untypically sedate innings, but according to the *Evening Echo* 'he batted with great authority and scored freely enough to keep the scoreboard ticking over'. Fletcher, who hit one huge six off John Spencer, made an unbeaten 46, while Hardie, McEwan and Lilley also passed 20.

Sussex set off like a train in pursuit of their target of 200, with openers Peter Graves and Gehan Mendis taking the score past 50 in the tenth over and reaching 108 before the former was caught behind by Smith off the bowling of East. Graves' departure for 55 sparked a 'startling slump' that saw the visitors collapse to 153 for 7 in the 32nd over. Mendis, Pakistan star Javed Miandad, and England batsman Paul Parker were among those to perish as Pont, Lever and Phillip all got among the wickets.

It was left to Fletcher's expert field placings to seize the day for Essex, leaving the Sussex pair of Tony Pigott and Arnold Long unable to score quickly enough to reach their target. Sussex ended on 190 for 7, nine runs short.

As a strange aside, the scorecard published in the *Evening Echo* suggested Essex had, in fact, lost by three wickets!

On the same day, Trevor Bailey expressed his surprise at John Lever's omission from the England squad for the first Test against India. Lever had taken 65 first-class scalps by that stage, putting him at the head of the country's leading wicket-takers.

According to Nigel Fuller, writing in the *Echo*, 'Lever was considered by many as a certainty for the match starting at Edgbaston in three days time.' Instead, the selectors stuck with the trio of seamers who had served them at the World Cup, namely Chris Old, Bob Willis and Mike Hendrick. The decision left former Essex captain and England Test player Bailey stumped.

'I find it hard to believe Lever is not included in the party. He's done everything possible to deserve and justify a recall, be still he's overlooked. It doesn't make sense to me. If someone had produced comparable form with the bat, there's no way they'd have been left out. I'd have definitely had Lever in for either Old or Willis, neither of whom really impressed in the World Cup.'

Quoted in the same article, Lever himself was his usual magnanimous self, admitting: 'I didn't bowl very well in the recent Test trial against the Indians so I can't have any complaints.'

Just a day later, Lever's patience and understanding would be rewarded when Old – a doubt for the previous week's Benson and Hedges Cup semifinal with a rib injury caused by a violent sneeze – was forced to withdraw from the England squad with a groin problem. Lever heard the news in a phone call from Lord's requesting him to report for duty at Edgbaston. It came midway through the final afternoon of Essex's ten-wicket championship win over Sussex. 'It came as a complete surprise but I'm delighted to be back in the reckoning,' said the bowler.

It turned out to be a day of double celebration for Lever as his wickets helped Essex complete a ten-wicket championship victory over Sussex at Southchurch Park – a success that stretched their lead over second-placed Somerset to 60 points.

Before the game begun, speculation was rife that Pont would make way for Acfield to take advantage of the slow Southend wicket. As it happened, however, the young all-rounder would keep his place on what turned out to be yet another seamer-friendly surface. All 20 Sussex wickets to fall would be taken by the unstoppable seam trio of Lever, Phillip and Turner.

Beginning the final day 49 runs behind with just four second innings wickets standing, Sussex were all out for 204, setting Essex just ten runs to secure their seventh championship win of the summer. While it was Lever and Phillip who completed the success, it had been the batting of Gooch and Denness on the first day that had set the platform. The duo ensured Sussex skipper Arnold Long paid for losing the toss by putting together a magnificent stand of 170 for the first wicket – the biggest of the summer for Essex in the championship

– in 55 overs. Gooch hit 86 while, at the other end, Denness hit 16 fours in a chanceless 136 before being stumped by Long off the bowling of Chris Waller.

McEwan and Fletcher continued the run spree before the latter declared the Essex innings at 338 for 5. There was little sign of the carnage to follow as Kepler Wessels and John Barclay safely negotiated their way through to the close. On the second morning, it was a different story. Once the opening pair had been parted with the score on 28, Lever, Turner and Phillip tore through the remaining batsmen, reducing a sorry Sussex to 143 all out. Fletcher asked opposite number Long to follow-on and the second innings followed much the same pattern as the first. Again, Lever and Phillip, who returned match figures of 8-97, were the chief tormentors as Long's men subsided to 82 for 5. Chris Phillipson launched a brave rearguard action before he was trapped leg before by Turner for 42. Shortly thereafter, Denness and Gooch knocked off the meagre total required for victory in less than two overs.

Lever now had 72 first-class wickets for the summer, stretching his lead over his rivals still further and thoroughly impressing the watching *Guardian* correspondent Henry Blofeld, who wrote that it was was 'no wonder the England selectors looked no further than Lever to replace Old' for the First Test against India at Edgbaston.

In Birmingham, Lever would have to contend with fulfilling 12th man duties for Mike Brearley's side. The England captain kept faith with the tried and trusted Willis, Botham and Hendrick, leaving the Essex man to do little more than carry the drinks as his three rivals bowled their country to a thumping innings and 83 runs success.

Gooch, in contrast, had a ball, making 83 from just 109 balls as England piled up 633 for 5 in their first innings. Boycott made 155, future Essex player Geoff Miller 63 not out, and Gower a stupendous unbeaten 200. Strangely, India's Kapil Dev would take all five wickets to fall.

In reply, England's seam trio took seven wickets between them as India were shot out for 297. Asked to follow-on by Brearley, Botham took five wickets and Hendrick four as the tourists made just 253 second time around. While Lever was understandably disappointed to miss out, not just on a Test cap, but also the chance to play for Essex in their important championship game against Nottinghamshire, Gooch was able to celebrate yet another famous win.

THE CRUCIAL GAME

With Lever and Gooch on England duty, Essex welcomed Nottinghamshire to Southchurch Park the following day, 11 July, for a crucial County Championship match without their best bowler and batsman. The visitors, boasting New Zealand all-rounder Richard Hadlee – who could have joined Essex himself in 1977 – and South Africa captain Clive Rice, posed a serious threat.

Lilley and Acfield were brought in to replace the missing England stars. The enforced changes appeared to make little difference as the young opener shared an opening stand of 66 with Denness. Following the departure of McEwan for 13 with the score on 106, however, Essex's innings subsided alarmingly. While the top nine batsmen all reached double figures, only Denness, Lilley and Fletcher made more than 20. As a result, Hadlee's 4 for 49 helped to dismiss the home side for a relatively moderate 240.

Nottinghamshire's other overseas favourite, Rice, then compounded Essex's misery by scoring 86 out of his county's 300 all out. Trevor Tunnicliffe added 56, Michael Smedley 34, the marvellously named Basher Hassan 32, and Hadlee 31 to give their side a 60-run first innings advantage. On a pitch offering turn and bounce to the spinners, the visitors' lead was more than useful.

By the close of play on the second day, Nottinghamshire's slow left-armer Mike Bore, Hadlee and Rice had reduced Essex to 111 for 5 – a lead of just 51 with half of their batsmen back in the pavilion. When Fletcher fell to Bore for 43 early on the third morning, the game appeared to be all but up. The visitors were on the verge of a famous victory, but they were to be stunned by two unlikely pairings.

Norbert Phillip had made just 119 runs in his previous ten championship innings as he strode out to bat with Essex precariously placed on 80 for 5. Stuart Turner, meanwhile, had failed to pass 50 since opening the season with a brutal 102 against Kent. The duo may not have been in the greatest of form, but their partnership now paved the way for a dramatic victory. They employed a mixture of defence and aggression to put on 66 for the seventh wicket, extending Essex's lead to 119 before Phillip was caught by Hassan off Bore for 40. Turner continued, though, reaching an unbeaten 68 and sharing a vital last-wicket stand of 42 with Acfield. When Essex were finally dismissed, they had totalled 229 – an advantage of 169.

Nottinghamshire had been set 170 in a little over four hours to record a shock victory over the title-favourites. They looked well on their way when Hassan and Smedley steered them to 87 for 1. By then, Fletcher had tossed the ball to his spin-twins East and Acfield. The unlikely room-mates would not let their skipper down.

KEITH FLETCHER: 'I used to always field close and as captain you lead from the front. The places I fielded I was likely to get hit. If I was to stand there and take the blows I expected other people to do the same thing. If I wanted someone to come in there they would. You can pressurise batters and kid them into all sorts of things. Even if the ball isn't turning you can kid them it is. I'd say to Ackers and Easty "just turn one or two balls an over and we'll do the rest around the bat". They kept it tight and we would get them out.'

From a position of strength, the visitors collapsed in what turned out to be a horror show on Friday the 13th. Acfield had Hassan caught by Hardie for 49 and bowled Smedley for 16. East then removed Rice, Tunnicliffe, Kevin

Mackintosh and Hadlee – the last two for ducks – before Acfield returned to get rid of Eddie Hemmings, Bore and Peter Hacker to leave Nottinghamshire all out for 123. Essex had won by 46 runs and stretched their lead over second-placed Somerset to 60 points.

Writing in *The Guardian*, David Frost described Essex's eighth championship victory in 13 matches as 'an astonishing feat of escapology'. For Acfield and East, it had been a chance to prove their worth after a strangely frustrating opening to the season.

While Lever, Phillip and Turner had taken wickets galore, the spinners had found their work limited on the green, damp pitches. At last, they had felt needed. In Essex's hour of need, the duo had well and truly stepped up to the proverbial plate. Both returned their best figures of the season so far – East took 5 for 56 and Acfield 5 for 28.

RAY EAST: 'Bowling Notts out was the big game for Ackers and I. We did bits and pieces in the championship but it was John Lever who would have the ball. I went from taking 90 wickets the previous season to not even half of that. I think it's all relevant to the amount of overs you bowl. If you bowl 400 overs you expect to get 40 wickets so it's one every ten. I think I bowled 800 in 1978 and only 400 in 79 so it was relevant. We had people who could do a job when required. We had a balanced side which helped us. These days you rarely see two spinners playing in a side. We had two opening bowlers, two spinners, Turner as the extra seamer and then Goochie and Pont who could bowl a bit. It was a balanced cricket side.

'We did feel a little bit out of it at times. I could bat a bit and got a few runs which kept me in it in some games. At the end of the day we were always important as were needed to bowl and runs were a bonus.

'David and I were totally different bowlers. He was more of a run-saver who would tie a batsman down and say "you make a mistake". I was prepared to toss it up and get hit to take wickets and that dovetailed nicely. We came from different backgrounds but became great friends. There was good-natured banter. Sometimes he felt he should be bowling when I was bowling and vice-versa. At the end of the day if we won the game and Ackers took seven wickets and I only got two I would be as happy for him as I was for winning the game. I wasn't the kind of person who, while he was bowling, hoped he got smacked around the ground and didn't get a wicket.

'I did feel sorry for him when he got left out and he got left out a lot. I think he wasn't, and he would admit it, one for getting many runs and wasn't as good in the field. You always say these days, and I say it to my youngsters at school, if you have three strings to your bow it is better than two. If you've the same ability with bat and ball as the next chap but can field better you will get in. I felt sorry for him when he didn't play because of the state of the pitches as much as anything else. We were playing on green pitches. But there were spells when he would play in one-day games and I wouldn't, so there were times when I was left out for him. He couldn't bat in the context of county cricket, but if you saw him in club cricket you'd think he could bat.'

DAVID ACFIELD: 'The match against Nottinghamshire was the big game because they were only just behind us. I put on 40-odd with Stuart Turner and then we won the game by about the same number of runs. Ray and I had hardly bowled at all before then but then we bowled them out. I took 5 for 28 and Ray took five wickets as well. That was *the* game.

'Rooming with Ray was a madhouse. It worked because we did it for 20 years and we're still great mates. It worked in a strange sort of way. They did try to separate us at one stage but we moaned so much that, in the end, they decided to put us back together again. That was better, really, because we'd always moan. We were great mates but of course we were rivals. Of course sometimes only one of us would play. He tended to get the nod at that stage because he batted better than I did and he bowled left-arm turning away from the bat which was always going to be better. He tended to get the nod and it was only from about 1981 onwards that I started to get the nod instead.

'We were both unloved, though, and there was an immense amount of piss-taking against us. We christened ourselves the "Seamers' Sweater Carriers" because we never bowled and used to just be there to shine the ball. We were the "SSC" from 1979 and so we went on like that from there. We were a little clique on our own, Easty and myself.'

Essex were momentarily brought back to earth by Northamptonshire, who recorded a five-wicket John Player League victory at Wardown Park, Luton, on Sunday, 15 July. By then, though, the championship leaders could have been forgiven for having turned their attention to the little matter of the Benson and Hedges Cup final.

THE FINAL COUNTDOWN

With all eyes turning towards Lord's, the major talking point moved from the availability of tickets to Essex's team selection. Denness, fresh from a useful innings of 44 in the defeat by Northamptonshire, was pushing hard for a recall at the expense of young Lilley. Acfield, meanwhile, had given captain Fletcher a timely reminder of his talents in the improbable win over Nottinghamshire. The skipper, renowned for his rock-solid decision-making, had two tough choices to make.

Nigel Fuller, writing in the *Evening Echo* on 16 July, labelled Fletcher's quandary over his choice of opening batsman 'a ticklish problem'. The reporter, rightly as it turned out, plumped for the venerable Scotsman: 'My guess is that Denness, with his vast experience to go with his current form, will get the vote over Lilley.'

The following day, Fletcher himself was clearly less sure of his own choice than Fuller. Both batsmen, the skipper pointed out, had reason to believe they should be involved in Essex's first-ever major final.

'I think it's the toughest decision I've had to make as skipper. For once I can put up a good argument for both players. While Alan has not put it together recently, he's turned in some good performances in earlier rounds to help get us into the final. Mike, on the other hand, has been in good nick recently and cannot be ignored. I console myself by being thankful for having two such fine players to choose from. But that doesn't make my job any easier. For I know whatever conclusion I arrive at, someone will be left bitterly disappointed. This is a game in which everyone wants to play. That's only natural. But unfortunately, someone has got to miss out.'

Fletcher revealed that he would wait until Friday, 20 July, the day before the final, to make his mind up. Until then, Lilley and Denness would be forced to wait on tenterhooks. The former had won a gold award for the 70 he made against Sussex in the group stage and also plundered a fine century against the Combined Universities, while Denness had scored heavily in recent weeks. The pair, along with the rest of the squad, were given Wednesday and Thursday off, ostensibly to relax, but more likely to ponder on whether or not they would be part of the team that would grace Lord's.

KEITH PONT: 'Keith Fletcher was a wonderful tactician but, and I've said this to his face, when it came to diplomacy and his players he was crap. He was one of those players who just didn't know how to tell you what was going on. I walked out to the field at Ilford and there were 12 of us as he hadn't told us what the team was. I knew I was 12th man but he hadn't said anything so I walked out and said where do you want me to field? The answer I got was why don't you **** ***, you're not playing! I said 'oh, I didn't realise'. He did the same thing for the next game and I stood up on the bannisters and leant across and shouted out to him as he went on the field: 'I presume this means I'm not playing then!' So, there was always this business about what Keith Fletcher was really like.

'For me, tactically he was just amazing. I found his ability to judge the set up brilliant. Dealing with players wasn't his greatest asset, which I think was borne out when he went to England and his dealings with players perhaps wasn't the best. I liked him very much, though.'

Meanwhile, the country's finest cricketing scribes were making their own minds up about who would prevail that Saturday afternoon. The finest of the lot, John Arlott, believed Fletcher's men had what it takes to dismiss Surrey's challenge. In a piece entitled 'Essex at last?' the great writer made a strong case for the bridesmaids to finally bury the ghosts of the past 103 years. While Arlott was convinced Essex had the stronger of the two teams, he also pointed out the importance of the fact that both Robin Jackman and West Indian paceman Sylvester Joseph were struggling to be fit for the final.

'Essex, of course, are favourites to beat Surrey in the Benson and Hedges Cup final in front of a full house at Lord's today, and thus win the first major honour of their 103-year history. Their chances look even stronger for the fact that Surrey's two opening bowlers, the West Indian Sylvester Clarke and Robin Jackman, are doubtful to play. Even if they are passed fit, the strain and pressures of the one-day game are such that an injury could be revived … Essex are well-equipped at all points; and they have been long over-limit experts without ever winning one of its chief prizes … They are a fit side, their fielding is always good, and Fletcher is as shrewd a captain as any.'

Attention was taken away from the final briefly by two other news items concerning Essex. Both were of the positive variety. Firstly, following a bumper week in 1979, general manager Edwards confirmed that Southend's Southchurch Park would again host festival cricket in 1980. The thrilling championship win over Nottinghamshire had been the highlight of a superb week by the seaside, and the town's cricket fans would have plenty more to cheer about the following year, Edwards forecast. The second announcement was equally, if not more popular. Lever was to be awarded a benefit year to begin the new decade.

Friday 20 July, the day before the final, saw Essex's players report to the County Ground for a pre-match meeting and for Fletcher's all-important team announcement. Or, at least, that is what the squad thought. Instead, the captain decided to wait until the morning of the game to name his final eleven. The agonising wait for Denness, Lilley and Acfield would endure for a further 24 hours. Fletcher explained to Nigel Fuller in the *Evening Echo* that he wanted to gauge the conditions at the Home of Cricket to give his team the best possible chance of success.

'I don't want to be caught on the hop by naming the side too soon. I don't know what conditions await us tomorrow and I want to take a long, hard look at the pitch before coming to any decision.'

Fuller speculated that, if Fletcher found the Lord's wicket to be 'firm and true', Lilley would get the nod over Denness, whose game was better suited to a green, more unpredictable surface. The captain himself also dispelled any suggestion that Surrey's perfect Benson and Hedges Cup record against his team had left the bookmakers' favourites nursing an inferiority complex. In contrast, Fuller found Fletcher in bullish mood.

'We beat them in the Gillette Cup last year and have had our fair share of success against Surrey in John Player League matches. It just so happens that everything has gone their way when we've met in the B&H but that's no reason to get all jumped up. This is another day; another match. And, while I honestly believe Surrey are a much-improved side and one to be respected, we've also come on a bit. We haven't reached the final and got to the top of the championship table by accident. We are there because we've worked hard together and are a darn good team. And I'm confident we'll confirm the point tomorrow, although we fully expect Surrey to make it tough for us.'

Fuller himself, like Arlott, was convinced that Essex would emerge as winners on their big day. The reporter, who went on to cover the county's ups and

downs for a further 30 years, even made a bold prediction of how things
would pan out at Lord's, writing 'I'm tipping Essex to end their long, long wait
for success by getting home by 40 to 50 runs or three or four wickets'. He
would prove to be a pretty accurate prophet.

SUCCESS AT LONG, LONG, LAST

Saturday, 21 July 1979 was a bright, if slightly cloudy mid-summer's day in
north-west London. Lord's was packed to the rafters, with Essex supporters
outnumbering their Surrey counterparts in all parts of the famous old ground.
Surrey captain Robin Knight won the toss and, as tradition dictated even in
those early days of one-day cricket, invited Fletcher's men to set his side a target to chase.

DAVID ACFIELD: 'Ray was picked because he was a better batsman and
a left-arm spinner. It was simple. What it meant was that I never played in a
Lord's final, even though I played in semi-finals, quarter-finals and everything.
The Boundary Club wanted to put on a dinner this summer for the Benson
and Hedges Cup victory but I'm not going. All I can remember is it being a
bloody miserable time of my life. I didn't enjoy it and I don't want to keep on
pretending that I did. I've done my bit. For 30 years I've turned up and smiled
sweetly but I've got to the stage [where I won't do it anymore].'

Essex fan Francis Ponder wouldn't miss the game for anything and could-
n't wait for the action to begin. He was pleased to see Denness chosen ahead
of Lilley in the side. 'The nerves weren't there on the day. It was a beautiful
occasion and when you see your team bat first and things go well it eases the
mind. We felt Essex could beat anybody but Surrey had some damn good players. I didn't want to see Lilley open. I knew which one was the better cricketer
out of the two. Denness was your England international and was a class act. I
thought Lilley was in the team because he was Gooch's mate! Lilley was a good
one-day player, though. He did a good job, as did Pont, but was never going
to be a fixture in the team.'

STUART TURNER: 'That day was just amazing. It always used to get me,
walking down the stairs at Lord's and out onto the field with a full crowd there.
It made the hairs on the back of my neck stand up on end. All the overseas
players will tell you that there is nowhere like walking out at Lord's and actually playing there. To walk down the steps and through the Long Room and
see all the old boys sitting there on a chair half-dead – it's a magical place. I'm
now an MCC member and it's also a great place for meeting people as well that
you haven't seen from one year to the next.'

With a light breeze blowing across the outfield, Gooch and Denness –
Fletcher had plumped for Denness's experience over Lilley's exuberance, ending the youngster's record of having played in every round – were greeted by
a crescendo of noise as they emerged from the Long Room, walked down the
pavilion steps and onto the outfield. The vast majority of the thousands of

Essex supporters who had searched long and hard for tickets had been successful. For one day, Lord's was Chelmsford. Surrey didn't know what had hit them.

In his book *A Cricketer's Cricketer*, Lever wrote: 'I had never heard anything like it from an English crowd. It was more like Eden Gardens, Calcutta, than St John's Wood.

RAY EAST: 'It was felt if you lost the toss at Lord's and were put in you stood no chance. It was a dream come true playing at Lord's. Having played there numerous times before with 1,000 people dotted around, to go there in front of a full house was something I will never forget. There was the roar when Gooch and Denness came down the steps to go and bat which was incredible. We had the majority of supporters there.'

KEITH FLETCHER: 'Lord's is my favourite ground. I enjoyed playing there more than anywhere else, whether it was for Essex or England. I still go to watch Test matches and there is nothing like the atmosphere on the first morning. The atmosphere is unbelievable. Calcutta when it has 115,000 takes some beating but Lord's has everything.'

Francis Ponder was one of them making the noise: 'It was a lovely July day and I will always remember Gooch and Denness walking down the steps and onto the pitch. There was this unexplainable roar. You normally get your segments of fans in certain areas of the ground, but this just seemed to hit you from all around. It seemed like we outnumbered the Surrey fans ten to one. The day was perfect.

'I saw what was probably the best batting I have ever seen from an Essex pair when Gooch and McEwan were together. The power of Gooch hitting the ball here, there, and everywhere, and the wristy, classy strokeplay of McEwan. It was brilliant to watch. McEwan was one of the best signings Essex ever made. He treated the fans for years to come. From 166 for 1, I thought we'd have to be bad from here on in to lose.'

Gooch, in the form of his life, hit three early boundaries as Essex rattled along to 21 without loss in just three overs. Denness, too, was hitting the ball with a cleanness and confidence. Surrey, for whom Joseph had failed a pre-match fitness test, were already on the back foot. The removal of the former England captain with the score on 48, caught by David Smith off the bowling of Hugh Wilson, provided no respite for the fielding side, with McEwan merely picking up where Denness had left off.

Wilson twice beat the South African's outside edge, but it would not be long before the prolific McEwan found the boundary with a pair of imperious off-drives. Gooch, at the other end, settled in to play a long and, as it turned out, match-winning innings. The England opener caressed the ball around the wide open spaces, while McEwan spanked and heaved Surrey's already weary bowlers to all parts. The partnership reached 118 in just 26 overs by the time the pair sat down for lunch with the scoreboard showing 166 for 1.

Shortly after the interval, however, Wilson made the breakthrough, having McEwan caught behind by Jack Richards. By then, though, the damage had been done. McEwan had scored 72 from 99 balls, hitting ten fours in his 96-minute stay at the crease. His partnership with Gooch had mustered 124 runs.

RAY EAST: 'Gooch had no nerves. I always watched when we batted. Any game, I would watch 99 per cent of the balls bowled. Others would turn off and go in the dressing room and read, but I was a compulsive watcher. I could tell how everyone got out, the sort of shot they played and how they scored their runs. Watching Gooch was wonderful. We took the mick out of him all the time for the way he was with his kit. He was such a big chap physically, a big striker of the ball, and watching him getting changed and putting his pads on was funny. When he got out he would get really deflated.'

Fletcher was next man in, and any hopes Surrey might have had of slowing Essex's serene progress were quickly ended as 'The Gnome' kept up the impressive run-rate. A Jackman over disappeared for 17, as Essex flew past the 200-mark. Gooch hit two towering sixes before his captain perished, bowled by Roger Knight for 34 from just 30 balls, to leave Essex 239 for 3. While Hardie made only 4 and Phillip 2, Gooch's imperious innings meant the shortage of runs at the other end made little difference. After hoisting Wilson for his third and final six, the bowler finally gained his revenge, but not before Gooch had made a majestic 120 from 141 balls.

GRAHAM GOOCH: 'If I had to pick out two or three innings in my career, that would be one of them because scoring runs in Test cricket and one-day internationals was great but, being brought up in the Essex family way and being that it was the innings that helped us win that first trophy, it was always going to be a standout moment, especially given what had happened with us being the bridesmaids so often.'

Pont launched a late assault of his own, hitting three boundaries in a rapid unbeaten 19 and when Essex's innings finally ended, Fletcher's men had reached a formidable 290 for 6 – the highest total in the competition's seven-year history. Surrey would need a minor miracle to break Essex's hearts yet again.

BRIAN HARDIE: 'I think in a way it was probably one of Goochie's finest hours. Your first hundred in a game like that is always going to be a special one. It took the pressure off us. Ken McEwan did likewise, as did Mike Denness at the top of the order. They set a big total for the bowlers to bowl at and it put all the pressure on the opposition.

'I had a superstition when I batted at number five that I never used to watch the first little bit of the innings. Once the first wicket fell, I would watch. I was sitting in the back of the dressing room and I heard this massive cheer go up and I presumed we had lost a wicket, but it was just the reception for the first runs. Everyone outside of Kent wanted Essex to win because we had never won anything before.'

KEITH FLETCHER: 'You're always nervous in a big game. It's about how you control those nerves. On this day we managed to hold it all together. Nerves are a huge thing. I still find Goochie amazing because he is never nervous. If I batted now in a village game I would be nervous going out to bat but he never had any and is the only player I have known like that.

'There was nobody better than him for Essex. McEwan was the closest. He could still play now. He prepared in his own way but that was mental preparation. You prepare yourself for the job you are going to do and everyone has a way of doing that. Goochie would work at his game in the nets. There weren't nets at the ground when I first started playing. You had a few catches at 10.30am and you went out and played. Goochie had the nets when he played and he worked on his game and all credit to him. Ackers would throw me a few and then I'd go in and get mentally prepared.'

JOHN LEVER: 'I didn't watch much of it. If I saw 3 overs, that would have been it. Every cricketer, they are always going to be superstitious. I wasn't watching and we were doing well. I was walking around the changing room, falling asleep, reading magazines. You knew when a wicket went down. I said it was like playing in India when you knew the Indians had taken a wicket. You knew it was time to put the pads on and didn't have to watch the game.'

The score eased the flutters in the stomachs of the Essex fans. Ponder was pleased Essex didn't fall away after Gooch and McEwan's partnership. 'The impetus needed to be kept up and Fletcher did it. All the players did their bit. I was with two friends and my brother and we said to each other that 290 was going to take some getting.'

KEITH FLETCHER: 'We did expect to win at 290. We had a chat at lunchtime when Kenny McEwan was batting and he said it's a flat wicket and we were going to have to get a big score, as 260-odd was gettable so we decided we had to keep going. In those days 290 was a huge score, not these days.'

Alan Butcher and Monte Lynch attempted to start the Surrey innings the same way Gooch and Denness had begun for Essex, but their strokeplay and, in particular, running between the wickets was less assured.

RAY EAST: 'After about three overs I hadn't touched the ball and I said to someone "I can't feel my hands", I was that numb and nervous. I had to have a ball hit at me quite hard to feel it. I hadn't played in front of 25,000 in England. I had in India on a private tour on a 125,000 capacity ground. There was a continual buzz and shouting of "Essex" and our names.'

Lever nearly ran out Lynch with his boot as the openers attempted a risky single, but it would not be long before the left-arm magician would claim his first scalp of the afternoon, having Butcher caught behind by Smith for 13. Lynch would soon follow, snapped up by McEwan off the bowling of East, who had been introduced into the attack early by the innovative Fletcher.

JOHN LEVER: 'I didn't like Lord's. The slope would put me off. It's easy to make excuses as it is the same for every bowler, but at one end I used to fall away a bit and bowl it down the leg side, and at the other end it took me onto the pitch a bit. As a left-armer you didn't get any leeway in those days, they were quite strict.

'The nerves were under control until we took the field and that same roar went up. It put the hairs on the back of your neck up. After two overs, I felt as though I had settled down. In the first over I didn't feel my feet hit the ground. It was strange, everything seemed in slow motion.'

KEITH FLETCHER: 'We would always celebrate when we took a wicket and were used to getting 20 a game. We were slightly different to, say, Jim Laker when he took 19 wickets and his team-mates would come up and shake his hand. We knew how to get excited.'

From 45 for 2, though, if Essex thought they would stroll to a comfortable victory, they would be much mistaken. New Zealander Geoff Howarth and captain Knight set their stall to chase down their distant target, playing with a freedom that would put Surrey ahead of their opponents at the 30-over mark. Knight passed 50 in just 60 deliveries – eight faster than McEwan earlier in the day. Essex needed to break what was turning into a threatening partnership. Finally, with the score at 136, they did just that.

JOHN LEVER: 'There were lots of nerves and then there was a little spot in the middle when Knight and Howarth started to smash us around and they were going very well and I walked past Mike Denness and I said "we're tossing this one away", and he said "no, no we'll win this". It wasn't even a gee up. It was just a passing comment. We went on and Ponty got a good wicket – Smith took a great catch and we went on from there.'

Pont was the man to strike, thanks to a superbly acrobatic catch from wicket-keeper Smith. Knight went for an on-drive, edged, and the Yorkshireman flew to his right to pluck the ball out of the sky. Suddenly, the tide had turned, but not before Howarth had taken 14 from a wayward Turner over.

With Knight back in the pavilion, Lever returned to the attack and put the brakes on the Surrey charge. While Howarth slowed, having been dropped in the deep by Denness, David Smith attempted to up the ante. When Howarth skied a Pont delivery into the sure hands of Fletcher for 74, Essex moved a step closer, but there was still work to be done. Again, an Essex bowler seized the moment, with Phillip removing both Smith for 24 and Pakistani Intikhab Alam – in the team for the injured Joseph – for 1.

KEITH PONT: 'Fletch was looking to take me off. One of our bowlers was going to take some stick when they were chasing 290. Fletch was looking to change me and just as he was going to I got a wicket and then another one. The catch was the big moment for me. Intikhab Alam hit it about two miles vertical. I ran away from the wicket and caught it as it came over my shoulder. It looks easy watching it on tape.'

Graham Roope, batting at number six, made a brave attempt to get Surrey back into the match, but his 39 not out from just 32 balls was rendered a meaningless cameo as Jackman, Richards, Pat Pocock and Wilson all had their stumps rearranged.

Surrey were finally bowled out for 255 with three overs and two balls remaining. Essex had won by 35 runs!

JOHN LEVER: 'In recent years I have played a bit of county cricketer's golf with Hugh Wilson, who came in at the end and really it was all over by then and he said to me "I knew you were going to bowl me a yorker". It went to plan. It was quite a nice sight. When that stump went out of the ground, the relief on the whole lot – looking around the whole side – the relief was fantastic. The ball went through and the stumps went everywhere and I jumped in the air and got three foot off the ground. That moment has stayed with me. When I floated back down, by that stage the crowd were nearly on. They were all lining up and there were hundreds of orange-jacketed staff and they weren't going to stop them.

'Fletch was the first person to me and we managed to get off and up to the balcony fairly quickly and you looked out and the whole ground was covered in supporters. There were Essex flags and Essex signs. It was quite something. Fletch was hoisted on to Brian Hardie's shoulders and we were thinking we are going to have a good night tonight. However, we were completely knackered. We were drained and couldn't raise a gallop. After a couple of beers the tiredness took over and we didn't arrange anything. We were perhaps a bit superstitious. For finals after that, we did make arrangements. The whole emotion which started at breakfast, getting to the ground early, practicing, having more catches than normal, nets and everything else took so much out of us. They took ages to bowl their overs so the game finished late as well.'

RAY EAST: 'We just ran off as soon as the final wicket was taken. We didn't look around or pat anyone on the back, it was just off. Then it was standing on the balcony with the cup. It did sink in eventually what we had achieved. Everyone had been talking about us having not won anything. In some ways, the aftermath of the cup win was an anti-climax because it had taken so much out of us. We stayed in the dressing room and drank the champagne.'

KEITH FLETCHER: 'The noise and the atmosphere of that day is something we will always remember. As far as Essex were concerned, for a one-off day that was by far the best. Even after we won other things that was still the number one as far as I was concerned.'

The party was well and truly beginning for Essex's thousands of fans. For Francis Ponder, it was an opportunity to make it on to the hallowed Lord's turf: 'It was a cracking game of cricket. They kept plugging away all the time and it wasn't until Essex took the three quick wickets that it was over. One minute it was "we are going to win this", then it would be "we're not going to do it". Sitting in the stands we thought someone was going to come through and score again for Surrey and rob us again. They pushed us hard all match but never got their noses in front.

'From the moment we won it there was a mass of fans running across the ground. It was lovely running across Lord's. I wasn't one of the first but I made it across to get a view of the presentation. The stewards were never going to keep us off. All they could do was rope us off to stop us getting near to the pavilion. The Essex fans were singing and chanting throughout the day and then it was singing and dancing at the end. The fans and players were rewarded.

'There is nothing better than going to Lord's and seeing your team win a final. I have seen them win finals and I have seen them lose finals and to win your first final in front of a packed crowd made it the best day. I've watched finals on TV and there is nothing like being there. It's all about the little moments, like when Gooch hit the ball on top of the Mound Stand. The noise which greets these moments sticks in your head forever. You want to be there watching when your team is winning, though, not losing. I wish I had been in the media at that time to have had access to them because it must have been great to have spoken to the players. We waited for the crowd to disperse and then wandered down to London Zoo where we parked. We ate what was left in our food rations and made our way home talking about what a great day it had been. It was one of the best sporting days of my life.'

After receiving the trophy and Gooch a thoroughly deserved gold award in front of their jubilant supporters, and enjoying the statutory glass of champagne in their Lord's dressing room, the Essex players and their wives and girl-friends headed for the Victoria Sporting Club in Knightsbridge for a special dinner arranged in advance by Lever to 'celebrate in style'. The bowler himself pictured the scene in *A Cricketer's Cricketer*.

'I still cannot remember how we organised the bill although I think the club might have ended up paying it. But it did not seem to matter at the time. I do recall that it was not a long night because the players were all so exhausted that once they had eaten and had a few beers they just drifted away. The enormity of the occasion had finally got to them.'

While Essex's players partied, at least the early part of the night away, the great Arlott was penning his own personal tribute to the victors. He was in no doubt that the right team had prevailed in an article printed in *The Guardian* on Monday 23 July: 'More than a century of Essex cricket reached its highest peak when they beat Surrey by 35 runs to win their first major honour – the Bensons and Hedges Cup – at Lord's on Saturday. They achieved it in the most entertaining of these finals and with the highest total ever made in them. They hold out the possibility of completing a double by taking this season's Schweppes County Championship – which, in county cricketers' minds, is the highest achievement in the game – as well; but for the moment they savour a prize most gallantly won.'

Arlott was also hugely impressed with the match-winning innings played by Gooch, as well as the roles played by seven of his colleagues. The writer's admiration for so many Essex players was testimony to the great team ethic that existed in the county's ranks: 'The outstanding performer was Graham Gooch, whose century was the first ever scored in a Benson and Hedges final, and in whom Trevor Bailey, delightedly as well as justly, gave the gold award. Essentially, though, this was a team performance. Mike Denness, Ken McEwan, Keith Fletcher, John Lever, Norbert Phillip, Ray East and Neil Smith all made important contributions.'

The players were getting their heads around what they had just achieved. It would be the greatest moment of the careers of many of them.

BRIAN HARDIE: 'The game went so quickly. You are so into the intensity of the occasion so it flies by. I remember turning my back when the ball went up in the air and Keith was getting underneath it to catch it off Howarth, who had been going well. I remember just hearing the sound of the crowd celebrating and I knew he had held it. I'm not sure you enjoyed it. You must have done but you don't remember because you were so focused on what was going on.'

While they were indeed able to savour their prize, Essex's players were not able to celebrate too long and too hard. Instead, they had to be up in Colchester the following afternoon for the visit of Yorkshire to Castle Park. Unsurprisingly, the home side's bleary-eyed players were unable to rouse themselves to complete their second victory of the weekend, going down by nine runs in a low-scoring contest.

East took 5 for 20 – his best figures of the summer – in a match reduced to 38 overs per side as Yorkshire were restricted to 142 for 8, but even that meagre score proved too much for Essex. Hardie made 34 and Turner 20, but the hosts were bowled out for 133 with five balls remaining. While the defeat was disappointing for the 6,000 spectators who turned out to cheer on the new Benson and Hedges Cup holders, the players themselves suffered a hangover from their exertions of the previous day.

In *A Cricketer's Cricketer*, Lever admitted the players' minds were elsewhere. The John Player League was not in their sights, but the Schweppes County Championship most certainly was: 'Not surprisingly, we lost our John Player League match against Yorkshire at Colchester the next day but that did not seem to matter, either. All that concerned us was the championship and I am sure we would have gone on to win [the championship] even if another side had got anywhere near us. We were a long way in front, we were playing good cricket and, with the confidence of having our first trophy under our belts, we were ready to go on and complete the job.'

Lever's was a view shared by the experienced Denness, who knew exactly how to win the County Championship, having done so as captain of Kent in 1970. Indeed, the experienced Scotsman told the *Evening Echo* that the 1979 Essex side was better equipped to secure the title than their neighbouring county had been nine years previously.

'This Essex side is much stronger than the Kent side of 1970. It has more bowlers with penetration and individual batsmen with greater style and class. Those are qualities which are essential throughout a gruelling season and I'm convinced they'll see us to the double. As skipper at Kent, I put the emphasis on doing well in one-day competitions because we had so many all-rounders – rather than specialists – to do well. It's a completely different story at Essex. Here, I regard any success in limited-overs competitions as a bonus, with the championship the main aim. And after our win against Surrey I can't see anything stopping us. We are already more than 50 points clear and the lads are more confident than ever.'

While victory at Lord's was sweet for Essex's players and supporters, it was also vitally important for the county's finances. Victory earned Keith Fletcher's men a first prize of £6,500, while Essex would also receive a windfall from the ticket sales at a sold out Home of Cricket.

News also broke on 25 July of an unexpected £10,500 bonus for Fletcher and his players in the shape of a bet placed at the onset of the 1979 season by Chelmsford-based insurance brokers Jardine Mathieson. The company had wagered £1,500 on Essex at odds of 7-1.

The captain himself, though, was more concerned about silverware than any financial benefits. Speaking to the *Evening Echo*'s Nigel Fuller at Lord's after lifting the Benson and Hedges Cup, Fletcher made it clear that he was focused on one prize and one prize only – the County Championship trophy.

'Winning the county title will give me an even greater thrill. That's what the game in this country is all about. I regard the winning of any one-day competition as the icing on the cake. The real prize has got to be the championship title. That is where consistency and class tells. You can only win that by being the best team in it – and that's what we want to be. And, remember, while limited-over competitions are comparatively new, the battle for the championship has been going on for over 100 years. So to win it for the first time would be something extra special.'

With a huge lead to defend and on a high, following their Lord's triumph, Fletcher continued by stating that he fully expected his players to complete the job in the three-day game. Now they had got over the hump and removed the monkey from their backs, Essex were ready to win again: 'The pressure has been on us to win something for the last few seasons. Now that we've succeeded, we are able to approach the last few weeks in a more relaxed frame of mind. But that doesn't mean we will become complacent. The Lord's success, if anything, just makes all of us more determined than ever to land the county title.'

THE FINAL FURLONG

With confidence high and so many of their major players in fine form, Essex returned to County Championship commitments on Wednesday, 25 July at

Dean Park, Bournemouth. The seaside town had been part of Hampshire until 1974, when a reorganisation of county boundaries had seen it moved into Dorset. However, Dean Park had been hosting first-class cricket since 1980 and was the venue for Hampshire's first county championship success in 1961. The previous summer, the county had also wrapped up the John Player League crown at the same location.

July 1979 was a different matter, though, as a rampant Essex relished their return to three-day cricket. Hampshire won the toss and opted to bat first. It would be a decision home captain Bob Stephenson would live to regret. In the *Evening Echo* Nigel Fuller summed up another memorable morning for John Lever both accurately and succinctly: 'In sultry conditions which enabled him to swing the ball a lot, he reaped a haul of 7 for 40 as Hampshire were shot out for 128. Incredibly, it was the eighth time this season he has taken five or more wickets in an innings and took his summer's total to 79 – far ahead of his nearest challenger.'

Lever was ably supported by Turner, who took 2 for 24, and Phillip, who returned figures of 1 for 44. It had not looked like Essex would enjoy such a productive day early on as West Indies great Gordon Greenidge steered Hampshire to 40 without loss, but the removal of the opener, caught behind by Smith off Lever, sparked a horrific collapse. Yet again, Essex appeared well on the way to another comprehensive championship victory.

Midway through the afternoon, it was Essex's turn to bat. With Denness forced to turn back for home halfway to Bournemouth with what was later diagnosed as a viral infection, an unexpected opportunity was handed to McEvoy. Unlike so many of his colleagues, the youngster had endured a tor-rid summer, totalling just 28 runs in five championship innings to that point. Unfortunately, his poor run would continue as he was caught by Michael Bailey off the bowling of Mike Taylor for 9.

Thankfully, Gooch's rich vein of form would continue, as he 'was able to demonstrate the power and range of strokes which have made him England's most exciting batsman' according to Fuller. The opener made 70, hitting 12 boundaries before being caught by wicket-keeper Stephenson off the bowling of Malcolm Marshall. Gooch shared a stand of 61 with McEwan and Essex had lost just three wickets as they passed Hampshire's total to end the first day on 151 for 3.

The second day started poorly for the visitors, however, as Marshall removed Fletcher for 20 and Phillip for a duck. All of a sudden, Essex were 208 for 7 and looking as if they may throw away all the good work they had done the previous day. Anyone who thought the champions-elect may be shot out did so without considering the combined talents of Hardie and East.

The pair put on 114 for the eighth wicket, with East making 48, having been dropped at slip on just 5. Hardie would go on, though, making a season's best 146 not out. In an innings spanning four hours and 22 minutes, the Scot would show his full range of talents and shots in leading Essex to a commanding 380 all out.

BRIAN HARDIE: 'I didn't look at it that I scored runs when it mattered. I just did what I could do and happened to score quite a few runs that year. I don't know what the statistics were but I think everyone in the team did reasonably well. I only got about three hundreds that season – I suppose I must have run out of partners! That innings really sticks out in my mind and I've been asked about it many, many times. Malcolm Marshall was coming on to the scene and, after we'd bowled them for about 120-odd – John Lever bowled them out like he did most of the season – he came on to bowl on the second morning with us three wickets down and had a purple patch and ran through our team. We got down to number nine and Ray East came in and scored nearly 50. I took Marshall so that Ray could stay away from him and we managed to do that quite well. JK came in, and then David Acfield, and we got a good score. I was really pleased with that innings because that was a real test, not only to face Marshall but also to keep the strike away from the tail-enders.

'Marshall learned how to bowl in county cricket. All these fast bowlers who come over initially try to bowl it short to scare you, or try to bowl it full to get you out, but he learned to bowl a consistently good length with swing and pace. If he didn't take a wicket, rather than getting angry and trying to knock your head off and losing control, he became the most consistent quick bowler in county cricket.'

Trailing by a mammoth 252 on first innings, Hampshire set about reducing their arrears in determined fashion. Hardie marred his memorable day by dropping the prolific Greenidge before the West Indies man had got off the mark. The error appeared to be a costly one as Greenidge passed 50 in sharing an opening stand of 117 with John Rice, who made 49. Once East removed the former for 67, however, Hampshire collapsed like a pack of cards for a second time.

While the seam bowlers had done the damage first time around, it was Essex's spinners who took centre-stage in Hampshire's second innings. East and Acfield combined to take nine of the ten wickets to fall, the other falling to Phillip. 117 for 0 quickly became 147 for 5 as the room-mates got to work. Acfield removed Rice and Trevor Jesty on the second evening before returning the following morning to get rid of Stephenson, Nigel Cowley and Taylor to finish with figures of 5 for 61 from 30 metronomic overs. Acfield's fourth wicket was his 600th in first-class cricket.

East, meanwhile, took the wickets of David Rock, David Turner and Marshall before Phillip found the edge of Michael Bailey's bat to end Hampshire's meek resistance. Essex had won, yet again, this time by the huge margin of an innings and 33 runs.

While his team-mates were able to celebrate another success, Gooch had a separate reason to be happy. The England opener's supreme run-scoring had earned him an invitation to take part in a unique competition to find the world's best batsman. The event, sponsored by brewers Courage, would see the Essex man joined by Clive Lloyd, David Gower, Barry Richards, Greenidge, Asif Iqbal, Zaheer Abbas and Ian Chappell in a two-day challenge at The Oval in mid-September.

The eight would be faced by a stable of the world's best bowlers – namely Michael Holding, Andy Roberts, Richard Hadlee, Imran Khan, Max Walker, Derek Underwood, Ray Bright and John Lever. The batsmen were drawn in pairs at the quarter-final stage, with Gooch up against Lloyd in his opening round match. The rules were simple – score as many runs as possible before losing your wicket. The winner would take home a £5,000 first prize.

While Gooch and Lever had the pleasant thought of a big end-of-season pay-day in their minds, it did not distract them from the job in hand – namely, securing the County Championship title as soon as possible. First up were County Championship and John Player fixtures against Gloucestershire at Colchester, to complete their commitments in July.

In the one-day game, staged on Sunday, 29 July the visitors, boasting the combined talents of Pakistani opening batsmen Sadiq Mohammad and Zaheer Abbas, and captain Mike Procter, lost out to Essex in a thrilling game reduced to 21 overs-a-side by rain. Mohammad and Abbas looked every inch the international cricketers they were as they took the Gloucestershire total past 50 in just the ninth over. The score had reached 83 by the 14th over but it was then that man-of-the-match Pont made his first impact, catching Mohammad off the bowling of Gooch for 37. Moments later, the all-rounder had swung the match in Essex's favour by having Abbas caught by East at mid-off for 50 and bowling Procter for a duck. With their momentum gone and their best batsmen back in the pavilion, Gloucestershire could muster only 127 for 6 from their 21 overs.

Essex's reply started poorly, very poorly, however, as David Partridge, David Graveney, Phil Bainbridge and a certain John Childs – who would go on to enjoy a successful 12-season stay with Essex between 1985 and 1996 – reduced the home side to 75 for 6 with just six overs remaining. Pont took centre-stage yet again, joining forces with Turner to secure another fine success for his team. Writing in the *Evening Echo*, Nigel Fuller described the afternoon's events:

'Hitting out boldly, they put on 31 in just four overs before Turner, whose innings of 20 included one six, fell to a catch on the mid-wicket boundary. But even then, Essex looked doomed to defeat when the last couple of overs arrived with 22 still needed. But it was the signal for Pont, now in partnership with Neil Smith, to seize control. They gathered 15 runs from that David Partridge over, Pont providing the highlight with a massive drive for six. And then the pair squeezed victory in Mike Procter's final over to leave the visitors wondering just how the game had slipped away from them.'

The championship game was equally fascinating but, again, Essex would come out on top. Success at Castle Park saw Fletcher's men extend their lead in the table to a seemingly untouchable 80 points. There would surely be no catching them now.

Essex's latest win again owed much to the swing of Lever and the spin bowling of Acfield. Gloucestershire won the toss and elected to bat first. 36 overs later, they had been skittled out for just 92, with Lever taking 4 for 37, Acfield 2 for 4, and East a remarkable 2 wickets for just one run in five near-perfect overs. Only Andy Stovold, with a dogged 47, and the extras column would reach double figures.

The hosts' reply was equally fraught, with Essex collapsing to 37 for 6. Veteran paceman Brian Brain was the chief architect of the home side's demise, taking five of the six wickets to fall on his way to figures of 5 for 33. Yet again, however, an Essex batsman would ride to the rescue when his side needed him. This time, it was Phillip, who reached his first half-century of the season in making a vital 62. When Essex were finally bowled out, they had reached the relative safety of 170.

Gloucestershire's second innings was a much more solid effort than their first, with Stovold hitting 52, Abbas 29, and former Cambridge University student Alastair Hignell 30 as the visitors reached 138 for 2. 46 runs ahead of the leaders, the West Countrymen appeared to be on course for a challenging total. That was until the entrance of another Cambridge man.

Acfield would bowl 40 overs, almost unchanged, removing six Gloucestershire batsmen with a combination of unerring accuracy and no little skill. Hignell, Procter, Bainbridge, Partridge, Graveney and wicket-keeper Adrian Brassington would all fall to the quiet man from Chelmsford. In three championship matches, Acfield had taken 20 wickets. From a position of relative strength, Gloucestershire subsided to 205 all out. Essex would need 128 to secure their tenth championship win of the summer.

The victory charge would start slowly, however, as Gooch and McEwan departed for 7 and 1 respectively to leave Essex floundering on 28 for 2. The experienced pair of Denness and Fletcher settled the nerves with a stand of 61 before another mini-collapse left the home side 119 for 6. East and Turner were not to be denied, though, and Essex got home with four wickets to spare. Turner completed the victory by driving Graveney for six. It was yet another memorable exclamation mark on the leaders' already unforgettable season.

Despite seeing his team take yet another giant step towards their inaugural championship triumph, captain Fletcher was quick to play down suggestions that the title was already sewn up. Whether he was being 100 per cent serious, concerned about Essex's tradition of throwing away seemingly unassailable positions, or simply trying to guard against complacency, the skipper was loathe to concede that it would take an implosion of gigantic proportions for them to slip up.

'The race is far from over. Anything can happen over the next few weeks and we've still got a lot of work ahead.'

Whatever Fletcher's true feelings, Essex ended July as they had begun it – with back-to-back victories. It was August and the County Championship, though, that the players' thoughts had already turned to. The headline in the *Evening Echo* on the final day of the month said it all: '*The Untouchables*'.

Keith Pont is interviewed by BBC television after being named
Man of the Match in the Benson and Hedges Cup semi-final against Yorkshire

Chapter Seven

August 1979

THE PITCH FROM HELL

A month of destiny or a month of fate? One trophy was already gleaming in the cabinet, but would another be on its way? The 103-year drought was over but the big one was still waiting to be claimed. Of course, Essex possessed an almost unassailable lead and only a disaster of biblical proportions could see them caught. However, in sport, anything is possible.

Having squeezed past Gloucestershire on the curious-looking pitch at Colchester, Essex were faced with the task of overcoming Middlesex and extending their 81 point lead.

KEITH FLETCHER: 'The pitches are prepared a lot more these days. If you played at somewhere like Colchester they might not even have a heavy roller there, so the wicket would certainly turn. I didn't like it so much if a seamer could keep going through the top, which happened often. People like Derek Underwood would take 16 wickets in a match when the ball was flying over your shoulder off a length. That was the major difference between 1963 through to the 1980s – the wickets were more bowler friendly and now they are batter friendly. I see batters now who average 40-odd and I think in the 1960s they may have averaged 22 or 23.'

In the build-up to the game, groundsman Eddie Neath held his hands up and admitted he blundered with the preparation of the Castle Park pitch. Essex may have won, but they were given a scare, especially by the visitors' spinners. The state of the pitch came as a blow to Neath, despite Essex strengthening their grip at the top. He told the *Evening Echo* the 'experimental' pitch was produced for a reason.

'I made a mistake – and it hurts. It was an experiment which went wrong and I'm not happy about it.'

The experiment involved flooding the pitch for five days before the match and rolling it while it was still wet, according to Neath. He explained he did this because of events in the John Player League clash with Yorkshire a week earlier. In that match, the seamers, even when coming off a shorter run, made the ball fly all over the place from regular lengths and spectators saw 18 wickets fall for 275 runs.

'It was largely because the bounce was so uneven,' said Neath. 'So, in an effort to eliminate the problem, I gambled on rolling the pitch while it was still wet to try and flatten it out.'

The pitch became a nightmare for batsmen, causing 36 wickets to fall for 596 runs, meaning Essex lost an extra day's gate money. Neath was amazed by what he was witnessing: 'I just couldn't believe it. It looked such a good track

for batting. Mike Proctor obviously thought so too or he would not have elect-
ed to bat. Certainly Sadiq [Mohammed] did. After looking at the pitch on
Saturday morning, he remarked that the side batting first should get 300 plus.
It goes to show just how difficult it is to read a pitch. And to prepare one.'

Essex and Middlesex were prevented from finding out what the pitch had
in store for them on the first morning of the championship match when rain
again came sweeping in. What lay under the covers remained a surprise until
3pm when all was revealed. The delay was not what Essex wanted, as they were
keen to get on with proceedings to edge ever closer to the title. Neath and his
fellow groundsmen spent time sweeping water from the covers in a bid to get
the game going. When play did begin, Essex had to make do without their two
top stars. Lever, the country's leading wicket-taker on 84 wickets, and Gooch
were both reporting to Lord's for England duty.

GRAHAM GOOCH: 'You need match-winners and John had made his
Test debut in 1976 when he was 27. He probably played for eight or nine years
before then and he had matured into a class bowler. He had a great first tour
in India and got seven wickets in his first innings. In county cricket he was a
guy who always wanted the ball in his hand and would always bowl all day if
you wanted him to. In fact, it was difficult to get the ball out of his hand. He
had that priceless ability to be able to move the ball around and the stamina to
keep going. He was the single biggest factor in us winning the championship
in 1979, 1983 and 1984. John Lever bowled people out.

'John should have played more Test cricket. What tended to happen was
that John was always picked for tours and did well, but in England they didn't
play him. Hendrick, Old and Willis were picked instead. He should have played
more in his heyday. He was the best county bowler and the best left-armer I've
ever seen. He was a fantastic bowler. His appetite was second-to-none, too. JK
was a number-one guy. He would have a good social time but every day he'd
be out there bowling his heart out for Essex.'

Into the vacuum stepped McEvoy, desperate to score some runs at first-
team level, and all-rounder Pont. Middlesex were also weakened by England
call-ups. Skipper Mike Brearley and left-arm spinner Phil Edmonds were their
absentees.

Like Gloucestershire's Mike Procter, Fletcher was left regretting his decision to bat on the uncertain Castle Park wicket. Just up the slope from the
ground is the town's Roman castle. The area was once a battlefield and, with
the state of the wicket, it was as though mines had been laid under the grass
and the town was under siege again.

Essex were shot out for their lowest total of the summer – an embarrassing 106. The pace of West Indian Wayne Daniel and seam of Mike Selvey were
the weapons. Daniel's searing speed on such a wicket was always going to cause
problems because of the inconsistent bounce, while Selvey's movement off
the pitch was exaggerated by the unevenness of the surface.

However, the Essex batsmen did not help themselves. They contributed to the miserable total by playing poor strokes. As unpredictable as the wicket was, it was not unplayable. McEvoy's wretched run of low scores continued, having been picked to replace Gooch. When he, Denness and Fletcher had come and gone, Essex were 9 for 3 – Fletcher repeating his first innings duck against Gloucestershire. Selvey took all three wickets in the space of ten balls.

Hardie and McEwan went about proving the wicket was not too bad by displaying some expansive shots. When Daniel pitched short, Hardie made ample room to hook and pull the West Indian with confidence. The determined Scot showed his gutsy character by scoring 41. Once Daniel bowled McEwan for 24, the innings failed to last much longer.

Daniel was loving it. He went on to take his best figures of the summer, ending with 6 for 38. Only Turner reached double figures from the other batters. On paper, 106 looked bad. On the pitch, it looked even worse. The manner in which Essex folded was so out of keeping with the performances which hoisted them to within touching distance of the title. Middlesex openers Mike Smith and Mike Gatting lived dangerously but survived the remaining six overs before the close.

Essex's search for an early breakthrough on the second day did not go according to plan. The pitch calmed and Smith and Gatting were able to repel Essex's pace-spin combination, employed to try and find a way back into the match. The openers passed 50 handsomely, as the boundaries flowed. Essex had to wait until Middlesex were on 76 before East made the breakthrough. Although he removed both openers, Middlesex were able to breathe easily. They had plenty of time to build a big lead so risks were unnecessary. The steady rate was emphasised by Clive Radley – normally a free-scoring player, who lasted 50 overs for 55.

In a match that was slipping from Essex's grasp by the hour, there was one reason to smile. Skipper Fletcher brought himself on to bowl as Middlesex plodded along. Trying to speed the game up, Fletcher loosened up and replaced the front-line attack with his leg-spin. And what a decision it proved to be! Coming on after Middlesex reached 200, he took the last five wickets to fall, finishing with figures of 5 for 41 – the best of his career. It was not enough to prevent Middlesex building up an advantage of 193 in their first innings, though, after they were all out for 299 in more than 105 overs.

KEITH FLETCHER: 'I was a good benefit bowler. When I was young I used to bowl but I didn't bowl much when I was playing for Essex, as Robin Hobbs was playing. He was a far better leg-spinner than me. I took 50-odd first-class wickets so there were a few mugs around! I used to enjoy bowling but I would have liked to have bowled at myself – I would have fancied scoring a few runs.'

RAY EAST: 'The thing about Fletcher as captain was he restored confidence in you. If Botham and Viv Richards were at the crease he would go and perch himself at silly point and I had a ball in my hand thinking if I bowl it in the wrong place they are going to kill him. But that was how he did it. He used to say to me when they had a spinner on, get in there and get some runs. He was prepared to lose to win. If he had persevered with his leg-breaks he would have been good but he didn't bowl enough. I was quite happy that when he wanted a declaration he could chuck it up and get hit.'

Hopes of salvaging even a draw were dealt a big blow when openers Denness and McEvoy were out before bad light halted play 45 minutes before stumps were due to be drawn, leaving Essex 30 for 2.

Four runs were added on the final day when Daniel had McEwan caught at slip by Roland Butcher. The deficit stood at 176 and Essex were staring at a heavy setback. Fletcher, Hardie and Pont did their best to hold up a first defeat of the season in the championship. Fletcher and Pont both struck half-centuries, but a spell from Norman Featherstone resulted in four wickets in five balls to end Essex's chances of preserving their unbeaten record.

Smith and Gatting polished off the 36 runs needed with no problems to seal a ten-wicket victory. The pessimists may have sensed Essex were on the slippery slope, and that defeats and high hell were all that would follow. Essex's history of coming close and making a mess suggested they should get those necessary points as soon as possible, but in reality one defeat was not going to cost them the title.

At Lord's, Lever and Gooch were named in the England side for the Second Test against India. Lever's patient wait had to last a little longer, however. He bowled seven balls on the first morning when the players were taken off the pitch because of bad light. Not a big fan of the Lord's slope, Lever recorded reasonable figures when play resumed, but in the context of the innings, he was thoroughly overshadowed by Botham, who took 5 for 35. Lever did remove last man Bishen Bedi, but it was not the impact the country's top wicket-taker planned on making, having forced his way back in.

With India 96 all out, England went on to build a huge lead. Gooch was one of the few to miss out, bowled by Kapil Dev for 10. When India restarted, 323 behind, their task seemed hopeless. It was Lever's chance to bowl his country to victory. Dreams do not always come true, though, and India produced a fantastic rearguard to save the game. They finished on 318 for 4. Lever dismissed centurion Gundappa Viswanath, but two wickets in the match was not what he was hoping for after being selected in place of the injured Bob Willis.

THE TITLE DECIDER?

There was no break for Essex between championship matches, as the players faced the possibility of another couple of days in the field.

JOHN LEVER: 'It was such a busy season and it's very easy to moan because cricket at that time with all the three-day games and one-day games, you got very little break, and we were in the field a lot. A good side is in the field a lot because you have to take 20 wickets to win a game and we seemed to be fielding all the time. The lads didn't moan because we were winning and that is the strongest emotion of all.'

Nineteen-year-old Gary Sainsbury was included in the Essex squad for what was being dubbed the 'title decider' between the leaders and second-placed Worcestershire. Essex were determined to put the disappointment of defeat to Middlesex behind them. Sainsbury earned a place in the squad, following a heroic display for the second eleven. The left-armer, from Ilford, claimed 8 for 8 off 9 overs against Middlesex.

Fletcher decided to tinker with the Essex line-up. The team had been settled for months, with the only changes generally taking place when Gooch was on international duty and a choice between spinner Acfield and all-rounder Pont, depending on the look of the pitch.

This time, Fletcher made wholesale changes to the batting order. McEvoy, so short of runs, was dropped down the order to number six, where he was deployed behind Pont, who had earned promotion following his 59 against Middlesex. Hardie moved up to open with Denness as Lilley remained out in the cold in the three-day game.

BRIAN HARDIE: 'I had opened before and that seemed to be my natural position. The previous season, Keith said to me that he wanted Graham to open and me to drop down to number five. What that did is make Graham into a more technically correct player because, to be an opener, that's what you have to do. For me, it loosened me up as a cricketer. To bat at number five, it takes away the anxiety of facing the new ball. It gave me a better all-round game and it relaxed me more and I was able to not worry about going back to open when Goochie was away with England.'

Essex were seeking the stability that was lacking so badly at Colchester and Hardie and Denness were seen as the most likely to give a solid foundation. Sainsbury was the man to miss out, despite the potential he had shown in the second string. This meant Essex would rely heavily on spinners East and Acfield to share the brunt of the bowling.

The toss was important on a wicket which would become a bone of contention for Fletcher by the end of the match. He called wrong and Worcestershire chose to make first use on a surface expected to offer more to the bowlers as the game wore on.

The last thing Essex needed to restore confidence was to spend a long day in the field, but opener Alan Ormrod made sure he would not be making any sprints to the boundary until at least after the tea interval. Ormrod scored more than 23,000 first-class career runs, based on patience and unwavering concentration. What he lacked in flair, he made up for by staying at the crease and frustrating the opposition for as long as possible. This was not to say he was totally reliant on occupying the crease to make a name for himself. While he dropped anchor against the Essex bowlers, he also hit the bad ball to the boundary.

Ormrod batted for five hours, aided by useful contributions from Phil Neale (25), Edward Hemsley (27) and Younis Ahmed (37). Worcestershire had no difficulty gaining maximum batting points, as Ormrod showed rare aggression after tea. East and Acfield bowled 70 overs between them. The former was given a pasting after the interval when his three overs cost 41 runs.

East was given something to cheer about when Ormrod's stay finally ended, stumped for 134 and Essex's fourth bowling point came off the last ball of the innings. Worcestershire were quite content to have scored 353 for 9 against the league leaders. It was a feat made easier by the absence of Lever, as Essex used four bowlers, with Pont not called into action. Hardie and Denness were untroubled during the remaining 20 overs, posting an unbroken stand of 49 to leave the match evenly balanced at the end of the first day.

Vanburn Holder, who would stay in the game after his playing days by becoming a first-class umpire, put the brakes on Essex's progress on the second morning. Essex were on 75 when he struck with the first of a double blow, leaving Essex further away than they hoped to be of claiming a first championship title. Hardie was trapped LBW, and McEwan, starved of runs, continued his poor run of scores when he was bowled for 7. Heavy cloud appeared, which did not help the Essex cause. The seamers found extra swing and the innings disintegrated.

Jim Cumbes was a true all-round sportsman, playing cricket in the summer and football in the winter as a goalkeeper for the likes of Aston Villa and Coventry. He showed he was adept at taking wickets as well as saving shots. At the other end, Gifford was extracting plenty of turn from the wearing wicket and Essex came to a virtual standstill. Fletcher and Pont went in the teens, McEvoy suffered a single-figure fate again, and Essex were all out for 185 by 4pm.

Worcester captain Gifford enforced the follow-on. The shape of the match changed little when Essex began for a second time. Two hours' play remained, and in that time Essex lost four wickets. Hardie and Denness put on 46 for the first wicket – at least hinting at an Essex revival. But John Inchmore was on the way to his best figures in two years, taking out the Essex top order.

Overnight rain delayed the start of the final day. No rain dance or prayer could save Essex as the clouds lifted and play began at 2pm. Three more wickets fell within an hour and Worcestershire completed victory by an innings and 22 runs shortly afterwards. McEvoy fought doggedly for 28 in the middle order, but Essex made just 146.

The malaise had fully set in, according to the pessimists and harshest critics. If one heavy defeat was not enough proof, two made it a fact. None of the character, talent and belief shown earlier in the season had so far been on display in August. Instead, it was replaced by a side seemingly low on confidence, lacking penetration without Lever, and giving their wickets away cheaply when batting. The lack of Gooch was an obvious loss. But the psychological impact was such that Essex were without the bully at the top of the order – the bats-man who, in scoring fast runs in an uncompromising fashion, was effectively saying to the bowlers 'You have no chance against us'. Essex were no longer the unbeatable kings of the championship. They could be defeated on any given day like the rest of the mere mortals.

Their challenge of winning the championship was now a tougher proposi-tion. The lead at the top was 71 points and Worcestershire had a game in hand. Essex faced a break until 18 August when they travelled to Northampton. In the meantime, Worcestershire would face Kent and Gloucestershire, while Essex went face-to-face with the Indian tourists.

Fletcher tried to ease the worries of the fans – fans too used to seeing the team stumble at the last hurdle. In the *Essex Chronicle* he assured the support-ers his side had not lost their way and did not intend to. 'I am sure we can get it together to produce at least a couple of results in our last five games, and that would surely be enough to ward off the challenge of Worcestershire or anyone else for that matter.'

Fletcher hoped the game against the Indians at Chelmsford would provide Essex with the chance to boost morale, away from the pressure cooker of the championship. There was also a financial incentive – £2,750 bonus if they could win. The Holts Trophy Sponsorship covered matches against the Indians, with £5,500 to be shared by counties who beat the international team. Gloucestershire were the only side to have done so before Essex's attempt.

The tourist fixture gave the Essex batters a chance to score runs, badly lacking during the previous two championship games. The Chelmsford wick-et would also provide the batsmen with better consistency than at Colchester and Worcester. Fletcher vented his feelings on the pitches in his column:

'It will be a change if we can get on to a wicket that is a little more con-ducive to batting than some we have encountered in the last fortnight. There was not too much encouragement in that department at Colchester, and at Worcester, in our last game, the toss virtually decided the match. Apparently they had had so many wickets that had been too good, they tried to produce one that would bring a result and in the event it was a slow turner on the first day. Then by the second and third days, the ball was coming through at all sorts of varying heights.'

Fletcher was keen to use the break to take stock and rebuild. However, it also robbed them of the chance to create a bigger lead and assure them of the title. He knew that when Essex were back in championship action, Gooch would be away on international duty, so their batting issues would have to be rectified without him. It was not clear whether Lever would be required for England. Willis was expected to return to the reckoning, and Old was also pushing for a place. If Lever was not available for Essex, it would mean

Sainsbury would be considered again. Fletcher talked up the youngster in the press and said he would have been selected at Worcester, had the pitch been more reasonable.

The Chelmsford crowd was treated to some thoroughly entertaining cricket in the summer of 1979. Championship games featuring big hundreds, opposition sides bowled out nearly twice in a day, stunning catches and action-packed John Player League encounters. Now they were treated to seeing some of the biggest names in cricket facing their own heroes.

The Indians were in the process of rebuilding. Beaten in the First Test by England, they had showed they were no pushover in the Second Test. A habit of drawing in the tour matches had arisen. Games against Northamptonshire, MCC, Hampshire, Leicestershire, Minor Counties, Somerset and Derbyshire all ended in a stalemate prior to them coming to Chelmsford. The Indians chose to use many of the games for batting practice, often after rain had left a positive result difficult to achieve.

Batting and spin bowling were synonymous with Indian cricket. Sunil Gavaskar, whose record number of Test hundreds (34) stood until Sachin Tendulkar surpassed it in Delhi in December 2005, was regarded as the finest opening batsman to have graced the game. More than 1,000 runs scored during the summer proved he was adept in English conditions, as were Yashpal Sharma and Viswanath.

The Indian spinners did not enjoy the best of times. Bedi, Venkataraghavan and Chandrasekhar accomplished little, with Venkataraghavan weighed down by the captaincy. The bowling workload fell on the young shoulders of Kapil Dev. The 20-year-old all-rounder was relied upon to bowl more than expected due to the lack of form shown by the spinners.

Before the game at Chelmsford, it was revealed that Pont would be jetting off to South Africa in the winter. The all-rounder was appointed professional of Northerns, a club side in the Cape Town area. Struggling to become a first-team regular, Pont was keen to experience cricket abroad at a club where he was expected to score heavily and take a lot of wickets. He paid tribute to team-mate Denness in the *Evening Echo* for what he had learned from him.

'I've learned a lot from him over the last few months. His tactical knowledge and dossier on the way opponents play is fantastic. More than anyone, he has taught me the need for self-discipline at the start of an innings. I'm an aggressive batsman by nature and like to thrash the leather off the ball. But on Mike's advice, I've calmed down a lot and am concentrating more.'

This was prominent in the Benson and Hedges Cup semi-final when his vital knock of 36 took 25 overs.

THE TOURISTS COME TO CHELMSFORD
The eyes of the selectors were on Lever when Essex and the Indians made their way out onto the pitch. An excellent performance would give them a

headache on whether Willis should be recalled or not. Yet Lever had saved his worst performances of this memorable season for the representative matches. A poor showing for the MCC had been joined by the two wickets at Lord's in the Second Test. It was an unfortunate record for a bowler who so many believed was the one of the best in the country.

Fletcher chose to bat on a slow wicket but Essex made a terrible start. Gooch was out for a duck and Denness for one, as the tourists went about trying to exploit the gulf between a county side and an international outfit. They might have dismissed a former England captain and a future one, but another future leader of the England team was on his way to the middle. Fletcher led by example, preventing Essex from being bowled out for below 100.

McEwan had amassed just 59 runs in his previous six championship innings, and had not passed 50 in the championship since his masterclass against Derbyshire when he smashed 185. This time, he made it to 16 when he fell to Bedi. Essex were 55 for 7 and alarm bells were sounding. Their highest score in the last four innings was 225 and it looked unlikely they were would achieve half that number.

KEN McEWAN: 'The great thing about cricket is that it is a great leveller – when things are going your way, make sure you make the most of it, because for no reason, things can change quickly. I recall a time when I just could not get going – it got so bad that on a flat pitch, we were bowled out before lunch for 52 and had to follow on. My contribution was 0. I was soon in again and managed another 0 – a pair before lunch! What made it worse for me was that we managed to score 500 in the second innings and saved the game. I cannot say that I was looking forward to the next day – we were playing Sussex at Chelmsford. Little did I know that I would make my highest score of 218, but in the following four knocks I managed centuries. I went from rock bottom to floating in the clouds.'

Then Smith joined Fletcher and the wicketkeeper heaved to good effect, adding 90 with the captain.

KEN McEWAN: 'It was a bit unfair to refer to the lower order as clouting louts, the exception being David Acfield. He played the most perfect forward defensive, except against Sylvester Clarke! The clouting louts certainly clouted us to a lot of success.'

The last three wickets fell for one run on a day when the Indian spinners got it right. Bedi took 2 for 19 at less than one run per over. Chandrasekhar took 4 for 30 and Venkat's 28 overs went for next to nothing. It was an extraordinary display of control, as Essex's 146 had spanned 81 overs. Hardly riveting for the spectators, but they were able to witness spin bowling at its supreme best.

India's opening overs had a familiar feel to them. Phillip blasted out dangermen Gavaskar, Chauhan and Vengsarkar, proving the 'rough diamond' could mix it at the top level. Sharma and Amarnath led the recovery, seeing

India through to the close at 109 for 3. Lever was not making the inroads expected and on the second day, Sharma reached his century, while Amarnath struck 55. Lever ended Sharma's fun for 111 and Venkat declared with India 69 ahead.

Gooch and Denness made a better fist of facing India's opening bowlers, putting on 72 for the first wicket. At the end of the second day, Gooch was out for 46 and Fletcher followed for 6. When rain threatened to ruin the possibility of an exciting climax on the final day, Fletcher tried to create a result by improvising. Light drizzle delayed the start by an hour and Fletcher sent in Smith, initially as nightwatchman, but now to throw the bat at everything. He added 58 with Denness at a run-a-minute before Chandrasekhar had the Scot caught at slip for 58.

McEwan became the first Essex batsman to pass 1,000 runs that summer and he then deposited Bedi over the boundary for six, with Essex in a hurry. It was the beginning of a sustained attack by McEwan, who took the Indians apart, hitting 68 in only 41 minutes. He was on course for the fastest hundred of the summer until he was bowled by Bedi. Fifty of his runs came in boundaries during a stand of 82 with Smith. Pont then carried on the assault. Pont may have told the press he was more studious over his batting now, but he was still able to launch the ball when required.

Essex's 295 for 6 declared set India a target of 217 to win in two hours, plus 20 overs – approximately 50 overs. The game was perfectly set up by Fletcher. If India went for the runs, they would ultimately lose wickets and Essex would be in with a chance of claiming the prize money, as well as a much-needed victory.

Party-poopers India wanted none of it. The Third Test at Leeds would start three days later so the tourists chose to use the Essex bowling as practice. To be fair to them, recognised batsmen Vengsarkar and Gaekwad were respective victims of a swollen knee and a stomach upset, while all-rounder Kapil Dev pulled a neck muscle. When the injuries were taken into account, India were essentially left with eight fit batsmen and a Test match in the back of their minds. Therefore, Chauhan, Amarnath and Sharma batted out 43 overs, seeing India through to 132 for 2. When Lever enticed Gavaskar to edge to Smith, Fletcher may have smelt victory – and prize money – but it was the only moment when Essex were in with a chance of winning. Fletcher bowled himself, removing opener Chauhan, while Gooch was also used ahead of the frontline bowlers. It was a disappointing end to what could have been an exciting climax.

At least McEwan was no longer enduring his personal nightmare. If Essex were to go on and win the championship, they would need Gooch and the South African, or one of the other batsmen to produce a big innings or two. McEwan had not topped 30 in 11 previous innings. The season had started so well for him – 836 runs in his first 13 knocks. Then the runs dried up – 160 in 11 visits to the crease. He told the *Evening Echo* that he was beginning to wonder when his luck would turn:

'One expects a bad patch from time to time, but mine seemed to be going on for ever. I was getting more than a little worried by it. Mind you, I started fearing the worst just before Colchester Festival Week. I don't know why, but it always seems to mark the start of a bad patch. I've been playing there for six seasons now and have only managed a top score of 52. And it's usually taken me a little time afterwards to get in decent nick. Still, that's in the past. I'm just relieved to be getting some runs again and can only hope there's a few more in store between now and the end of the season.'

Another batsman was enduring the opposite sensation to McEwan during the India match. While McEwan was relived to be out of his rut, Hardie was stepping into one. He was the unfortunate recipient of a pair against the tourists, an embarrassing feat no one wished to be associated with. However, the run gods would not be harsh on him for long.

Worcestershire were drawing with Gloucestershire while Essex were in action in the tour match, which meant Essex still had a 61-point lead going into their trip to Northampton. A game in hand meant a maximum 20 points would clinch the championship. Worcestershire began their clash against Derbyshire at Derby on 18 August – concurrently with Essex at Northampton. Derbyshire had experienced the thrill of winning a championship game only once all summer, so Essex sensed Worcestershire would not be slipping up.

The Title is Won … at Last

Good news for Essex fans arrived when Lever was named 12th man in the Third Test for England. He was released from his duties and sped down the country from Leeds to Northampton to spearhead Essex's push for the title. Just 11 wickets short of a century, the sight of Lever was a huge boost for Fletcher's faltering team. Gooch was away with England so Fletcher banked on the experience of Hardie to open with Denness, ahead of McEvoy or Lilley. Turner was passed fit after being troubled by 'housemaid's knee' – an inflammation of the small sack of fluid (the bursa) in front of the kneecap.

STUART TURNER: 'I played until I was 43. I was lucky with injury. I had some niggly ones but nothing too important or too bad. It was only towards the end of my career that I started to pick some up but they were to do with my age. Back then, we just played through injuries. Of course, if they were too bad we couldn't, but with the little niggles and everything you just got on with it. In 1979 I had a couple of strains here and there but nothing that kept me out. If you had a niggle, the physio would perhaps organise a cortisone injection and get you back on the field. It wasn't recommended to have too many of those but that was the way it was then. Now, they have psychologists and dieticians and this guru and that guru and it's totally different.

'We played day-in, day-out. We played a lot more cricket than they do nowadays and I just don't know why we didn't get the injuries. I think John Lever probably played through things like stress fractures. Towards the end of my career I had both of my knees washed out through arthroscopy but that was just for wear and tear. I had various things floating about. Our fitness was the result of the influence of Brian Taylor. He was hard as nails and would gruffly tell us about physiotherapists that "good players don't need 'em and bad players aren't worth them". That was his stock comment.

'The fitness regimes now are quite rigorous but I personally think I was as fit as the modern-day players are now. We did start introducing far more rigorous fitness regimes when we started to win things. A couple of professional footballers would come in and do sessions with us and we used to train with Chelmsford City when they were based in New Writtle Street next door. We used to do a lot of sprints and running and things. I used to enjoy the fitness side of it and I felt it made a hell of a difference. I didn't have any problems with my weight either. You used to dread picking up an injury in the early days because you didn't want to be left out. When you only had 12 or 13 players on the staff, you couldn't afford to get injured.'

An overcast and damp morning led Fletcher to ask his side to bowl on the first morning. It was a decision vindicated when Northamptonshire lost three wickets in the first half an hour and were 99 for 5 at lunch. Lever and Phillip were instigating the damage until Peter Willey came to the fore.

A fearless man, specialising in backs-to-the-wall situations, Willey was perfect to have in at 9 for 3. He saw his side's star man, Allan Lamb, caught at bat-pad off Phillip, and Northamptonshire were in danger of falling under the Essex steamroller, which was slowly chugging back to speed. Enter Willey, who would go on and play 26 Tests for England before being another to stay in the game as an umpire. He watched his team-mates flounder all around him, coming and going for single-figure scores. If he scored 50, his innings would have stood out. That he finished on 131 out of 224 said it all.

Turner's 5 for 70 gave him his best figures of the season and Essex now needed to rid themselves of any concerns over their batting, which had been creaking in recent weeks. By the close of play on the first day, they were well-set on 82 for 1. Hardie notched his first run for three innings, but added only another ten by the time he was LBW to Pakistani Sarfraz Nawaz, the master of reverse swing, who was at the peak of his powers. The paceman came into the county season on the back of taking 9 for 86 against Australia in Melbourne.

When McEwan and Denness continued the innings – the day after Essex had beaten Leicestershire in the John Player League – it was all looking dandy. Full bowling points were achieved and, although Worcestershire bowled Derbyshire out for 194, Essex need not have worried about what their rivals were up to. McEwan was scoring runs freely but lost Denness (31) when the score was 118. Fletcher's requirement was to see Essex through to a lead of around 50. It failed to materialise. McEwan (70) was the second of Sarfraz's six victims as Essex folded to 199 all out. The last seven wickets fell for 56, but Fletcher survived the lethal bowling of Sarfraz to remain unbeaten on 52. Only five of the 20 points needed to ensure the title (4 bowling, 1 batting) had been claimed, which meant Essex could earn only 17 points for winning.

Worcestershire were busy piling up a massive lead at Derby. Phil Neale struck a century in his side's 328 for 9 declared. They were soon ravishing Derbyshire's batting line-up, bowling them out for 158.

Northamptonshire's second innings went smoothly to begin with. Lever dismissed Larkins and Williams, but Cook and Lamb took the total above 100 with no further wickets lost. Come the end of the day, the game had a different complexion to what it had worn eight hours previously. Lamb dug in and struck 66, but Essex gradually worked their way on top. Turner was doing his benefit no harm and timed his best figures of the season for the second time in the match to perfection – taking 5 for 56 to give him ten wickets overall. It was an outstanding feat by Turner, who was never to repeat his ten-wicket heroics again for Essex. The county maestro was always there, bowling from the end no one fancied, being brought on at difficult times, and basically doing the dirty work that rarely earned the plaudits. This was his day, and his season in the spotlight.

STUART TURNER: 'It was a real buzz for me. It was the first time I'd taken ten wickets in a match. I'd come close a few times but to get ten wickets in the game when we won the title was special.'

Northamptonshire were 174 for 8 at the end of the second day – a lead of 199. If Essex could take the two remaining wickets early on the final day, it would allow more than enough time to score the championship-clinching runs. Northamptonshire were not going to roll over and hand Essex the title on a plate, though. They added a further 29, setting Essex 229 to lift their second trophy of the summer.

Five hours were left in the day, and rain was delaying Worcestershire's attempts at gate-crashing the Essex title party. Patel and Gifford were bowling out Derbyshire for a second time as Hardie and Denness made their way to the wicket.

If Essex were to make a smooth passage to victory, they needed a decent opening stand to settle the nerves. With the batting having failed so emphatically during August, a betting man may have fancied Northamptonshire when the final innings began. Victory was Essex's to mess up. The closest they had ever been to winning the coveted prize. Just hold firm, don't do anything stupid, and build towards the required total. Those were the thoughts running through the minds of Fletcher and his players.

An opening stand of 113 all but did it. Denness proved once more why Essex made the correct choice in going for experience over youth, stroking his way to 51 and supporting Hardie. McEwan looked in the mood for getting the party going when he smote a monster six over mid-wicket, but soon afterwards he was trapped in front of the stumps by Willey. Northamptonshire's firepower was significantly reduced when Sarfraz went off injured. It was as though everything was falling into place for Essex.

In Fletcher and Hardie, Essex were in safe hands. Winning a title is a job for the skipper and there was no way Fletcher was going to give up the opportunity of guiding his side home. The nerves diminished and the excitement grew as Essex edged closer and closer. In a summer when Gooch starred for England in the World Cup and McEwan played some of the most exquisite innings seen by an Essex player, it would be easy for everyone to forget about the role of players like Hardie and Turner. But it was they who plotted the course for victory.

By the time the last 20 overs were called, Essex needed 30 to win. Fletcher edged to slip with the score at 210, but he had seen his side move close enough to know they would be victors. It was a shame he could not walk off at the end, knowing he had scored the runs which claimed the club its first championship, but Fletcher's legacy would not be forgotten. Pont joined Hardie and, instead of rushing Essex to their target, he helped Hardie claim his third century of the summer, making his memory of the match even more special.

KEITH PONT: 'The record book says Brian scored a hundred and I was eight not out, but what it doesn't show is I blocked out a maiden while Brian was on 98 so he could score his hundred. I told him "For God's sake get it this over as I can't wait much longer"!'

BRIAN HARDIE: 'It had been a funny game and the wicket had kept low and there had been a lot of LBWs. It looked like being a stiff task to get the runs in the fourth innings. However, Northamptonshire's overseas bowler Sarfraz Nawaz went off injured, which reduced their bowling options. I think their heads went down a bit and, while it was nothing spectacular, we were able to bat and get the runs. There was no real pressure in terms of time or from their overseas bowler. It wasn't easy, but his absence made the chase easier.'

Essex won by seven wickets, with 9.3 overs to spare and claimed 17 points. They had done it. Or had they?

Events at Derbyshire were shrouded in controversy. Worcestershire bowled out Derbyshire for 158 in their second innings and began their reply at 5.50pm under the impression they had four overs to score the 25 runs required. Worcestershire captain Gifford claimed umpires Dave Halfyard and Tom Spencer had told him this. However, as the innings started, a phone call to Lord's revealed the umpires had made a mistake and misinterpreted the regulations. In fact, Worcestershire were given only two overs to score the runs and they fell eight short so their game was drawn, thus handing Essex the title. Gifford contacted Lord's to try and get a ruling that the match be extended for a further ten minutes – a request which was turned down.

Meanwhile, Essex were left waiting at the other end of the phone for confirmation of the Worcestershire result. When the news arrived, the celebrations began. Champagne had been brought up to Northampton by general manager Edwards in the boot of his car and the corks were popped amid the relief and jubilation that the wait was finally over. No longer were Essex the side who could not win anything. No longer were they the side everyone was expecting to slip up. They were winners. Double winners. Kings of the country and county champions.

BRIAN HARDIE: 'We had to wait for the result to come through from Worcester to confirm that we had won the championship and we also had to drive home, so there was no real chance of popping loads of champagne corks. However, Stuart Turner and my car sponsor came round to my house that evening and we had a few beers to celebrate.

'My nickname was "Lager" because I came into the dressing room and my seat was at the other end of the dressing room from the door. We had a dressing room attendant who left, and there was a Hong Kong policeman called Martin Cowley who was on leave and said he would do the job for the summer. He would do the drinks list every day and most people would change their drink every day but he just used to look down to me and say "Lager?" and I'd reply "Lager" and the name just stuck. The nickname was more to do with my choice of post-match drink than the quantity!'

STUART TURNER: 'We had a few drinks in the dressing room to celebrate. It was part of the 12th man's duties to take the drinks order at the start of the day. Nowadays it's probably energy drinks and the like but back then we'd have pints of lager or bitter. He'd have a scorecard and against your name he'd write down the type of drink you wanted. Very few of them would have a soft drink. It was always a pint of something. Because we were at Northampton, we had a few drinks and then we drove home. It would have been very different if it had been playing at home.'

KEITH FLETCHER: 'We all had to travel back from Northants, so we couldn't get on the champagne. It would have been nice if we had won it at Chelmsford, then we really could have given it a crack!'

As the drama on the field finally abated, attention switched to the Wantage Road dressing rooms. The protagonists were Keith Pont, Ray East and, if the rumours are to be believed, a plague of rats. The infamous rat tale is best told by the players, but not the animals, involved.

KEITH PONT: 'They had wooden stairs that went down to the showers so we took brooms down there. If someone saw a rat we'd be after it with a broom. Some were cowards and wouldn't go down there – they'd get changed and showered at the hotel. People were throwing things up into the dressing room from the showers so they would think it was a rat, but it was the end of a broom. It was causing chaos in the dressing room. We would bang the side of the shower and then shout "get out you bugger! I found one, I got it!" The only rodents that night were in the Essex dressing room! There were a lot of rats in there and a few furry things running around!'

RAY EAST: 'Keith Pont and I saw something. We thought it was a rat, while having a shower down in the cellar after the game. It was a rickety old pavilion and in those days the showers were down the bottom. It appeared to run around and Ponty got most excited and tried to kill it. I was trying to get out!'

A cool £8,000 swelled the Essex coffers, plus £120 for each of their victories and £5 per bonus point. Added to the £6,500 for winning the Benson and Hedges Cup, and £660 for the three zonal wins, the much-needed prize money was flowing in at long, long last. In Fletcher's column in the *Essex Chronicle* he talked of the great feeling of being crowned champions. He reckoned he and his team always had the experience and, above all else, the ability to win it.

'Why are we the county champions and such clear-cut winners at that? Well, it has to be because ours is clearly the best side in the country at the moment. It has been a tremendous all-round team effort, and in match after match players have chipped in with vital contributions. There have been bad days and disappointments; that is inevitable. There has been pressure and a lot of hard work to do. But the rewards make it all worthwhile. I could not ask for a more willing bunch of blokes and our bowlers, in particular, have always kept at it.'

Fletcher's view on his bowlers is significant. He recognised, along with many observers, that they missed very few matches, unlike a whole host of other bowlers up and down the country. All bowlers suffer aches, pains and strains, but, while some play through them and no doubt do their body untold damage, others refuse to bowl at the slightest hint of discomfort. Turner took ten wickets at Northampton with a sore knee. At times, Lever was not 100 per cent fit but continued to bowl and was rewarded with his wealth of wickets and selection for England. The general level of fitness achieved prior to the season and the long runs led by wicket-taker in chief Lever both paid off. They may not have been enjoyable at the time, but Essex could look back and see how valuable they had been.

An instant thought after the title had been won was the relative age of the team. It was not young. Gooch would be around for years, but question marks remained over the longevity of the likes of Turner, Fletcher and Denness. The youngsters were being given a go but, in the championship, McEvoy and Lilley had made little impact. And what would Essex do if Lever and Gooch were away for long periods and either Turner or Phillip were injured?

Such thoughts were only fleeting, as it was a time of celebration and joy. Essex stood as the best side in the country and the side would remain intact, certainly in the short term. The congratulations were coming in thick and fast and the players' telephones were ringing non-stop.

JOHN LEVER: 'The difference between us finishing the job off or toss-ing it away was having won the B&H Cup. You do it once and you can do it again and it will happen again. It was the big monkey off our backs. We were confident we were going to go on and win the championship. You played sides that were languishing near the bottom and they didn't have a lot of fight in them. They had the odd top England or overseas player who might be a prob-lem, but you felt once we were on a winning track it was going to happen.'

Victory at Northampton made it difficult for Essex to celebrate properly. Had the title been claimed in front of their own fans, no doubt Chelmsford would have been jumping for days on end. The spectators would have poured onto the pitch and the players would have been chaired off the field as heroes, before saluting the crowd from the balcony and lapping up the adulation. Instead, Northampton was nigh-on empty.

JOHN LEVER: 'We had to drive home and were split right the way around the county. We all disappeared to different parts of Essex. I went down the Travellers Pub in Woodford Green and bought a bottle of champagne.

'We had put Essex on the map and feel quite proud of the fact we had sort-ed this side out from everything else that had gone on before. There were so many civic receptions, and everywhere we went there was this huge feeling towards us as a side. The nice thing was we were respected as a decent bunch of blokes. I don't think anybody disliked us as a side. Anybody and everybody was clambering for a piece of the action. If we all had agents then we could have cleaned up. The players flew the flag for Essex in quite a nice way. The legacy was the number of members the following year reached all-time highs. We must have had 8,000 or 9,000 members.'

As few Essex fans were at Northampton, it was a strange experience, knowing they had won their first title. Francis Ponder was waiting for BBC updates each hour, while other fans around the country were relying on the air-waves: 'It was a pity they did it in front of one man and a dog at Northampton instead of doing it at Chelmsford or any Essex ground where there would have been a full house. I remember Peter Edwards saying they used to sell more scorecards in a day at Colchester than they did in a whole week at Northampton. That's how poorly cricket was supported at places like that. There was a cricket line you could phone up later on, but in 1979 we were wait-ing for every sports bulletin from the BBC [Radio 2] to see what the score was. You couldn't wait for the next bulletin to see where it had moved on to. It was an anti-climax but great at the same time. We won it so easily which made it a bit surreal.

When the dust settled, it was announced Denness was offered new terms to stay at Essex. The opener was at the end of his three-year deal and the Essex committee was keen to keep the side together. Denness was delighted to stay on and forecast the beginning of a golden period for the club, with more silverware to follow. The sage veteran would be proved right.

The former England skipper had enjoyed a new lease of life after leaving Kent and scored heavily enough throughout the season to retain his place at the top of the order, despite Lilley producing scintillating one-day form at the start of the campaign. Denness spoke to the *Evening Echo* about his thoughts on the future:

'We've proved what we are, the best-balanced side in the country. And I firmly believe more trophies lie ahead in the immediate future. The title, coupled with the achievement of winning the Benson and Hedges Cup a month ago, can only send the players into the future with even greater confidence. Certainly this is a better all-round team than the Kent one which I led to the County Championship nine years ago. It has so much strength in all departments and, more importantly, is one that can be kept together for a few more seasons.'

For Denness, he was relatively new to the club, whereas the likes of Turner, Fletcher, East and Lever had endured the miserable years. They had toiled away for no reward, trekking up and down the country, playing in howling, cold winds on wickets resembling minefields and chased umpteen balls to the boundary, taking blows to the body from fast bowlers and wondering when, and if, their time would ever come. They had been part of the days when opponents would see Essex as easy pickings, just another game on the circuit. Those days were over. The dedication, effort and leadership resulted in them now being the big-guns.

The gulf between Essex and the rest of the counties was there for all to see in the league table. Champions with four matches still to play, Essex had tasted victory 11 times. No other county had won more than five. It was not a sneaky, streaky title victory. Essex won it by a street.

Awards for Essex players and the team were frequent in 1979. Lever's deluge of wickets gave his personal coffers a boost, as well as a title to cherish. He already claimed £400 as winner of two of the first three Wilkinson Sword/Sun Demon bowler awards for hitting the stumps more often than any other county bowler. He was also well on the way to winning £1,000 for being the 'Demon Bowler' of the season. The awards were aimed at encouraging attacking cricket. For the batsmen there was the chance to be richer for hitting the most boundaries. Gooch and McEwan had already been recipients of such awards that super summer.

It is easy to forget, amongst the drama of the game at Northampton and the makings of history, that Essex were at their walloping best in the John Player League at Grace Road, against Leicestershire. In the present day, it is hard to imagine a championship-deciding match to be split in two by a meaningless 40-over game. But Essex were forced to slip out of three-day mode and assume their one-day mindset after the first day at Northampton. Fortunately, the journey from Northampton to Leicester is not the longest, although it was by no means ideal at such an important and tense time.

Essex made steady progress to 164 all out. Denness opened with Lilley but neither made a significant contribution. McEwan top-scored with 45, while Pont (35) and Hardie (29) gave Essex a score they could defend. The pace and swing of Phillip and Lever totally blew Leicestershire away. They shared six wickets for only 25 runs to inspire Essex to an easy 60-run triumph.

CRICKETING TED

Away from the action, but nonetheless part of the media circus, was a tale close to a certain lady's heart. Those possessing an open mind would point to the effect an extra member of the Essex team had on the season. Hocus pocus maybe, but a Teddy bear just happened to arrive on the scene at the beginning of the 1979 season. Five months later, and Essex were double winners. Coincidence? Or just plain nonsense?

A chance meeting between a club official and Doris Cook brought about the relationship between the little bear known as 'Cricketing Ted' and Essex County Cricket Club. The coming together of Doris and the club would bring her fame and a life-long appreciation from players and fans alike.

It all started when Doris was at the Brentwood Leisure Exhibition with fellow members of the Little Warley Childerditch Women's Institute. They were arranging their handicrafts when her latest creation was spotted. He was dressed in Essex cricketing whites, complete with a bat. So impressed were observers by Doris's creation that she was asked to make another as a mascot for the team. Having gone 103 years without winning anything, Essex were willing to try anything to change their luck. Cricketing Ted went on to receive plenty of television coverage and adorned the cover of David Lemmon's account of the season after the trophies finally belonged to Essex.

For Doris, it was a reward for the exquisite creations she had spent hours producing over the years. Her fascination with Teddies had started at a young age and with her needle expertise allowing her to make her ideas a reality, she went on to win dozens of awards in Women's Institute competitions.

It wasn't just Teddies she created – dolls and patchwork quilts were also given her artistic touch. Teddies were her favourite, though, and she brought delight to hundreds of children by producing the furry friends which varied in size and shape. Children from as far away as Bangladesh were to benefit from Doris's Teddies. She heard of the endeavours of British Airways staff, who were raising money to start an orphanage there. The BA pilots and cabin crew took some of her 'Pyjama Teds' to give to the children to cherish and look after.

Many Teddies all over Essex were saved by Doris, who undertook the roll of 'head surgeon' at what was Bon Marche, but later became McDonald's, in Brentwood. The family firm was owned by Margaret Hutchings and when she realised Doris liked making teddies, she asked her to take on the role of Teddy Doctor. *The Brentwood Weekly News* went to speak to Doris after hearing of the amazing effect her Cricketing Ted appeared to have on Essex's season. The Brentwood resident said she sewed hundreds of limbs and eyes back on during her time at Bon Marche, while sitting by the window happily sewing away.

Sadly, Doris Cook has since passed away, but her Cricketing Ted is remembered as being a big part of Essex's success in 1979. Of course, Teddies don't win trophies. Unless they're very good at cricket!

Essex and Cricketing Ted were to experience scenes of ecstasy when their fans were given the opportunity to welcome the heroes home. Surrey were the visitors to Chelmsford in the championship on 25 August – four days after the title victory was confirmed. A big crowd turned out to acclaim the returning stars and a carnival atmosphere would provide the backdrop for the players to bask in their collective glory.

A telegram arrived from Essex County Council congratulating the players: 'Heartiest congratulations to you and your team on a wonderful achievement. Essex is proud of you, even though it took a century to become champions. Best wishes for continued success from all at County Hall.'

CHELMSFORD WELCOMES THE HEROES

Although the season was now over in terms of prizes to be won, with the John Player League out of their reach, Essex were not about to give up their habit of winning. Fletcher made a point of saying before the match that his side would not relax now they had the title sown up like a Doris Cook Teddy. Instead, with four matches to go, they wanted to compete as hard as ever and win every one of them. Future opponents could expect no favours. Gooch was back from England duty to bolster the batting, meaning Fletcher had to choose between Acfield and Pont for the final place, with Pont getting the nod.

DAVID ACFIELD: 'I found being an off-spinner extremely frustrating. Even in that year, we won the game at Northamptonshire where we won the title and I played in that one, and when we came back, I'd played in 17 or 18 games, but I was left out for the last game at Chelmsford so I was not even part of the accolades of going round the pitch in front of the members. You will have to forgive me, but I find looking back on some of this quite hard work. I played for 20-odd years and I had a lot of great fun and it was good but I had some tough times being left out of sides. Selection is extremely difficult and you can get caught up in it. Certainly in my case, I suppose, you start to wonder, having had a Cambridge education, what you are carrying drinks for. I was thinking "What am I carrying drinks for on a wet day at Hull?" I always found it very difficult to be twelfth man. I couldn't see the point in being there. I always found it very difficult to be left out of the side but, very often, we used to deliberately leave grass on the pitch so that only one spinner was needed most of the time. I just think people do forget that, in professional sport, there are a hell of a lot of kicks you have to take.'

For Surrey, it was a chance to extract revenge on Essex for their defeat in the Benson and Hedges final. They must have been sick of the sight of Essex celebrating and lifting trophies.

Essex won the toss and decided to bat first in front of the large crowd. Gooch was out cheaply, McEwan went for 22, and Fletcher followed for 4, but Denness and Hardie treated the masses to an array of attacking shots before lunch. The most poignant moment of the morning was the reception skipper Fletcher received when walking out to bat – and back to the pavilion soon after. He may have failed in this innings, but he was a cricketing god in the eyes of Essex fans for bringing them so much cheer.

Denness (61) and Hardie (76) added 83 for the fourth wicket, and while Pont went for 7, Phillip struck his highest knock of the summer. When Turner and Smith went in quick succession, Essex looked to be falling short of the magic 300 mark and full batting points. Phillip took it upon himself to get Essex as close as possible, heaving the ball to all parts in reaching 66. East and Lever added the runs needed for Essex to obtain the final batting point, which came from the last delivery of their 100 overs. Surrey made it through the last seven overs unscathed before the match was put on hold until the John Player League fixture with Middlesex was completed.

Middlesex were without the cricketing brain of Brearley, West Indian express Wayne Daniel, and Featherstone – the man who hurried through the Essex line-up earlier in the season. Essex took advantage of Middlesex's weakened team to rout them in front of another partisan crowd.

The visitors elected to bowl on a wicket suggesting it might seam. Lilley scored 28, as Essex moved to 77 for 3. Then Hardie and Fletcher got to grips with the Middlesex bowlers, adding 52 in eight overs before Fletcher was stumped four runs short of his half-century. Hardie continued to hit out, receiving useful support from the ever-willing Pont and Turner. A total of 189 for 5 was above par, with Lever, Phillip and Turner licking their lips at the opportunity to bowl on a strip providing movement.

It was a typical crushing Essex performance. Middlesex were reduced to 43 for 7 at one stage as Turner ripped through the visiting batsmen. He finished with 4 for 18, while Pont took a couple of wickets and East finished the game off, giving Essex victory by 99 runs. Remarkably, Lever was left wicketless, but it mattered not.

August Bank Holiday Monday brought in another full house as the crowds came to see if Essex would pull off one of their steamroller-esque innings victories. Unfortunately, the day did not turn out that way.

Later made an MBE and an OBE, Geoff Howarth had held up Essex's assault on the Benson and Hedges Cup, striking 74 at Lord's six weeks previously. It merely delayed the inevitable, and Essex fans were hoping he was just doing the same here when he went on a run spree. Watchful to start with, he took 20 minutes to get off the mark before blossoming. The New Zealander hung around for three hours to strike 11 boundaries in his 103. As at Lord's, skipper Roger Knight was his main accomplice, adding 113 for the third wicket. Both were victims of Turner's nagging doggedness. The all-rounder was enjoying a golden spell with the ball, having almost single-handedly bowled out Northamptonshire to lift the title, and given Essex a massive victory against Middlesex in the John Player League. As a result, Surrey went from 159 for 2 to 192 for 6. Graham Roope frustrated the Essex bowlers, taking his time in accumulating 61. He was one of Lever's three wickets, while Phillip also took three and Turner, the pick of the bowlers, returned an impressive haul of 4 for 61 from 24 overs.

Essex led by 13 as they went out to bat on the evening of the second day. With maximum bowling points bagged, they were keen to see out the day and build a lead big enough to defend, while scoring quickly enough to give themselves time to bowl Surrey out on the final day.

However, joy turned to despair when Gooch, McEwan and nightwatchman East all fell before the close, leaving Essex 44 for 3. For East, it was rare when he did not perform his role up the order successfully. He was caught off the bowling of Robin Jackman – one of his 87 victims during the season, the best haul among Surrey's bowlers.

It left Denness and Fletcher to pick up the pieces on the final morning. Fletcher began positively, scorching a drive to the boundary for the first four of the day. Denness was more subdued, as though he could foresee what was to come. Hugh Wilson forced Fletcher to edge into the slips when on 13 and five runs later Essex suffered another setback. Hardie was on four when he too edged into the slips, this time off Jackman. The Surrey bowlers were extracting plenty from a pitch favouring the seamers. The tide was turning in their favour, but whatever their bowlers could do, Essex's could do just as well, if not better.

Pont joined Denness to try and steer Essex out of trouble. They moved Essex past the 100-lead mark, as Denness, seeing the trouble his side were in, broke loose. Then a dramatic slump ensued. Roope replaced Jackman and the change worked a treat as he dismissed Pont, Phillip and Denness before the score could move past 87. Worse followed when Smith was caught in the gully to give Jackman his third wicket. He then wrapped the innings up by having Lever caught behind. Essex stumbled to 101 all out.

The bounce was becoming more and more variable as Surrey set about chasing the 114 needed to win. Despite conditions helping Essex's seamers, they would still have to bowl incredibly well to stop Surrey from winning.

But this was Essex and this was 1979. This was the side which could bowl teams out for pathetic totals, a side containing Lever, who would go on and claim his 100th first-class wicket of the season during the innings.

The drama was unrelenting. Surrey appeared to be coasting home at 35 for 1. Then Lever started his demolition work. He captured the important wicket of first innings century-maker Howarth and ended the resistance of Alan Butcher. Smith caught Graeme Clinton to give Lever his century of wickets and suddenly Surrey were 61 for 6. Lever was mobbed by his team-mates and deservedly so.

DAVID ACFIELD: 'If you are going to win the championship you always need one bowler to take about 100 wickets and JK took 99 in the championship that summer. It was always going to be a seam bowler because, as a spinner, you were never going to bowl enough to take 100, unless you have a drought like we did in the summer of 1976 when the ball turned square.'

Called up for England at The Oval the following day, Lever was far and away the best seam bowler on the county circuit at the time. He bowled unchanged throughout the innings as Essex fought back in style. Phillip lent support, taking 4 for 19 in 12.5 overs, while Turner took two wickets in an over to see Surrey bowled out for 99 – 15 runs short of their target. The day belonged to Lever, though, who finished with 4 for 54 from 20 overs. His fitness and the adrenaline from the occasion saw him carry on to the end, despite the aching limbs of a long season.

The match encapsulated why Essex were champions. Full batting points, and 20 wickets taken – mostly by the seam bowlers, utilising the friendly conditions. Once on a roll, they would not surrender.

Chelmsford would see only one more championship encounter in 1979. It came straight after the win over Surrey, with Northamptonshire the visitors on 29 August. Three changes were made to the Essex side – two of them enforced. Gooch and Lever were on England duty, and Fletcher decided to bring Acfield back in for Pont. McEvoy was given another chance, in place of Gooch, and Sainsbury made his first-class debut in Lever's place.

The wicket was looking good when Northamptonshire won the toss and chose to bat. The lack of Lever in the Essex bowling ranks showed, as Northants were able to score freely. Phillip caught Geoff Cook off his own bowling when the opener miscued trying to hook the West Indian. Wayne Larkins was going well, though. He struck 91, taking a liking to openers Phillip and Sainsbury, who was not to enjoy any success in his first bowl for the club in the championship. Allan Lamb hit 69 and there were contributions all the way down the order for the visitors, who gained full batting points, declaring on 314 for 7. Acfield was Essex's most successful bowler, taking 2 for 66 from 30 overs.

Hardie opened with Denness, as Fletcher continued to use McEvoy in the middle order rather than at the top, as he had done earlier in the season. Denness was out early for 4 and Essex closed on 59 for 1.

When play resumed on the second day, Essex lost the wickets of McEwan (30) and Fletcher (2) with only 27 added to the overnight total. Hardie, though, was having no such trouble, moving towards his third half-century in as many matches. The battling Scotsman was joined by McEvoy. Time was running out in the season for the youngster to make an impact. Fletcher was persevering with him ahead of Lilley in the batting ranks, but the runs were not forthcoming. He put on 56 with Hardie and looked set to finally build a big score, but was trapped LBW by Alan Hodgson for 24. It was a blow to McEvoy, who was so prolific in second eleven cricket, yet was unable to transfer his run-scoring ability when it came to playing for the first team.

KEITH FLETCHER: 'He was just, if brutally honest, not quite good enough. He could field and catch and if he was ten per cent better he would have been a good county cricketer.'

Phillip and Turner were out in quick succession and Essex were 189 for 7 when Hardie edged Griffiths to slip on 93. He was the second Essex batsman to pass 1,000 runs for the season – following McEwan to the feat.

Full batting points were a long way off when Smith was joined by East at the wicket. In a spell suitable for today's Twenty20 cricket, the pair literally teed off. They were together for 14 overs, smashing 91 runs. Smith's blitz featured three sixes and a four from one Hodgson over and he went on to launch a couple more sixes. His 63 took 78 minutes and East was a willing foil when it came to fun and fireworks at the crease. He smashed 47 to take Essex past 300 when it seemed impossible only an hour earlier.

The scales were tipped completely in Essex's direction come the end of the second day. Sainsbury took his first wicket when Geoff Cook was LBW for a duck and it marked the start of another period of Essex domination. This time, they showed they did not need Lever to bowl a side out cheaply. Turner took five wickets – again – by the close, as Northamptonshire teetered on 135 for 8.

Phillip ensured the visitors did not hang around long the following morning, taking the two remaining wickets in three balls. Essex needed 149 for their 13th victory of the season. Denness and Hardie put on 29 for the first wicket when Hardie was bowled by Jim Griffiths. Tim Lamb helped himself to four wickets, including Denness for 30. McEvoy failed to make double figures and Phillip, batting ahead of Turner, was also out before the target was reached. Fletcher was the guide, seeing it through to the end. He fittingly brought the game to a close by hitting Cook for six to bring up his half-century.

In the Fourth Test, Lever was overlooked again, but Gooch was doing his county proud. Still searching for his maiden Test hundred, he fell short again, striking 79 in the first innings and 31 in the second, as the match ended in a draw.

August had been a rollercoaster month for Essex. It was the month they needed to get out of the way – preferably with the title already in the bag. It began with them floundering, as predicted by the cynics. But they settled down and reached their cricketing Holy Grail. The batting hit a rocky patch but Hardie hit form at the right time, while Fletcher and Denness helped them through. If June was Lever's month, then it can be said August belonged to

Turner. His performances with the ball were superb, taking 23 wickets, including three five-wicket hauls. The figure may pale in comparison to Lever's deluge in June, but Turner stepped up his game when he was needed, and to take ten wickets in the title-winning match is an achievement up there with the best.

Fletcher's call for Essex not to take their foot off the pedal was answered. Two wins from two in the championship, and one from one in the John Player League. The month was over. August 1979 – the month Essex became championship winners for the first time in their history.

Stuart Turner, John Lever, Graham Gooch and Mike Denness celebrate
the Benson and Hedges Cup final win over Surrey at Lord's

Chapter Eight

September 1979

With the County Championship in the bag and the John Player League title out of their reach, September was a huge anti-climax for Essex. The month began with a trip to the cricketing outpost of Grace Road for a championship fixture against Roger Tolchard's mid-table Leicestershire side.

DAVID ACFIELD: 'Park grounds do tend to turn more and seam more. Chelmsford has always been flat. Generally pitches on the park grounds did something and we were a good side when the ball did something. We were a rubbish side at Leicester for example, because it didn't do anything, we were bored, we didn't like the people and they didn't give us decent drinks. I didn't mind playing there but it was a funny place to go. It was a very big ground and it was always empty. They were boring people and we used to go out and clap ourselves on to the field.

'We were a bad side when nothing happened. I did a lot of bowling in those days and would just say to myself "I'm going to bowl 30 overs and go for 70 runs" and that was it. On flat, slow wickets, we struggled. Brian Davidson of Leicestershire always got a hundred against us at Leicester but never got a run against us at Chelmsford because the wicket bounced a bit more there.'

In a near carbon-copy of their previous three-day fixture at home to Northamptonshire, Essex failed to bowl their opponents out in the first innings. With Barry Dudleston, John Steele and Chris Balderstone all making half-centuries, Leicestershire made 310 for 7 in their allotted 100 overs.

After reaching 98 for 1, the champions' reply collapsed like a pack of cards. Only Denness, who made 45, showed any real resistance as spinners Nick Cook and Jack Birkenshaw took three wickets apiece to bowl Essex out for just 167.

Leicestershire took the bull by the horns in their second innings, piling on the misery for Essex's bowlers by reaching 226 for 1 before declaring 369 runs ahead. A victory target of 370 was always likely to be a near-impossible one for the visitors to chase, and so it proved. On a turning pitch, the hosts' slow bowlers again did the damage, with Cook recording figures of 6 for 57 from 26 accurate overs, as Essex subsided to 172 all out. Birkenshaw and left-arm Balderstone took two wickets each as Fletcher's men were beaten by 197 runs.

DAVID ACFIELD: 'We played a ridiculous game at Leicester and it was in the time when we'd come off after 100 overs and we were way behind on the over rate. I remember saying to Fletch that I was damned if I was paying his fine, so we actually got through 100 overs by something like 2.40pm. Lever bowled off one pace. We turned the game into disrepute really but we got our over rate up that way. We played a daft, absolutely crazy game.'

Amazingly, considering their travails at Leicester, Essex were able to ignore their championship struggles to secure a thrilling one-wicket victory over Worcestershire at New Road in their penultimate John Player League match, which was scheduled between the second and final days of the Leicestershire defeat. At Worcester, fine spells of bowling by Pont and Turner restricted the home side to 199 for 6 from their rain-affected 39 overs, with Indian Younis Ahmed making 90 not out. Essex appeared to be cruising to their eighth Sunday success in 15 matches when Pont and Fletcher carried the score to 159 for 3.

However, as at Leicester, the batting collapsed, with two calamitous run outs accounting for Phillip and East. With the last pair, Turner and Lever, at the crease ten runs were still needed. The pair showed all their experience, however, to steer Essex to victory from the final ball of the innings.

The day after falling to a heavy defeat at Leicester, Essex's battle-weary players made the long journey north to take on Yorkshire at Scarborough in their final championship fixture. Unfortunately, the champions could not end the season with a victory, but they came mightily close.

RAY EAST: 'It was always a very social occasion at Scarborough. We met Rory Bremner once in the hotel, and him and Ian Pont – Keith's brother – were mimicking people. There is always a different atmosphere playing in Yorkshire as they love their cricket. Wherever you played them there was always a big crowd – especially Scarborough.'

KEITH PONT: 'Rory and Ian were doing Richie Benaud impersonations in this hotel. Next thing you know, everyone in the bar is doing it and it went on for the whole night. It was so funny.'

Essex appeared to have put themselves into a strong position, as McEwan hit a sublime 124 to lead his county to 339 for 9 declared. Gooch made 69 and captain Fletcher a round half-century, passing 1,000 first-class runs for the season when he reached 34. Graham Stevenson was the pick of Yorkshire's bowlers with four wickets, but it would be his less-heralded batting that would make the headlines.

Yorkshire replied with 329 for 6 in 97 overs before declaring, with Richard Lumb making 110 and both Lever and East finishing with three wickets each. Essex ended the second day on 62 for 1, with a draw looking by far the most likely of outcomes.

On the third morning, however, Arnie Sidebottom and Phil Carrick ripped through the champions' batting line-up, with the latter taking five wickets with his slow left-arm tweakers. Essex were all out for 154, setting Yorkshire 165 to end their season with a win.

With Turner in magnificent form, Yorkshire's victory charge appeared to have hit the buffers when they were reduced to 95 for 6 and then 134 for 9. Unfortunately for the champions, however, the final breakthrough would just not come.

With number eleven Geoff Cope nursing a nasty finger injury suffered taking a catch off Gooch the previous day, it was left to fast bowler Stevenson to score the majority of the 31 runs needed for victory. He did just that, making an unbeaten 23, while Cope made a brave 5 not out.

Essex's season ended on Sunday, 9 September with something of a damp squib in the form of a narrow John Player League defeat to Glamorgan at Chelmsford. In a match reduced to 38 overs a side, Glamorgan captain Alan Jones won the toss and decided to bat first. It proved to be a good decision, both collectively and personally, as Jones went on to make an unbeaten 86 out of a decent total of 194 for 4.

In reply, Essex lost wickets at regular intervals, falling to 83 for 5 and 135 for 7 before wicket-keeper Smith launched a late bid to end the summer with a victory, making 32. It was not enough, though, as the home side were finally dismissed for 180 with seven balls remaining.

While the final fortnight of the champions' season had not been memorable, the preceding four months most certainly had been. Essex's double success served as a springboard for a decade of dominance in the domestic arena. Essex would win five more championship titles between 1983 and 1992, in addition to a further four one-day trophies. The reputation as county cricket's bridesmaids had been dispelled by the heroes of 1979. Everything that followed can be attributed to the leadership of Keith Fletcher, the far-sightedness of Peter Edwards, and the efforts of a group of players whose efforts the Essex supporters will never, ever forget.

KEITH FLETCHER: 'We were a good enough side and just obviously had to play well. That we did. We passed it with five games to spare. You look at the scorecards and we bowled every side out twice and weren't giving any easy declarations. There were no false matches. Wherever we went we took 20 wickets. It was really pleasing. Hampshire had won it in the 60s and they had won it on about seven or eight declarations and everyone says that is false. We actually won it by bowling sides out.

'We were a long while in the field and you accept it because we were winning and enjoying it. If you get 350 and bowl sides out twice there is nothing better, there is nothing better than winning. You say you play cricket for the love of it, yes you do, but you go out there to win the game. That is it. If you lost it then fair enough, you hold your hands up and say the opposition played better. Losing is not my idea of cricket.

'It made it the most special season I played in. It was the catalyst for going on and winning more silverware during the next 12 years. We were the best side for 10-15 years after 1979. Just for a day, the cup final was the one I would remember for a long time, but the championship was more important. That day at Lord's was magnificent.

'Winning in 1979 helped me gain recognition as a captain so I was able to go on and captain England. From that year, right up to when I retired, we were winning things. For ten years we were the best side in the land and it helped. At the time they tried Beefy (Ian Botham), David Gower, Boycott. Things hadn't gone that well so I was called and asked if I wanted to captain in India.'

KEN McEWAN: 'I am proud to have contributed to Essex's success during the 1970s and 1980s, but the great thing about our side was that everybody contributed to our triumphs. I was recently doing a spring clean at home, when I came across letters and cards I received from loyal Essex people wishing me well when I decided to return to South Africa. Reading them again after 24 years certainly made my eyes water. I was very fortunate that Essex offered me the opportunity to fulfil my dream as a kid and be able to play cricket every day, and for accepting me as their overseas player. After all, I was a rookie. I have many wonderful memories and wonderful friends from Essex.

'Winning the championship was so special. Towards the end of my career in South Africa, I was playing for Eastern Province and we won our championship, and the Currie Cup, also for the first time after 100 years. Those were all special moments.'

KEITH PONT: 'I was capped [by Essex] in 1976, which was a momentous year for me. It means an awful lot to be capped as you are recognised by your own county as being someone who has performed. But 1979 will always be remembered by me for the final and semi-final which was my day and winning the trophy at Northampton, being there at the end with Brian.'

RAY EAST: 'The cup was the biggest for me. It was the first one, and playing in front of the big crowd is unforgettable. Obviously the championship is harder to win. There were only half a dozen games to win the cup. We did win the championship again, but having won two trophies, and them being the first ones we won, made it the best year of my career.'

JOHN LEVER: 'The season of 1979 meant nearly as much to me as playing for England and that seems a strange thing to say but it was the emotions of winning the one-day game and we'd got so close on so many occasions and thrown it away, not that the opposition had beaten us, it was we had thrown it away and we had to overcome that mental barrier. I always feel that Mike Denness's calming influence and stabilising effect had a lot to do with us going that extra yard to winning the game. He had been with a successful side and all we had ever known was getting to somewhere near glory and tossing it away.'

DAVID ACFIELD: '1979 was the one that mattered to me because in 1979 I played in every zonal match in the Benson and Hedges and then, because Ray East was fit again, I never played in the final. For me, the championship was the one that really mattered. It's the one the players want to win and that is not a cliché because it is a test of your all-round abilities. You learn how to win. I remember when I was commentating on the Essex v Notts final and Richard Hadlee said that to me, and it was very perceptive. You have to learn how to win and then you can get over that final hurdle. From then on, once you've done that, you can do it again quite easily, but getting that first one is hard work.

'I think it was the case that we had a side for all seasons. Keith Fletcher used to say that we could play on any pitch. We were very strong as a seam attack but if we got on a turning pitch we had two spinners to bowl the other side out. We had a very powerful batting line-up and everyone chipped in at the right time. Keith would drum into the batsmen that it was their job to see off the likes of Malcolm Marshall so that he was worn out by the time he got to the tail and we would get runs, so that's what we did. If you look at any of the games where I put on runs it was because they had worn out the fast bowlers. My job as a number 11 was to keep an end up while the batsman at the other end scored the runs. It didn't matter if I got nought. I judged it by how many runs we put on together.'

GRAHAM GOOCH: 'The year 1979 is a special memory for me. I've never, ever heard a roar like when we went out to play in that B&H Cup final in 1979. It was like the whole ground was Essex. It was a good game of cricket, too. It was a good day for us winning our first trophy, but also in the manner that we won it. It was fantastic because we'd had all those years of near-misses. It was nice to get that off our backs.'

The victorious Essex squad with the Schweppes County Championship and Benson and Hedges Cup trophies.
Back (from left): Clem Driver (scorer), Keith Pont, Graham Gooch, Neil Smith, Norbert Phillip, Mike Denness, Peter Edwards (secretary). Front (from left): Ken McEwan, John Lever, Keith Fletcher, Tom Pearce (president), Ray East, Stuart Turner, Brian Hardie

Chapter Nine

Epilogue

1980 ONWARDS

After streaking clear of their rivals in the Schweppes County Championship and winning the Benson and Hedges Cup in 1979, 1980 was always likely to be a season of anti-climax for Essex. So it proved. In the championship, Essex began with a Gooch century and three first-innings wickets for Lever and Phillip against Glamorgan at Swansea. However, unlike the previous campaign, when Keith Fletcher's men ran through their opponents almost at will, the visitors were unable to bowl out the Welshmen a second time and were forced to make do with a draw.

In their second championship match, Essex were forced to bat for 126 overs in their second innings to hold on for a draw against Somerset at Ilford. Next came another Gooch century and a thrilling two-wicket win over Kent at the same venue. It appeared that Essex were up and running, but victory would be achieved only four times by the champions all summer long.

Instead, the team that had won 13 and drawn just four matches the previous summer drew a staggering 15 games in 1980. Although they would lose only three of 22 games, one fewer than in their championship-winning season, Essex would finish eighth, 98 points behind winners Middlesex.

The absence of Gooch, who played just eleven championship matches – scoring 766 runs at 51.06 with four centuries – due to his England commitments, combined with Lever's relative drop in form – 50 wickets in 18 matches at 28.70 – meant the defence of the title would always prove difficult.

Fletcher, McEwan and Hardie would all pass the 1,000-run mark in championship cricket, but only the South African – and the often-absent Gooch – would average more than 40 with the bat. East would be Essex's leading wicket-taker in the three-day game, snapping up 60, while Acfield (46), Turner (41) and Phillip (40) all chipped in, but it would not be enough.

Essex's defence of the Benson and Hedges Cup was more impressive, with Fletcher's men topping their group above Sussex, Glamorgan, Gloucestershire and the Minor Counties. 1979 finalists Surrey were vanquished again, this time at the quarter-final stage, thanks to McEwan's 95. The semi-finals saw Essex take on Worcestershire at New Road, where half-centuries from Denness, Gooch and McEwan were enough to see off the hosts by eight wickets, setting up a Lord's final with Northants. No fairytale ending this time.

Instead, in a match that went into a second day due to the bad weather, Fletcher's men lost a final they should have won. After bowling Northants out for 209, with England batsman Allan Lamb making 72, Essex looked on course to retain the trophy at 112 for 1 in reply. Pakistan fast bowler Sarfraz

Nawaz took three wickets, including those of Fletcher, Turner and Smith, Willey two in removing Denness and McEwan, and Tim Lamb the vital one of Gooch. Essex collapsed to 203 for eight to lose by six runs.

In the other one-day competitions, Essex failed to shine, reaching the quarter-finals of the Gillette Cup before falling to old adversaries Surrey by the slimmest of margins. Both counties totalled 195 at the County Ground, but Surrey advanced by virtue of losing fewer wickets as Essex were bowled out with a ball to spare.

The John Player League was a near-disaster. Fletcher's side won just six of their 16 matches to finish the season joint 14th, just one victory above bottom-of-the-table Glamorgan.

On a personal level, 1980 began well for Gooch as he was named as one of *Wisden*'s five Cricketers of the Year. The batsman who had led Essex to Benson and Hedges Cup glory and England to the Prudential World Cup final in 1979 was lauded for 'blossoming into one of the most exciting stroke-players in the game'. His innings of 120 at Lord's had the famous old Almanack gushing: 'Those who witnessed it will treasure the innings for a long time to come, and it set the seal on a remarkable season's work in the Benson and Hedges Cup.'

Another positive for Essex during the 1980 season was the emergence of two young cricketers who would play a huge part in the county's subsequent domination of the domestic game over the next decade – Derek Pringle and Neil Foster. All-rounder Pringle, who had joined the county in 1978 after impressing at Felsted School and Cambridge University, made eight championship appearances, while Foster, then just turned 18, made his debut in the early-season draw against Kent, taking three wickets in the first innings.

MORE TROPHIES
Essex bounced back to trophy-winning form in 1981, winning the John Player League for the first time. Fletcher's team won 12 of their 16 matches in the Sunday one-day competition, losing just three, to finish six points clear of second-placed Somerset. Essex's success was based on an all-round team effort. No fewer than six bowlers, including young Pringle, would take eleven wickets or more, with Lever leading the way with 18. Batting-wise, McEwan would lead the way with 496 runs, while Hardie made 448 and the enigmatic Phillip smashed 306 at an impressive average of 38.25.

Fittingly, Essex confirmed their title triumph with yet another victory over Surrey, this time in the shape of a 21-run win at The Oval on 13 September. Phillip made a superb unbeaten 80 before miserly bowling from East, Lever and Pringle ensured Surrey would come up short of their target of 204. A week previously McEwan made a vital 109 as Essex held off the challenge of Middlesex by three wickets with two balls to spare at the County Ground. In all, Essex won their final four matches to complete a memorable campaign.

Essex nearly returned to Lord's for a one-day knockout final for the third straight season, only to fall agonisingly to Derbyshire at the semi-final stage in the newly named National Westminster Bank Trophy (formerly the Gillette Cup). Going into the final over of a rain-affected match that went into a second day at Derby, the home side still required ten runs to win. Chasing a modest Essex total of 149 all out, Derbyshire's Bob Taylor and Paul Newman scrambled the run they required from Phillip's final delivery to send Essex spiralling to a defeat by virtue of the hosts having lost fewer wickets. Derbyshire would go on to win the competition, beating Northamptonshire in identical circumstances at Lord's that September.

In the championship, there was an improvement as Fletcher's men won eight and lost four of their 22 matches. However, an abundance of draws – nine this time – again put paid to Essex's title chances. They amassed enough points to finish fifth, 50 behind champions Nottinghamshire. Had Gooch been able to turn out for the county instead of his country, Essex might have secured enough victories to come closer to a second championship. The England batsman was in imperious form in 1980, recording five hundreds and four half-centuries in just 17 innings. In total, Gooch made 1,091 runs in nine matches at a superb average of 64.17.

Gooch was one of four Essex batsmen to pass 1,000 runs, with Hardie, McEwan and Fletcher all enjoying impressive seasons at the crease. With the ball, Lever took 78 wickets, while Acfield would weigh-in with 69 and East and Phillip 49 apiece.

One notable change during the 1981 season was the replacement of wicket-keeper Neil Smith with David East. The championship-winner enjoyed a relatively successful season with the bat, averaging more than 27, but this did not prevent him losing his place to the 21-year-old East for the trip to Edgbaston to face Warwickshire in early July. Smith would never play another first-class match for the county he had served for eight seasons.

The Benson and Hedges Cup was the only negative for Essex in 1981. Fletcher's team failed to reach the final for the first time in three years, finishing third a group won by Kent and also containing Somerset, Glamorgan and Combined Universities.

1982 proved to be a frustrating season for Essex and, in particular, Keith Fletcher. The man who had led Essex to three trophies in three summers had been rewarded for his cricketing nous and consistent batting by succeeding the retired Mike Brearley as England captain. Fletcher, who had been overlooked by England for 47 Test matches – a span of nearly four years – took charge of the national team for the tour of India in November 1981.

England lost the first Test of a six-match series in Mumbai by 138 runs, whereupon Fletcher opted for a more defensive approach to the remaining five matches, all of which were drawn. England flew home having lost the series 1-0.

In March 1982 Fletcher led the England team in Sri Lanka, where the batting of David Gower and Chris Tavare, and the bowling of John Emburey,
carried England to victory in the only Test in Colombo. Little did he know, but
Fletcher had both captained and played in his final Test match.

Chairman of selectors Peter May had decided to replace Essex's most successful captain with Bob Willis. With the shock of being sacked as national
team captain, Fletcher returned to Chelmsford to lead his county for a season
when he had expected to lead his country. As such, it was no surprise that he
was not at his inspirational best.

Despite his personal setback, Fletcher still managed 1,221 championship
runs at 40.70, while the availability of Gooch – banned from England duty for
three years after leading the 'rebel' tour to South Africa in March 1982 – gave
a huge boost to the batting line-up. The opener was in magnificent form, playing all 22 championship matches and making 1,597 runs at 44.36. In the
Benson and Hedges Cup, Gooch would smash 198 not out in the Group 'C'
victory over Sussex at Hove, a record that would stand until broken by Ravi
Bopara's unbeaten 201 in the Friends Provident Trophy quarter-final at
Leicester in June 2008. Despite Gooch's heroics, Essex would finish third in
their group and were eliminated.

While Gooch was in fine personal form, 1982 was a season of failure for
Essex as a team. In the championship, they finished seventh, winning just five
and drawing 12 of their 22 matches. The John Player League saw Essex end
the summer in fifth place, 22 points adrift of runaway leaders Sussex. The
NatWest Trophy momentarily offered dreams of another trip to Lord's when
Essex beat Kent at Chelmsford to reach the quarter-finals. There, however,
they slumped to 51 for 9 against Yorkshire at Headingley. And although Stuart
Turner and number eleven Ray East lifted the score to 132, the home side
romped to victory with nine wickets and 21 overs to spare.

1983 was a season when Essex well and truly hit the target, winning the
Schweppes County Championship for the second time. A year on from his
England debacle, Fletcher was fully focused on rediscovering his Midas touch.
With McEwan and Lever in the form of their lives and Gooch available for
the whole season yet again, due to his England ban, Essex won the title after
losing just five of their 24 championship matches, finishing 16 points clear of
second-placed Middlesex.

Ironically, considering the reason for Gooch's presence, it was McEwan
who led Essex to their second title with the bat, totalling 2,051 runs and finishing second in the national averages behind Viv Richards. Averaging 68.36,
McEwan was nigh-on unstoppable, recording eight centuries and seven fifties
and a top score of 189 not out in 35 innings. It was fitting that the South
African should be awarded a benefit for the following, 1984 season.

Lever was equally impressive on the bowling front, taking 98 championship
wickets at 16.80 apiece. Only Hampshire's Malcolm Marshall kept him off the

top of the national averages. 1983 was also the season when Neil Foster made his mark as a first-class cricketer, taking 51 wickets.

One date that neither Foster nor Phillip – who took 68 championship wickets himself – will ever forget is 30 May 1983. That day, Phillip returned sensational figures of 6 for 4 and Foster 4 for 10 as Surrey were bowled out for a humiliating 14 at Chelmsford. It was the lowest first-class score in the county's history. Amazingly, Essex did not win the match as Roger Knight's unbeaten century helped Surrey to secure an unlikely draw.

Overall, Essex's second championship triumph was a mirror opposite of their first. Then, they had led from the front: now, trailing the leaders entering the final month, Gooch hit top gear, hitting three centuries in the last seven matches to help his county to reach the summit of English domestic cricket for the second time in five seasons.

In his book *Champions!* secretary Peter Edwards waxed lyrical about the all-round talents of the club he had done so much for. 'To win the County Championship – and to be in serious contention in the one-day competitions – as Essex did last year, a side must have certain ingredients. Firstly, it needs a Captain who can give firm orders, who is respected by the players, and who can assess a situation and make quick decisions that may well turn a game. Keith Fletcher has all these qualities and has led his team extremely well. Secondly, the side needs top class strikers like Graham Gooch, Brian Hardie, Ken McEwan and the Captain who can score sufficient runs to give a well-balanced bowling attack a chance to win the game. Essex's new ball attack of John Lever, Norbert Phillip and Neil Foster, plus the spin of Ray East and David Acfield, and the two all-rounders Derek Pringle and Stuart Turner, have all given splendid support to their Captain.

'Leaving what I regard to be the best to last, what a magnificent summer young wicket-keeper David East had last year. His catching standing back could rarely be faulted and some of his stumpings were really superb. To my mind, David is the most improved wicket-keeper in the country and he proved it by winning a Gordon's Gin monthly award and then being voted Wicket-Keeper of Year 1983.'

Essex did not repeat their championship heroics in the one-day competitions, finishing joint-sixth in the John Player Special League table, and beaten by four runs by Kent in the second round of the NatWest Bank Trophy.

It was, yet again, the Benson and Hedges Cup where Essex showed their true colours in the shorter form of the game, beating Hampshire, Somerset, Minor Counties, Warwickshire and Kent to set up a Lord's final showdown with Middlesex. A superb spell from Foster saw Middlesex restricted to just 196 for 8, with Clive Radley's innings of 89 not out the only barrier between Essex and a seemingly comprehensive victory.

It did not seem to matter as Gooch (46) and Hardie (49) put on 79 for the first wicket. At 151 for 3, Essex appeared on course for another memorable win, despite the fine bowling of England spinner Emburey. It was another spinner, Edmonds, and seam bowler Norman Cowans, however, who turned the game on its head. Essex lost their last five wickets for just seven runs to be bowled out for 192. Amazingly, they lost a match that had been at their mercy by four runs. Unlike in 1979, there would be no County Championship and Benson and Hedges Cup double to display.

THE BEST TEAM IN THE COUNTRY
Unlike 1980, when Essex appeared to suffer a hangover from their championship success, the champions went from strength to strength in 1984, retaining their title and losing just three of their 24 matches.

But those statistics do not tell the whole story, as Essex's title win was anything but as straightforward as it had been five years previously. While the 1979 success had been a canter, Essex went into their final match in 1994 against Lancashire knowing they were powerless to stop Nottinghamshire from winning the title if their closest rivals could beat Somerset at Taunton.

Whatever happened, Essex needed to beat Lancashire to realistically give themselves any chance of lifting the championship trophy. They did so in style, thrashing the Red Rose county by ten wickets at Old Trafford. Future captain Paul Prichard, then just 19, and McEwan both scored centuries, while Lever, Foster and Pringle were all among the wickets to leave Essex the simple task of knocking off 13 runs for victory in their second innings.

With their side of the bargain completed, Essex had to rely on Somerset stopping a Nottinghamshire side containing the might of New Zealander Hadlee, South African Rice and England batsmen Chris Broad and Tim Robinson. A pair of sporting declarations from captains Rice and Botham left Nottinghamshire to chase 297 in 60 overs to win the match and snatch the title from Essex's grasp.

What happened next was summed up superbly in the 1985 *Wisden* Almanack editorial, written by John Woodcock. 'For the third time in six years and the second year running Essex won the County Championship, which was sponsored for the first time by the Britannic Assurance Company. They also took the John Player Sunday League. The Championship had a dramatic finish. With only two balls of the season left, it could have gone either way. Nottinghamshire, needing 297 to beat Somerset at Taunton and so hold off Essex, were 293 for nine. Going for the winning hit, Bore, Nottinghamshire's number ten, was caught by Ollis, a substitute fielder, five yards inside the long-off boundary. A week earlier Nottinghamshire, only a single point behind Essex with a match in hand, had looked the likelier winners.

'Although when the two sides met at Chelmsford in May Essex were well beaten, Nottinghamshire's form in the last week of the season was disappointing. For much of the campaign Gooch batted in truly commanding fashion for Essex, and as in 1983 the faithful Lever took over 100 wickets for

them. With the help of Fletcher's canny captaincy, and under an active administration, Essex are conducting an admirably efficient transition from one gen-
eration of players to the next.'

Aside from Somerset's late assistance, the incomparable Gooch had been
in his pomp in 1984, amassing 2,281 championship runs as Essex won the title
by 14 points. The opener hit seven hundreds and eleven fifties, but was not
named as one of *Wisden*'s five Cricketers of the Year, perhaps due to his ban
from international cricket, which would end in May 1985. As a bowler, Gooch
had also become a weapon, capturing 36 wickets at 21 apiece to supplement
the super-human efforts of Lever, who snared 106 victims, Foster, who took
78, and Pringle, who totalled 55.

The 1984 season marked a memorable end to the career of Ray East. At
the age of 37, the spinner retired after taking 1,010 first-class wickets at 25.54.
One of the finest slow bowlers never to represent his country, East also managed more than 7,000 first-class runs for the county he had played for since
1965.

Essex were unstoppable in the John Player Special League, winning 12 and
losing just one of their 16 matches to end the season eight points clear of runners-up Nottinghamshire and third-placed Sussex.

GRAHAM GOOCH: 'It worked in Essex's favour when myself and John
Lever were banned from playing for England [for three years] in 1982 [after
going on the rebel tour to South Africa]. We played every game for three years.
I'm not blowing my own trumpet but it was no coincidence that we won the
championship twice. We had the best bowler in county cricket playing every
game.

'The side evolved through the 1980s. The basic side stayed together until
the mid-1980s then people like Stuart Turner and Norbert Phillip were getting
on a bit. Neil Foster and Derek Pringle arrived on the scene in about 1982 or
1983 and they just came straight in for Norbert and Stuart so we had Foster,
Pringle and Lever. Stuart and Norbert still played in one-day cricket so they
were still a factor in that.'

The only disappointments in 1984 came in the NatWest Trophy, where
Surrey saw off Essex's challenge at the second round stage, and the Benson
and Hedges Cup. There, after finishing with a 100 per cent record in their four
group stage matches, Lancashire stole a four-wicket success at Chelmsford,
despite five wickets from the ever-improving Pringle.

ONE-DAY DOUBLE
Having won two trophies in 1984, Essex repeated the trick a year later, retaining their John Player Special League crown and winning the NatWest Trophy
for the first time. Despite their failure to win the County Championship for a
fourth time, there is no doubt that 1985 will go down as one of the finest season's in the club's history.

The NatWest Trophy final would be another memorable, nail-biting occasion for everyone concerned. Following their late collapse against Middlesex two years previously, Essex came perilously close to throwing away an even stronger position before holding off the challenge of Nottinghamshire – again – with just one run to spare.

Having made a challenging 280 for 2 – the highest final total in the competition's history – from their allotted 60 overs, thanks largely to a record-breaking opening stand of 202 between man-of-the-match Hardie (110) and Gooch (91), Essex appeared to have their opponents under the cosh when Nottinghamshire needed 20 runs off the final over. England batsman Derek Randall, approaching the twilight of his career at the age of 34, hit 18 from Pringle's first five balls. The veteran then holed out to Prichard off the final delivery, having made 66 from just 54 balls, and Essex held on to secure a thrilling success.

Amazingly, the day after these heroics, Gooch and Hardie put together an opening partnership of 239 in a John Player Special League fixture against the same hapless Nottinghamshire attack at Trent Bridge, paving the way for Essex's 44-run victory. Gooch made a savage 171, complete with 18 fours and three sixes, while Hardie played the perfect foil with a more sedate 60.

A week later, Pringle and McEwan scored half-centuries – the latter in his final one-day game for the club – as Yorkshire were beaten by two wickets at Chelmsford to secure the Sunday League title for the county for the third time in five seasons.

Essex were unable to complete a hat-trick of County Championship titles, finishing fourth. Again, Fletcher's men were extremely hard to beat, losing just two of their 24 matches, but a record of 14 draws meant they were unable to gather enough points to seriously challenge champions Middlesex.

There was also heartbreak in the season's other one-day competition, the Benson and Hedges Cup. Essex won all four matches, in a group containing Middlesex, Surrey, Sussex and Combined Universities, before beating Derbyshire and Middlesex for a second time to set up a final showdown with Leicestershire at Lord's

Gooch made 57 and McEwan a quickfire 29, but Essex's total of 213 for 8 looked too small to defend. So it proved as Leicestershire, led by an unbeaten 86 from Willey and 43 from Gower, got home with five wickets and three overs to spare.

The 1985 season would be McEwan's last as an Essex player. Having enjoyed a thoroughly deserved benefit the previous summer, the prolific batsman signed off his time at Chelmsford by passing the 1,000-run mark in first-class cricket for the 12th time in 12 seasons with his adopted county. In 282 first-class matches for Essex, McEwan made 18,088 runs at an average of 43.37, complete with 52 centuries, 82 half-centuries and a top score of 218. In one-day cricket, too, he was a potent force, plundering 8,351 runs at 34.79 with another 13 hundreds, 47 fifties and a top score of 162 not out. Without any exaggeration, McEwan was a run machine and one of the finest batsmen ever to pull on an Essex sweater.

At the age of 33, the South African returned to South Africa to the family farm in his native Cape Province. His replacement for the 1986 season would be none other than Australia captain Allan Border. Despite Border's own hugely impressive credentials, McEwan's boots would be big ones to fill.

Internationally, Gooch made his comeback to the England team in spectacular fashion, making a half-century and two centuries in his first three matches. Unfortunately, the Essex man's form was not enough to stop Australia winning the Texaco Trophy series.

It was a different story in the six-match Ashes series, which England won 3-1. It was a fantastic achievement, considering the national side had been 'black-washed' in the West Indies the preceding winter. Gooch's form was not sensational, but he did make a superb 196 in the final Test of the summer at The Oval, sharing a second-wicket stand of 351 with Gower as England won by an innings and 94 runs. It was a fitting climax to a memorable summer for both his county and his country.

After dominating the one-day game in 1985, Essex regained their position at the top of domestic first-class cricket a year later, winning a fourth County Championship in eight seasons, under new captain Graham Gooch.

Under Gooch, Essex would lose six of their 24 matches – three times as many as they had in 1985 – but a record of ten victories and just eight draws would mean the county amassed 287 points, 28 more than nearest rivals Gloucestershire. The signing of Border proved a masterstroke. The Australian made 1,287 runs in 18 first-class matches at an average of more than 51. Border would make four centuries and eight fifties to ensure that, run production-wise at least, McEwan would not be missed.

Paul Prichard would be the only other Essex player to pass 1,000 championship runs as the county's batsmen shared the burden of scoring. Gooch, Fletcher, Hardie, Lilley, David East and the emerging John Stephenson would all make more than 500, while Pringle and Foster also made useful contributions. Foster would also excel with the ball, taking exactly 100 championship wickets. The fast bowler, who had made his Test debut for England in August 1983, took five wickets in an innings ten times to lead Essex to the title. He was ably supported by spinner John Childs, who celebrated his second season since moving to Chelmsford from Gloucestershire by taking 85 wickets. The evergreen Lever snapped up 58 and all-rounder Pringle 41.

Of the class of 1979, Turner would play just one championship match in 1986. It would prove to be his last. After 22 seasons with Essex, the all-rounder took 1 for 72 and managed an unbeaten 25 in his final first-class appearance for the county he had served with distinction for more than two decades. He was a week past his 43rd birthday.

Essex came agonisingly close to winning the John Player Special League for the third time in four seasons and the fourth time since 1981, finishing four points behind winners Hampshire. In the end, a one-wicket defeat to Surrey at Chelmsford on Sunday, 24 August was to cost Gooch's men dear as their run-rate was far superior to that of the champions.

In the one-day knockout competitions, Essex never threatened to add to their trophy collection. The team negotiated the Benson and Hedges Cup group stage, only to fall to a three-wicket defeat by Nottinghamshire in the quarter-finals. In the NatWest Trophy, Northumberland were beaten but a Geoff Humpage-inspired Warwickshire ended Essex's challenge in the second round.

1987 was the final year of exclusively three-day cricket in the County Championship, but Essex were unable to mark the occasion by topping the table. Instead, Gooch's team finished a hugely disappointing 12th. The reigning champions won just two of their 24 championship matches, drawing 16, tying one and losing five. Captain Gooch averaged under 40, and only he and Hardie struggled past the 1,000 run mark. Without the influential Border and with Lever's legendary powers beginning to wane, Essex looked like a team in transition. Of the side that had won the title so gloriously in 1979, only Gooch, Fletcher, Hardie, Lever and Lilley remained.

That 1987 season would be the first of four without a trophy for Essex. Since 1983, the club had won six competitions and finished as runners-up in two more. On Sundays, the renamed Refuge Assurance League saw Essex end 14th, and they failed to negotiate the group stage in the Benson and Hedges Cup. In the NatWest Trophy, Northamptonshire proved too strong at Chelmsford in the quarter-finals. It marked the end of Essex's golden era. From 1988, four-day cricket was upon us.

When Essex won the double in 1979, it was about a group of men playing the game they love in front of thousands of fans watching the game they love. For many of the players, that summer offered an escape from rudimentary winter jobs, like the next man in the street. They played, they won, they were the best in the country. And they did it with a collective smile.

1979 ESSEX RESULTS

21, 22 and 24 April   University Match, Fenner's
Cambridge University drew with Essex
Cambridge University 197 all out (Turner 3/26, Pont 3/34) and 90 for 4
Essex 308 for 8 dec (Hardie 59, Fletcher 56)

29 April   John Player League, Edgbaston
Essex beat Warwickshire by 15 runs
Essex 174 for 8
Warwickshire 159 all out (East 3/20, Pont 3/41)

2, 3, and 4 May   Schweppes County Championship, Chelmsford
Essex drew with Kent
Essex 305 for 7 dec (Turner 102) and 43 for 9
Kent 250 for 8 (Phillip 3/37, Pont 3/44)

5 May   Benson and Hedges Cup Group C, Northampton
Essex beat Northamptonshire by three runs
Essex 230 for 5 (Gooch 83, Fletcher 65)
Northamptonshire 227 for 7

6 May   John Player League, Chelmsford
Essex beat Derbyshire by eight wickets
Derbyshire 114 all out (Pont 4/24, Phillip 3/20)
Essex 118 for 2 (Gooch 68 not out)

9 May   Schweppes County Championship, Lord's
Middlesex drew with Essex
Middlesex 265 for 6 dec
Essex 224 for 7 (McEwan 66)

12 May   Benson and Hedges Cup Group C, The Oval
Surrey beat Essex by seven runs
Surrey 207 for 6 (Lever 4/29)
Esssex 200 all out (Fletcher 72)

13 May   John Player League, Southampton
Hampshire beat Essex by seven wickets
Essex 172 for 6
Hampshire 173 for 3 (Lever 3/24)

16, 17 and 18 May   Schweppes County Championship, Chesterfield
Essex beat Derbyshire by an innings and 171 runs
Essex 335 for 4 dec (Fletcher 140 not out, Gooch 109)
Derbyshire 63 all out (Phillip 5/23, Turner 3/12) and 101 all out (Lever 6/52 and Turner 3/20)

19 May   Benson and Hedges Cup Group C, Chelmsford
Essex beat Combined Universities by 214 runs
Essex 350 for 3 (Gooch 133, Lilley 119)
Combined Universities 136 all out (Lever 4/18, Turner 3/33)

20 May   John Player League, Trent Bridge
Nottinghamshire v Essex (Match Abandoned)

23 May   Benson and Hedges Cup Group C, Chelmsford
Essex beat Sussex by seven wickets
Sussex 188 for 8 (Lever 3/33)
Essex 189 for 3 (Lilley 70, Gooch 66)

26, 28 and 29 May   Schweppes County Championship, The Oval
Surrey v Essex (Match Abandoned)

27 May   John Player League, The Oval
No Result
Surrey 88 all out (Phillip 4/26)
Essex 25 for 1

30, 31 May and 1 June   Schweppes County Championship, Ilford
Essex beat Glamorgan by nine wickets
Glamorgan 184 for 7 (Fletcher 3/44)
Essex 185 for 1 (Gooch 93 not out, McEwan 67 not out)

2 and 4 June   Schweppes County Championship, Ilford
Essex beat Lancashire by an innings and 132 runs
Essex 339 for 6 dec (Hardie 100 not out, McEwan 88)
Lancashire 84 all out (Lever 7/27) and 123 all out (Acfield 4/11)

3 June   John Player League, Ilford
Lancashire beat Essex by six wickets
Essex 127 for 9
Lancashire 130 for 4

6 June   Benson and Hedges Cup Quarter-Final, Chelmsford
Essex beat Warwickshire by 44 runs
Essex 271 for 5 (Gooch 138, McEwan 50)
Warwickshire 227 all out

9, 11 and 12 June   Schweppes County Championship, Chelmsford
Essex beat Leicestershire by 99 runs
Essex 303 for 9 (Denness 122, Smith 90 not out) and 181 all out
Leicestershire 232 all out (Lever 6/76) and 153 all out (Lever 7/41, Phillip 3.55)

13, 14 and 15 June   Schweppes County Championship, Edgbaston
Essex beat Warwickshire by an innings and 75 runs
Warwickshire 185 all out (Lever 8/49) and 134 all out (Lever 5/38, East 4/34)
Essex 394 for 7 dec (McEwan 208 not out)

16, 18 and 19 June   Schweppes County Championship, Bath
Somerset drew with Essex
Somerset 277 for 9 (Acfield 3/60, Phillip 3/70) and 284 for 7 (Lever 3/61)
Essex 302 for 8 (McEwan 71, East 70, Hardie 54) and 87 for 7

17 June   John Player League, Bath
Somerset beat Essex by nine wickets
Essex 120 for 9 (Fletcher 51 not out)
Somerset 121 for 1

20, 21 and 22 June   Schweppes County Championship, Chelmsford
Essex beat Derbyshire by an innings and 40 runs
Derbyshire 258 all out (Lever 5/72, Phillip 4/59) and 137 all out (Phillip 4/28, Lever 4/45)
Essex 435 for 9 (McEwan 185, Pont 77)

23, 25 and 26 June   Schweppes County Championship, Tunbridge Wells
Kent drew with Essex
Kent 318 for 8 dec (Turner 3/70, Lever 3/73)
Essex 20 for 1

27 June   Gillette Cup, Old Trafford
Lancashire beat Essex by 70 runs
Lancashire 247 for 5
Essex 177 all out

1 July   John Player League, Chelmsford
Essex beat Kent by nine wickets
Kent 117 all out (Phillip 4/24)
Essex 121 for 1

4 July   Benson and Hedges Cup Semi-Final, Chelmsford
Essex beat Yorkshire by three wickets
Yorkshire 173 for 9
Essex 174 for 7

7, 9 and 10 July   Schweppes County Championship, Southend
Essex beat Sussex by ten wickets
Essex 338 for 5 dec (Denness 136, Gooch 86, Fletcher 52 not out) and 12 for 0
Sussex 143 all out (Phillip 4/42, Turner 3/17, Lever 3/46) and 204 all out (Phillip 4/55, Lever 4/67)

8 July   John Player League, Southend
Essex beat Sussex by nine runs
Essex 199 for 5 (Gooch 77)
Sussex 190 for 7

11, 12 and 13 July   Schweppes County Championship, Southend
Essex beat Nottinghamshire by 46 runs
Essex 240 all out (Denness 65) and 229 all out (Turner 68 not out)
Nottinghamshire 300 all out (East 4/93) and 123 all out (Acfield 5/28, East 5/56)

15 July   John Player League, Luton
Northamptonshire beat Essex by five wickets
Essex 164 all out
Northamptonshire 165 for 5 (Lever 3/31)

21 July   Benson and Hedges Cup Final, Lord's
Essex beat Surrey by 35 runs
Essex 290 for 6 (Gooch 120, McEwan 72)
Surrey 255 all out (Phillip 3/42)

22 July   John Player League, Colchester
Yorkshire beat Essex by nine runs
Yorkshire 142 for 8 (East 5/20)
Essex 133 all out

25, 26 and 27 July   Schweppes County Championship, Bournemouth
Essex beat Hampshire by an innings and 33 runs
Hampshire 128 all out (Lever 7/40) and 219 all out (Acfield 5/61, East 4/48)
Essex 380 all out (Hardie 146 not out, Gooch 70)

28 and 30 July   Schweppes County Championship, Colchester
Essex beat Gloucestershire by four wickets
Gloucestershire 92 all out (Lever 4/37) and 205 all out (Acfield 6/56)
Essex 170 all out (Phillip 62) and 129 for 6

29 July   John Player League, Colchester
Essex beat Gloucestershire by three wickets
Gloucestershire 127 for 6
Essex 128 for 7

1, 2 and 3 August   Schweppes County Championship, Colchester
Middlesex beat Essex by ten wickets
Essex 106 all out and 225 all out (Pont 59, Fletcher 57)
Middlesex 299 all out (Fletcher 5/41, East 4/106) and 36 for 0

4, 6 and 7 August   Schweppes County Championship, Worcester
Worcestershire beat Essex by an innings and 22 runs
Worcestershire 353 for 9 (Phillip 3/55, East 3/128)
Essex 185 all out and 146 all out

11, 12 and 13 August   Tour Match, Chelmsford
Essex drew with Indians
Essex 146 all out (Fletcher 64) and 295 for 6 dec (McEwan 68, Smith 65, Denness 58)
Indians 215 for 8 (Phillip 4/50) and 132 for 2

18, 20 and 21 August   Schweppes County Championship, Northampton
Essex beat Northamptonshire by seven wickets
Northamptonshire 224 all out (Turner 5/70, Phillip 3/35) and 203 all out (Turner 5/56, Lever 3/71)
Essex 199 all out (McEwan 70, Fletcher 52 not out) and 229 for 3 (Hardie 103 not out, Denness 51)

19 August   John Player League, Leicester
Essex beat Leicestershire by 60 runs
Essex 164 all out
Leicestershire 104 all out (Lever 3/10, Turner 3/15)

25, 27 and 28 August   Schweppes County Championship, Chelmsford
Essex beat Surrey by 15 runs
Essex 300 for 9 (Hardie 76, Phillip 66, Denness 61) and 101 all out
Surrey 287 all out (Turner 4/61, Phillip 3/52, Lever 3/83) and 99 all out (Phillip 4/19, Lever 4/54)

26 August   John Player League, Chelmsford
Essex beat Middlesex by 99 runs
Essex 189 for 5 (Hardie 55 not out)
Middlesex 90 all out (Turner 4/18, East 3/9)

29, 30 and 31 August   Schweppes County Championship, Chelmsford
Essex beat Northamptonshire by five wickets
Northamptonshire 314 for 7 and 137 all out (Turner 5/39)
Essex 303 for 9 dec (Hardie 93, Smith 63) and 150 for 5 (Fletcher 50 not out)

1, 3 and 4 September   Schweppes County Championship, Leicester
Leicestershire beat Essex by 197 runs
Leicestershire 310 for 7 (East 3/80) and 226 for 1
Essex 167 all out and 172 all out (Hardie 59 not out)

2 September   John Player League, Worcester
Essex beat Worcestershire by one wicket
Worcestershire 199 for 6 (Pont 3/24)
Essex 200 for 9

5, 6 and 7 September   Schweppes County Championship, Scarborough
Yorkshire beat Essex by one wicket
Essex 339 for 9 dec (McEwan 124, Gooch 69, Fletcher 50) and 154 all out
Yorkshire 329 for 6 dec (East 3/54, Lever 3/74) and 167 for 9 (Turner 5/35)

9 September   John Player League, Chelmsford
Glamorgan beat Essex by 14 runs
Glamorgan 194 for 4
Essex 180 all out (Pont 52)

County Championship

1 match abandoned

Batting and Fielding	M	Inns	N/O	Runs	HS	Ave	100s	50s	Ct	St
David Acfield	17	15	9	55	12*	9.16			5	
Mike Denness	20	33	2	973	136	31.38	2	3	8	
Ray East	19	25	5	390	70	19.50	0	1	8	
Keith Fletcher	21	31	4	880	140*	32.59	1	6	19	
Graham Gooch	10	15	2	535	109	41.15	1	4	14	
Brian Hardie	21	31	5	1,111	146*	42.73	3	4	27	
John Lever	17	13	4	72	14	8.00	0	0	3	
Alan Lilley	3	4	0	46	35	11.50	0	0	1	
Mike McEvoy	7	12	0	108	28	9.00	0	0	11	
Ken McEwan	21	32	2	1,254	208*	41.80	3	5	18	
Norbert Phillip	21	28	4	417	66	17.37	0	2	6	
Keith Pont	11	17	2	292	77	19.46	0	2	6	
Gary Sainsbury	1	0							1	
Neil Smith	21	26	6	297	90*	14.85	0	2	48	3
Stuart Turner	21	28	4	525	102	21.87	1	1	14	

County Championship

Bowling	Balls	Maids	Runs	W	Best	Ave	5wl	10wM
David Acfield	2,720	132	991	39	6 for 56	25.41	3	0
Ray East	3,249	162	1,253	43	5 for 56	29.13	1	0
Keith Fletcher	135	3	85	9	5 for 41	10.62	1	0
Graham Gooch	144	4	75	1	1 for 21	75.00	0	0
Brian Hardie	30	0	39	2	2 for 39	19.50	0	0
John Lever	3,455	138	1,460	99	8 for 49	14.74	8	2
Norbert Phillip	3,139	123	1,445	66	5 for 23	21.89	1	0
Keith Pont	342	13	154	4	3 for 44	38.50	0	0
Gary Sainsbury	138	2	79	1	1 for 38	79.00	0	0
Stuart Turner	3,225	150	1,211	57	5 for 35	21.24	4	1

John Player League

Batting and Fielding	M	Inns	N/O	Runs	HS	Ave	100s	50s	Ct	St
David Acfield	6	2	2	4	3*		0	0	2	
Mike Denness	4	4	0	107	44*	26.75	0	0	0	
Ray East	10	6	1	14	10*	2.80	0	0	6	
Keith Fletcher	15	13	3	314	51*	31.40	0	1	0	
Graham Gooch	11	11	2	303	77	33.66	0	2	4	
Brian Hardie	15	12	1	285	55*	25.90	0	1	6	
John Lever	15	7	3	16	5	4.00	0	0	3	
Alan Lilley	15	15	1	219	31	15.64	0	0	3	
Ken McEwan	15	15	2	237	45	18.23	0	0	7	
Norbert Phillip	14	10	2	60	15*	7.50	0	0	0	
Keith Pont	15	12	1	265	52	24.09	0	1	5	
Neil Smith	15	9	4	86	32	17.20	0	0	4	4
Stuart Turner	15	11	3	146	20	18.25	0	0	9	

John Player League

Bowling	Balls	Maids	Runs	W	Best	Ave	5wI	10wM	Rate	Econ
David Acfield	288	6	150	4	1 for 12	37.50	0	0	72.00	3.12
Ray East	372	10	218	17	5 for 20	12.82	0	1	21.88	3.51
Keith Fletcher	5	0	5	1	1 for 4	5.00	0	0	5.00	6.00
Graham Gooch	102	0	79	2	1 for 22	39.50	0	0	51.00	4.64
John Lever	647	20	318	24	3 for 10	13.25	0	0	26.95	2.94
Norbert Phillip	554	9	332	15	4 for 23	22.13	2	0	36.93	3.59
Keith Pont	639	14	428	21	4 for 24	20.38	1	0	30.42	4.01
Stuart Turner	678	15	381	17	4 for 18	22.41	1	0	39.88	3.37

Benson and Hedges Cup

Batting and Fielding	M	Inns	N/O	Runs	HS	Ave	100s	50s	Ct
David Acfield	4	1	1	1	1*		0	0	2
Mike Denness	1	1	0	24	24	24.00	0	0	0
Ray East	3	0							1
Keith Fletcher	7	7	2	248	72	49.60	0	2	4
Graham Gooch	7	7	0	591	138	84.42	3	2	5
Brian Hardie	7	7	2	80	35	16.00	0	0	0
John Lever	7	1	0	9	9	9.00	0	0	0
Alan Lilley	6	6	0	249	119	41.50	1	1	1
Ken McEwan	7	7	0	237	72	33.85	0	2	3
Norbert Phillip	7	4	1	32	14	10.66	0	0	0
Keith Pont	7	5	3	112	36	56.00	0	0	3
Neil Smith	7	2	1	14	10	13.00	0	0	7
Stuart Turner	7	4	3	15	11*	15.00	0	0	1

Benson and Hedges Cup

Bowling	Balls	Maids	Runs	W	Best	Ave	5wi	10wM	Rate	Econ
David Acfield	231	8	112	5	2 for 14	22.40	0	0	46.20	2.9
Ray East	198	5	104	6	2 for 25	17.33	0	0	33.00	3.15
Graham Gooch	12	1	5	0						2.5
John Lever	448	11	248	19	4 for 18	13.05	2	0	23.57	3.32
Norbert Phillip	451	6	273	12	3 for 42	22.75	0	0	37.58	3.63
Keith Pont	390	3	292	6	2 for 67	48.66	0	0	65.00	4.49
Stuart Turner	462	11	262	10	3 for 33	26.20	0	0	46.20	3.4

Gillette Cup

Batting and Fielding	M	Inns	N/O	Runs	HS	Ave	100s	50s	Ct
Mike Denness	1	1	0	27	27	27.00	0	0	0
Ray East	1	1	0	1	1	1.00	0	0	1
Keith Fletcher	1	1	0	31	31	31.00	0	0	1
Graham Gooch	1	1	0	33	33	33.00	0	0	0
Brian Hardie	1	1	0	2	2	2.00	0	0	1
John Lever	1	1	1	2	2*		0	0	0
Ken McEwan	1	1	0	12	12	12.00	0	0	0
Norbert Phillip	1	1	0	4	4	4.00	0	0	0
Keith Pont	1	1	0	27	27	27.00	0	0	0
Neil Smith	1	1	0	6	6	6.00	0	0	0
Stuart Turner	1	1	0	18	18	18.00	0	0	0

Gillette Cup

Bowling	Balls	Maids	Runs	W	Best	Ave	5wi	10wM	Rate	Econ
Ray East	72	1	39	1	1 for 39	39.00	0		72.00	3.25
John Lever	72	1	51	0						4.25
Norbert Phillip	72	1	70	0						5.83
Keith Pont	72	3	25	2	2 for 25	12.50	0	0	36.00	2.08
Stuart Turner	72	0	44	1	1 for 44	44.00	0	0	72.00	3.66

15-Jun-79	P	W	L	D	Aban	Bat	Bowl	Pts
1 Essex	7	4	0	2	1	22	20	90
2 Hampshire	6	1	0	4	1	12	18	42
3 Northamptonshire	8	1	1	5	1	12	15	39
4 Somerset	7	1	0	5	1	10	14	36
5 Kent	6	1	0	5	0	10	12	34
6 Derbyshire	7	1	1	4	1	9	12	33
7 Sussex	6	1	1	2	2	7	13	32
7 Worcestershire	6	1	1	3	1	5	15	32
9 Warwickshire	7	1	2	3	1	5	10	27
10 Middlesex	7	0	0	5	2	11	14	25
10 Leicestershire	6	0	2	3	1	11	14	25
12 Gloucestershire	6	1	0	3	2	8	4	24
13 Nottinghamshire	6	1	0	2	3	4	7	23
14 Surrey	6	0	0	5	1	7	15	22
14 Yorkshire	6	0	0	5	1	10	12	22
16 Lancashire	8	0	3	5	0	4	16	20
17 Glamorgan	6	0	3	2	1	6	13	19

31-Jul-79	P	W	L	D	Aban	Bat	Bowl	Pts
1 Essex	14	9	0	4	1	41	46	195
2 Nottinghamshire	15	5	4	3	3	28	37	125
3 Kent	15	4	1	10	0	36	37	121
4 Somerset	14	4	0	9	1	35	34	117
5 Worcestershire	13	4	3	5	1	30	35	113
6 Hampshire	14	3	5	5	1	24	43	103
7 Leicestershire	14	2	3	8	1	36	42	102
8 Gloucestershire	15	3	3	7	2	29	35	100
8 Sussex	14	3	3	6	2	30	34	100
10 Yorkshire	15	2	2	10	1	34	41	99
11 Lancashire	16	3	3	10	0	27	35	98
11 Surrey	15	2	2	10	1	29	45	98
13 Northamptonshire	15	2	2	10	1	35	36	95
14 Derbyshire	15	1	5	8	1	35	38	85
15 Middlesex	14	1	2	9	2	26	36	74
16 Warwickshire	15	1	5	8	1	27	31	70
17 Glamorgan	14	0	5	8	1	23	38	61

Final Table	P	W	L	D	Aban	Bat	Bowl	Pts
1 Essex	22	13	4	4	1	56	69	281
2 Worcestershire	22	7	4	10	1	55	61	204
3 Surrey	22	6	3	12	1	50	70	192
4 Sussex	22	6	4	10	2	47	65	184
5 Kent	22	6	3	13	0	49	60	181
6 Leicestershire	22	4	5	12	1	60	68	176
7 Yorkshire	22	5	3	13	1	52	63	175
8 Somerset	22	5	1	15	1	56	55	171
9 Nottinghamshire	22	6	4	9	3	43	54	169
10 Gloucestershire	22	5	4	11	2	53	54	167
11 Northamptonshire	22	3	6	12	1	59	58	153
12 Hampshire	22	3	9	9	1	39	66	141
13 Middlesex	22	3	3	14	2	44	60	140
13 Lancashire	22	4	4	14	0	37	55	140
15 Warwickshire	22	3	7	11	1	46	51	133
16 Derbyshire	22	1	6	14	1	48	58	118
17 Glamorgan	22	0	10	11	1	35	58	93

Printed in Great Britain
by Amazon

19345818R00103